A Book bought to
Celebrate the Millennium,
the Jubilee Year - 2000 A.D.

Daniel J. O'Connor
St. Jude the Apostle

ROME RESHAPED

Also by Desmond O'Grady

Eat from God's Hand
A Long Way from Home
Deschooling Kevin Carew
Valid for All Countries
Rafaello! Rafaello!
Marriage Gamblers
The Victory of the Cross
Correggio Jones and the Runaways
The Turned Card

ROME
RESHAPED
JUBILEES 1300–2000

DESMOND
O'GRADY

CONTINUUM NEW YORK

1999

The Continuum Publishing Company
370 Lexington Avenue, New York, NY 10017

Printed in Australia

Library of Congress Cataloging-in-Publication data
O'Grady, Desmond, 1929– .
  Rome reshaped: jubilees 1300–2000 / Desmond O'Grady
  224 pp. 23 x 15 cm
  Includes index.
  ISBN 0-8264-1205-X (hc.)
  1. Holy Year — History. I. Title.
263'.9—dc21   99-28903
                          CIP

Acknowledgements
Thanks are due to the following for their help:
Mark Coleridge, Emilio Cardini, Terence Kennedy CSsR, Matthew Fforde,
Mario Fois SJ, Henry A. Kelly, Aharon Lopez, Margaret McGrath NDS, John
Navone SJ, Gerald O'Collins SJ, and Szezana Stojnic. The quotations of the
Divine Comedy are from Dorothy L. Sayers' translation (Penguin, 1949).

CONTENTS

JUBILEE 2000

For Victor, Riccardo and Tommaso,
arrows into the Third

INTRODUCTION

During each of the twenty-five Jubilee years since 1300, Rome, meaning both the city and the Holy See, has tried to reassert its centrality, its universal relevance, and it will do so again in the year 2000. Once more it will try to draw people towards it and give them something of its treasures.

What is distinctive about the year 2000 is that for the first time a Jubilee coincides with a millennium, which could inspire both kitsch religion and apocalyptic forebodings. The Jubilee shuns both as it aspires to ferry humankind into the third millennium by asserting that history is a meaningful journey. The millennium, of course, is a commemoration of Christ's birth; and, even though the traditional date is now known to have been miscalculated, it shows how Christianity succeeded in giving its sense of time to history.

In this book, Jubilees since 1300 are surveyed to see how Rome responded to various challenges. The year 2000 represents a new challenge in new conditions. The Jubilee will be celebrated simultaneously in all dioceses around the world, but Rome retains a significant role due to its example of historical resilience and willingness to be open to the future.

Christianity gave Rome its future orientation. Pagan Rome had a profound respect for tradition and a univeralist aspiration shown in its willingness to grant citizenship to outsiders. This meant that its frontiers could expand to the world's limits. *Urbi et Orbi* was an aspiration long before popes used the phrase.

1

But as Christians learned to look with equanimity at the fall of the Roman empire they saw a future, whereas pagans feared catastrophe. Jubilees exemplify this forward vision, for they affirm the possibility of a clean slate for humankind. The name derives from the Old Testament recommendation to hold a Jubilee every fiftieth year, in which Jewish slaves would be freed, debts cancelled and land returned to its original owners in a collective tribute to the Lord's sovereignty and the integrity of creation.

Its horizon of hope has helped Rome respond vigorously to many psychic traumas. Its links with Jerusalem provide two examples of these responses. The destruction in the year seventy of Jerusalem, site of the mother church of the first Christians, was a heavy blow, but Rome swiftly took over the role of arbiter. The center of gravity of the church had moved across the Mediterranean but Jubilee 2000 will reemphasize the primordial link with Jerusalem.

From early in the second millennium pilgrimages to the Holy Land increased. During the Crusades, pilgrimages became armed, but when in 1291 the last Christian stronghold, Acre, fell to the Muslims it was much more difficult to reach Jerusalem. Loss again of contact with its source was a further trauma for Christianity but once more Rome responded by establishing the Jubilee in 1300. The Jubilee provided a goal for pilgrims who previously would have gone to the Holy Land.

Pilgrimage is common to many religions; for Christians Rome has been its major focus. Those who come in the year 2000 will not find a religious museum but a city in which some live their faith fully in a setting which preserves much of the evidence of the history of the church and humankind. Against the remains of the pagan city, three strata can be distinguished: Europe's oldest Jewish community which preceded Christianity and was often disadvantaged under it; the catacombs which testify to the first Christians; and the churches built after Christianity was recognized early in the fourth century. Seven of them comprise the full Jubilee itinerary.

Since 1300, Jubilees have strongly influenced the development of Rome, and this is true to a certain extent also for that of 2000. The dual nature of contemporary pilgrimage to Rome, as a site of the faith and as a city, is described in the following chapters before surveying past Jubilees. The survey, a pilgrimage through church history, provides a perspective for the final section, a consideration of how Jubilee 2000 aspires to link the city with the world as never before.

ECCE ROMA!

TO BE A PILGRIM

What you are, I was,
What I am, you will be.
Pray for me. Do penance.
    Inscription on the tomb of a pilgrim in the
        church of St Prassede in Rome

D o those carrying plastic bottles of mineral water and wearing sneakers rather than donning sackcloth still count as pilgrims? It is more difficult to identify pilgrims nowadays than when they carried a staff, but earlier pilgrims often had multiple motives while contemporary travellers, despite a casual exterior, can have serious intentions. One of the earliest pilgrims to the Holy Land, the Spaniard Egeria, in 398, admitted that she was curious about exotic countries as well as religiously motivated. Pilgrimage has often been partly tourism.

Travel itself disposes towards transformative experience: the departure from the daily routine, difficulties overcome, attainment of the goal and the return home prepare people to recast the old self, whether the trip is to Lenin's tomb, Woodstock, a Vermeer exhibition or Victoria Falls. To do it in company, to share the experience, often augments the impact. But if travelers believe they have established contact with the divine and are purged of the weight of the past, the impact can change lives.

Pilgrimage is practiced in many religions. Some scholars claim that pilgrimages to both Jerusalem and Mecca have their roots in the pagan past, but Judaism, Christianity and Islam all look back to Abraham who heeded the voice of God calling him to set out on a pilgrimage of faith. The journey is the basic metaphor of the Bible because it presents humankind's experience of God as a creative dislocation. Jubilee 2000 will be a further chapter in the history of pilgrimage.

Pilgrimage to Jerusalem was one of the unifying factors in Israel after King David established his capital in this neutral site around the year 1000 BCE. With Mary and Joseph, Jesus went on pilgrimage to the capital. The tradition of Jewish pilgrimage has not been broken. In the seventeenth century a Jewish writer, Jemsel, gave memorable expression to the passion for pilgrimage: 'I was seized by a violent and insatiable desire to visit the places of God ... this desire to set out which had formed itself in my mind was so violent that it was impossible for me to remain in my own home, or to go about my accustomed business.'

The fifth of the five Pillars, or obligations, of Islam is a pilgrimage or Hajj to Mecca once in a lifetime. Hundreds of planes land daily at Jiddah airport during the pilgrimage season which follows Ramadan, the Islamic holy time of fast; each year over two million pilgrims participate, about a third of them women.

There is an Islamic legend that Adam and Eve were the first pilgrims to Mecca. Until earlier this century, many pilgrims still traveled to Mecca by caravans from cities such as Baghdad, Damascus or Cairo. In the fourteenth century, a Cairo caravan was composed of an advance guard, notables, treasury held in strongboxes, women, merchants, ordinary pilgrims, then the rearguard. Some caravans seemed endless: in Damascus in 1432, the 3000 camels of one returning caravan took two days and two nights to enter the city. Often the caravans traveled by night to avoid the heat.

Bedouins tried to extract money from pilgrims en route and even near Mecca itself. In 1049, 2000 Moroccans were killed outside the city gates for refusing to pay protection money. When trains were introduced, Bedouins raided them also. As Joseph Conrad's Lord Jim testifies, there were pilgrim ships; Thomas Cook obtained a monopoly of the Indian Ocean pilgrim transport. Some port authorities and merchants, as well as the Bedouins, treated pilgrims as sheep to be fleeced. At the Red Sea port of Aydhal, for a certain period, authorities hung by their testicles those pilgrims who did not want to pay a toll.

There were also real sheep, and goats, to be slaughtered. For Christians, Christ superseded animal sacrifices, but Muslims, like Abraham, still slaughter sheep and goats which have to be on hand in Mecca. Obviously a Hajj is a major feat of organization, not least because pilgrims, some of them infirm, have to complete a circuit of approximately 25 miles. In the eighth century the pilgrimage was already well organized, with forts and water supplies along the routes.

In the nineteenth century the British and French became worried that the Hajj was strengthening pan-Islamic, anti-colonialist sentiments. Other foreign powers were concerned by outbreaks of cholera during the Hajj. There was an epidemic in 1831; in 1865 cholera killed 15,000 pilgrims, another 60,000 died in Egypt and the disease spread to Europe. In less than thirty years there were eight epidemics before, in 1893, 33,000 of 200,000 pilgrims died at Jiddah, Mecca and Medina. This was a major factor in the eventual establishment of the International Health Convention which, in 1948, became the World Health Organization.

In 1916 the flag of Arab revolt flew in Mecca. With British and French help, Ottoman rule was thrown off but after eight years the Saudi regime took power and imposed the severe style of the Wahhabi current of Islam. Since then the kingdom has become oil rich, which some Muslims consider has had nefarious consequences for the sacred sites. Deaths during the Hajj have been frequent in recent years: in 1994, 1426 died because of a crush in a tunnel; in 1997, 343 died when a fire destroyed pilgrim tents; in 1998, 118 died on a bridge where there had been other victims a few years earlier.

The mosque at Mecca, a town of 450,000 inhabitants in a valley some forty miles east of the Red Sea, is the world's largest open-air temple, consisting of a forum surrounded by tiered arcades. Its white marble floor is 560 feet by 350. Pilgrims wheel seven times around the central Ka'ba, a huge cube of granite covered with an embroidered black cloth. It is the first of a series of rites which include a request to Allah for pardon for wrongs done. The Hajj rites have impressed many as a celebration of brotherhood—an experience aided by pilgrims donning a white garment of two seamless sheets which abolishes all distinctions. In 1807 Ali Bey wrote, 'The native of Circassia presents his hand in a friendly manner to the Ethiopian, or the Negro or Guinean; the Indian and the Persian embrace the inhabitants of

Barbary and Morocco; all look upon each other as brothers or individuals of the same family united by the bonds of religion, and the great part speaking, or understanding, more or less the same language, Arabic. No, there is not any religion that presents a spectacle more simple, affecting and majestic.'

Malcolm X said something similar after participating in the Hajj of 1964. Before going to Mecca, the American Muslim leader had seen whites as devils but there he realized they were part of a universal brotherhood. Since then, increasing numbers of American Muslims have undertaken the pilgrimage.

For Christians, unlike Muslims, pilgrimage is not obligatory, but they have been pilgrims at least since the second century. One example is provided by Hegesippus, a convert Jew, who came to Rome about 180 and wrote an account of his journey. At the Council of Nicea in 325, the bishop of Jerusalem told Helena, the mother of Emperor Constantine, that nothing was being done to identify, preserve or commemorate the sites of Christ's passion and death. Two hundred years earlier, to punish rebellious Jews, Emperor Hadrian had covered over Christ's sepulchre to build a temple to Aphrodite. This had preserved the tomb. Helena set out with a team to excavate and explore. She found the sites of Calvary, the Holy Sepulchre and, in Bethlehem, that of Christ's birth. Within seven years a pilgrim from Bordeaux travelled through Toulouse, Padua, Belgrade, Sofia and Constantinople, then, by military road, crossed through Syria to Jerusalem to visit these same sites and left a record of his trip. After Jerome, the monk who rendered the Bible into good Latin, transferred from Rome to Bethlehem late in the fourth century and established a monastery there, pilgrimages increased. Religious orders were established later to provide hospital and other services for pilgrims. In time some of their members took arms to ensure Christian access to Jerusalem despite the Muslim presence, but towards the end of the thirteenth century Christians could no longer reach Jerusalem and pilgrims sought other venues in Europe.

After the downfall of the Roman empire, the figure of St Peter, the Gatekeeper, was crucial for the conversion of the new peoples of Western Europe such as the Franks and the Anglo-Saxons and they expressed their gratitude by pilgrimages to his tomb in Rome. Some wanted to live and die there, to be near the one who would control the heavenly gates at the resurrection. Compounds were established for various foreign communities. Part of the one for Germans is still found by St Peter's in the German cemetery; the one for Anglo-Saxons was on a site on the Tiber bank where the Santo Spirito hospital now stands. Here various Saxon kings lived, beginning with Ines of Wessex in 726. Often the pilgrimages were not only to Peter's tomb but were also cultural because Rome was a school for chant, liturgy and church decoration.

As order and prosperity increased in Europe in the eleventh century, pilgrimages became more frequent, bringing so many formerly separate peoples into contact that it has been said that Europe was created by the interchange. Sometimes pilgrimage reinforced prejudice rather than fostered understanding, to judge by a twelfth century French pilgrim guidebook for Santiago di Compostella which claimed the Basques were so obnoxious they could only have descended from the Scots.

Pilgrimages to the Holy Land had been literal attempts to put one's feet in the footprints of Christ and this was the metaphorical sense of all Christian pilgrimage. In the seventh century, Irish monks, who were influential in continental Europe, introduced the practice of using pilgrimage as penance. It could also be undertaken in fulfilment of a vow, to seek a cure or give thanks for one, or even on behalf of another person: pilgrimage by proxy.

Following a decree of the Second Nicene Council in 787, that no church could be consecrated without relics, there was intense interest in them. Pilgrim sites competed to have a saint's remains. Many of them were robbed. In 1087 merchants from Bari, on Italy's Adriatic coast, took the remains of St Nicholas, on whom the legend of Santa Claus is based, from the island of Myra. Bari is still considered one of the major holy cities of Orthodoxy because it possesses St Nicholas' remains.

Some pilgrim sites lose their appeal, some have fluctuating fortunes, some are hardy perennials. Canterbury had a great vogue after Thomas Becket was murdered and buried there in the late twelfth century. Cologne too was an important goal because it held a relic of the Three Wise Men, but Santiago di Compostella, supposedly the burial place of St James the Apostle, has outlasted them. It emerged early in the twelfth century as a major center and it remains so today: the number of pilgrims has increased 25–fold in the past decade and many walk there along the historic pilgrim routes from France.

Sites in Padua, Assisi and Cascia are steady drawcards. The appeal of St Francis in Assisi is universal but perhaps an even greater drawcard is one of his early followers, the Portuguese St Anthony, renowned for helping people find lost objects. A Lisbon-born theologian and preacher, he is identified with Padua; in 1995 seven million went to his shrine there. Cascia in Umbria draws constant pilgrimages because of Rita, a mother and widow who became a nun and achieved sainthood. Padre Pio, the Capuchin clairvoyant and miracle worker who died in the 1960s, has since drawn millions to Foggia, south Italy. Likewise Medjugorje in Bosnia draws as many as the traditional Marian sites such as Loreto, Fatima and Lourdes, even though it has not yet received Vatican approval. Pilgrims do not necessarily wait for this: pilgrimage cannot be controlled, it is the travelling church—which is one reason why it can unsettle some churchmen.

As early as the eighth century some were suspicious of pilgrimages. In 735 an English missionary in Germany wrote to Cuthbert, Archbishop of Durham, about the need to check 'the practice of pilgrimage, for many, both men and women, go abroad for the purpose of living licentiously, without the restraint they would find at home, or are tempted by the vices of the cities of France and Lombardy to fall from the path of virtue.' An interlocutor in Thomas More's *Dialogue on the Adoration of Images* claimed the majority of pilgrims to Canterbury 'cometh for no devotion at all, but only for good company to babble thitherward, and drinke dranke there, and then dance and reel homewards.'

Geoffrey Chaucer's *Canterbury Tales* confirms that pilgrimage could be an occasion for having a good time. The Lollards, an English reform movement, criticized pilgrimage both as an excuse for licentiousness and for profiteering by clerical organizers. In 1407 a Lollard priest and Oxford scholar, William Thorpe, was tried for heresy by Archbishop Thomas Arundel of Canterbury. One of the charges was that Thorpe had preached against pilgrimage as unlawful, but in response he claimed to have distinguished between good pilgrimages and those in which, out of twenty participants, it was not possible to find 'three men or women that know surely a commandment of God, nor can say their Paternoster and Ave Maria nor their Creed readily, in any manner of language. And, as I have learned and also known some what by experience of these same pilgrims, telling the cause why that many men and woman go hither and thither now on pilgrimages—it is more for the health of their bodies than of their souls, more to have riches and prosperity of the world than for to be enriched with virtues in their souls, more to have here worldly and fleshly friendship than for to have friendship of God and of his saints in heaven!'

Thorpe further complained that pilgrims arranged 'to have both men and women that can well sing wanton songs, and some other pilgrims will have with them bagpipes—so that every town that they come through, what with the noise of their singing, and with the sound of their piping, and with the jangling of their Canterbury bells, and with the barking out of dogs after them—they make more noise than if the king came there—with all his clarions and many other minstrels.' The archbishop stood up for 'good, delectable' songs but Thorpe said that Christ's followers 'joy greatly to withdraw their ears and all their wits and members from all worldly delight and from all earthly solace.' Others criticized the luxury in which certain aristocratic pilgrims travelled, saying that a holy life rather than holy places were essential for salvation.

Before departure, pilgrims with means made a will which also specified how their goods were to be administered in their absence. During this time the goods could not be taken even by court order and feudal obligations were suspended. From early in the twelfth century, the typical pilgrim dressed like a friar in a sackcloth habit which sometimes had a cowl. Often the habit was grey with an embossed cross. A soft leather purse, containing a food tin and money, was attached to the belt. Pilgrims carried a metal-tipped staff, wore a large-brimmed hat and sometimes had a cape or scarf. On return from the more famous pilgrim sites, some carried on their hat a symbol or badge: from the Holy Land a palm leaf of Jerico; from Santiago di Compostella, which was near the Iberian inlets, a scallop shell, and from Rome keys. Pilgrims received a church blessing and from the eleventh century the staff was given in a ceremony which resembled those for knights bound for the Crusades. The pilgrim robe and accessories were attributed symbolic significance, as if the pilgrims had entered an order of the church. Indeed the German monastic reformer Wilhelm of Hirnau distinguished five groups in the church: bishops and priests; monks; laity; virgins; pilgrims and hermits. Some considered that, if it was impossible to become a monk, the next best thing was to be a pilgrim.

There were risks, however, in the calling. A saying warned that one should never advise anyone to marry, to go to a war or on a pilgrimage because they could turn out badly. Brigands lived from robbing pilgrims. There was an international Mafia at work: at the end of the Middle Ages, Germans marauders were active in north Italy and

English thieves robbed the pilgrims to Santiago di Compostella. On major pilgrim routes prostitutes offered a short cut to Paradise.

If not slaughtered by brigands, pilgrims could be fleeced by innkeepers and merchants. Monks had an obligation to offer hospitality, pure water and fresh bread to pilgrims. As pilgrim numbers grew they were forced to build hospices for them. One of the most famous was that of St Bernard (of Aosta), in the highest and windiest Alpine pass, which was functioning by 1080 and was used by most English, Irish, French and Flemish pilgrims. Its famous rescue dogs are now bred there for sale as pets. Inns provided for those who did not stay at hospices, but the perils involved are suggested by a fourteenth century French phrase book for English travellers: 'There are fleas in the dust under the straw mattress … I've scratched my shoulder until the blood runs' is one sample, and another mentioned mice.

Nevertheless pilgrims never stopped coming to Rome, Europe's most popular pilgrimage destination, although there was a decline towards the end of the first millennium and again in the mid-1280s. Major pilgrim routes, which were sometimes maintained by volunteers as a work of charity, ran through Lyons, then Siena or Bologna. The coastal road through Genoa was less frequented because of the danger of malaria. Hospices were situated at not more than thirty miles from one another as this was the maximum distance which could be covered on foot in a day. Only a minority came on horseback.

A pilgrimage such as that undertaken to the Jubilee of 1500 from Europe's northernmost diocese, Trondheim in Norway, was an education. Trondheim had an imposing cathedral, part Norman-Romanesque and part Gothic. The Jubilee pilgrims, in small boats, followed the route of fishermen taking their dried cod to market, navigating between islands and the coast to Bergen, a trading city dominated by German merchants. There they took an ocean-going ship for the 500 nautical miles to Hamburg. Then waterways led to the largest German city, Cologne, which was also one of Europe' s main pilgrimage sites. The cathedral, still incomplete in 1500, was begun in 1248 to house the relics of the Three Wise Men which had been robbed from Milan at the time of Emperor Frederick Barbarossa. Cologne had sobering memories of another pilgrimage: it was here that, on their return from Rome, St Ursula and her virgin-companions had been slaughtered because Ursula refused to marry the Hun leader. The martyrs' remains were in the city's churches.

Shortly beyond Cologne the group from Trondheim saw the first vineyards on the river slopes. There was also a succession of castles atop the hills and another stood on an island where the Moselle joined the Rhine at Koblenz. Next came Mainz, where Boniface, the Anglo-Saxon monk who had evangelized in this region in the eighth century, had been archbishop, and where, some thirty years earlier, the inventor of printing, Gutenburg, had died. In the distance could be seen the 142–meter high tower of the Gothic cathedral of Strasbourg which had been standing for sixty years.

The final port was Basel where fifty years earlier a council had elected the last rival pope (antipope) Felix V, who was the pious Amadeus VIII of Savoy. Close to the city was the Pilatus peak, so named because it was said that the spirit of Pontius Pilate wandered there in despair. Nearby, a war between Swiss forces and the Habsburgs, in which 22,000 lost their lives, was nearing its end, and beyond the Gothard Pass into Italy the French were fighting the Milanese.

The party from Trondheim avoided these dangers and arrived in Tuscany where olive trees showed that at last they had reached the Mediterranean. Florence was in turmoil. On 23 June the previous year Girolamo Savonarola, the Dominican friar who was a fierce critic of Pope Alexander VI and of local politicians, had been hanged then burned before the Town Hall. The Medici had been expelled, there was a fragile republic. The painter Sandro Botticelli was revered but was old and tormented by Savonarola's dire prophecies.

The trip from fjords surrounded by snowy peaks to sun-drenched Italy had been a cultural and historical education but the climax was still to come. Excitement must have grown steadily during the last 120 miles to Rome. Finally, from a slight rise in the road, they saw the brown walls and many domes of the capital of Christendom. The cry went up: *Ecce Roma!*

A RELIGIOUS THEME PARK?

Pilgrims in the past expected to find in Rome a holy city, but present-day religious tourists might suspect that Rome is a religious theme park or museum for inner-city churches are often empty. There is a plethora of churches because the inner-city population was halved to 140,000 in the thirty years between 1961 and the last census in 1991, and the decrease has since continued. In the twenty years to 1991, the total population remained steady at 2,775,000. The churches are not located where the people live. In some parts of the city's tacky periphery, Mass has to be celebrated in garages, apartments or halls. For the Jubilee there are plans to build in the periphery fifty churches, one of which is specifically to commemorate the occasion. The Californian Jewish architect, Richard Meier, won the international competition for the design of this church; a Japanese Shintoist, Tadeo Ando, was runner-up. A city mission prepared Romans for the Jubilee.

Christians in Rome are involved in fighting drug abuse and helping AIDS victims, immigrants, gypsies, the homeless and the aged, largely through the diocesan agency Caritas. Until his death in October 1997, Caritas was headed by Monsignor Luigi Di Liegro, who took courageous stands on behalf of the needy even if it brought him into conflict with the city administration. Among other examples of dedicated Christian groups in Rome are a parish which has built a church and a school for a 'twin' parish in Kenya and supplies also money and personnel. Another Roman parish has a similar twin in Mozambique. The Sant' Egidio Community works for peace in many trouble spots. Its representatives convinced the Mozambique government and rebels to negotiate, ending the civil war in the former Portuguese colony.

The Sant' Egidio community, founded by students in the late 1960s, was recognized by the Holy See in 1986 as an International Public Association of Laity. Eight thousand of its worldwide membership of 15,000 are in Rome, where it runs soup kitchens and helps the needy including immigrants, for whom it provides training courses. One of its aims is to reduce tension between groups, whether it be arranging financial help for victims of the Bosnian war, mediating in Algeria and for the Kurds, or establishing in Albania health aid centers and university-level training courses for administrators. The meeting of representatives of all religions to pray for peace which Pope John Paul organized in Assisi in 1986 gave rise to accusations of syncretism which dissuaded him from repeating the gesture, but the Sant' Egidio Community has followed it up by yearly inter-religious meetings in different European cities. That held in Bucharest in 1998 opened the way for John Paul's visit there in 1999.

The community continues a Roman tradition of combining concern for human needs with a universal perspective. The founder of the community, Andrea Riccardi, now a university professor of modern church history, wants to unite prayer life with social involvement. 'We aim to evangelize ourselves as well as those furthest from the church,' he has said, 'to serve the poor and work for peace, ecumenism and inter-religous dialogue by living in friendship among ourselves and towards the world.'

The history of Jubilees shows that the Holy See was often involved in dubious politics because of its possession of the Papal States, that some popes were unworthy and many acquiesced in deplorable nepotism, that there was prostitution and executions in Rome, and that its inhabitants had their share of faults. A character of Boccaccio adduced the vices of papal Rome as proof of the church's divine origin, saying that otherwise it would not have survived.

But the church in Rome, if it sometimes caused scandal, could also be edifying, as it had been in its first centuries. Augustine of Hippo contrasted the fanaticism of the Manichees, his first contacts in

Rome, with the charity and moderation of the Christians notable for 'charity in their speech, charity in their dress, charity in their looks. Charity unites them and inspires their acts.' He explained that when in Rome shortly before 388 he had known several Christian groups 'living in charity, sanctity and liberty,' each presided by a person 'eminent for character, prudence and divine knowledge ... they sustain themselves by their own hands. I was told that many practiced fasts of quite amazing severity, not merely taking one meal daily towards night, which is everywhere quite common, but very often continuing for three days or more in succession without food or drink ... With all this, no one is pressed to endure hardships for which they are unfit; nothing is imposed on anyone against their will; nor is anyone condemned by the others because too feeble as they bear in mind how strongly Scripture enjoins charity on all.'

Many pilgrims were grateful to Rome for preserving the faith and those from west, north and central Europe for having brought it to them. Its ritual satisfied huge congregations. At its center was the pope. A Scottish Presbyterian, John Moore, vividly described the solemn blessing by Clement XI at the closure of the 1575 Jubilee: 'It was a remarkably fine day. An immense multitude filled that spaceless and magnificent area [St Peter's Square]. The horse and foot guards were drawn up in their most showy uniform. The Pope, seated in an open portable chair, in all the splendor which his wardrobe could give, with a tiara on his head, was carried out of a large window, which opens in a balcony in front of St Peter's. The silk hangings and gold trappings with which the chair was embellished concealed the men who carried it, so that to those who viewed him from the area below His Holiness seemed to sail forward from the window, self-balanced in the air, like a celestial being. The instant he appeared the music struck up, the bells rang from every church, and the cannon thundered from the castle of St' Angelo in repeated peals.

'During the intervals the Church of St Peter's, the palace of the Vatican, and the banks of the Tiber re-echoed to the acclamations of the populace. At length His Holiness arose from his seat, and an immediate and awful silence ensued. The multitude fell upon their knees, with their hands and eyes raised towards His Holiness as to a benign Deity. After a solemn pause he pronounced the benediction with great fervor, elevating his outstretched arms as high as he could, then closing them together and bringing them back to his breast with a slow motion as if he had got hold of the blessing and was drawing it gently from heaven. Finally he threw his arms open, waving them for some time as if his intention had been to scatter the benediction with impartiality among the people.

'No ceremony can be better calculated for striking the senses and imposing on the understanding than this of the Supreme Pontiff giving the blessing from the balcony of St Peter's. For my own part, if I had not in my early youth received impressions highly unfavorable for the chief actor in this magnificent interlude, I should have been in danger of paying him a degree of respect very inconsistent with the religion in which I was educated.'

The Rome of Philip Neri, Ignatius Loyola and other saints delighted those pilgrims seeking a spiritual tonic. The Rome of austere Pius V (1566–72) impressed a widely-travelled Spaniard, Martin de Azilcueta, who, in 1567, after three years in the city wrote, 'I have seen devotions in other countries but as for that of the Romans I never tire of admiring it. It fills me with stupefaction for I cannot explain such fervor, such indefatigable piety on the part of all.'

Most Roman families were involved in religious guilds or confraternities which grouped members of a trade, such as stonemasons, or those who came together for a religious purpose such as helping the dying. The one most involved in Jubilees was the Arch-Confraternity of Pilgrims and Convalescents but it was not the only one to give hospitality to visitors. There were related confraternities elsewhere in Italy and beyond, and when their members came in their colorful habits on pilgrimage to Rome, members of the corresponding Roman archconfraternities would meet them at the city gates, accompany them to their residences and help them during their stay. All social groups were involved in the confraternities, some of which offered free accommodation to pilgrims. Several still function, although in an attenuated form.

The exaltation of pardon, which had its apotheosis in Jubilees, entered deeply into the culture and remains today. It was seen in the attitude to wrongdoers and in the comparatively humane prisons. Even the scurrilous *A Pilgrimage to the Grand Jubilee*, published in 1700, admitted 'Romans are very generous to the poor,' as is still true. The Englishman John Howard, who disclosed the miserable state of English prisons towards the end of the eighteenth century, spoke well of those in Rome.

In 1644 John Evelyn gave a laudatory report on the Christ Hospital complex in Rome. In the marble-floored infirmary, he wrote, 'the beds are very fair and in the middle is a stately cupola, under which is an altar decked with divers marble statues, all in sight of the sick, who may both hear and see Mass as they lie in their beds.' A school, quarters for orphans and others for five hundred girls, a 'fair and well-stocked' apothecary's shop, a monastery, convent and church completed what he called 'one of the most pious and worthy foundations I ever saw.' Rome hospitals were probably the best in Europe and there were other fine charitable institutions.

A booklet of 1592 by an Englishman who had been a prisoner in Rome had this tribute: 'Any [needy] Christian ... shall be relieved, with all those necessities whereof he is destitute, as apparel, meat and drink, and some money, though it be but little; if he is sick, then shall he be put into hospital where he shall be choicely attended upon, having good lodging, dainty diet, and comfortable physic for the restoring of his health, whether he be Papist or Protestant.'

Despite Romans' shortcomings, some have always given exemplary witness to the Gospel. This is true today also even though, in a larger city, it is not easy to discern it. Neither is it easy to understand the city's past as something other than a curious collage unless one discovers how to read Rome.

READING ROME

Go thou to Rome, at once the Paradise,
The grave, the city and the wilderness.

P. B. Shelley, *Adonais*

THE JEWISH CHAPTER

The Christian presence in Rome is a story of initial intermittent persecution followed by triumph; the Jews have a longer story with many trials and tribulations, often at the hands of Christians whose attitude towards them was wildly ambivalent. In medieval times they were often treated quite well: their skills and industry were appreciated and they were able to build a synagogue. Between 1130 and 1138 there was a Jewish rival pope, Anacletus II, a grandson of a converted Jew of the rich, powerful Roman family, the Pierleoni.

The treatment of Jews worsened during the Renaissance and even more during the Counter-Reformation. The belief that 'perfidious Jews', as the Good Friday liturgy had it until John XXIII removed the phrase, were Christ-killers who continued perversely to resist conversion created a culture of contempt. They were not treated better in many places beyond the Papal States, but every quarter of a century Rome celebrated a Jubilee, which in theory should have meant better treatment. The Jubilee looked back to the Old Testament recommendation to release people from burdens, yet for over three centuries Jews continued to be locked each evening in a walled ghetto or, as it was called, an enclosure.

Although no longer obliged to do so, some of Rome's 15,000 Jews still live in what is called the ghetto. Now it has no walls and the term is applied to an area larger than the original site. That was confined to four city blocks behind where the synagogue now stands opposite the Tiber island. It was a proto-Manhattan, as buildings had nowhere to go but up: there were seven-storey buildings accommodating about 3200 inhabitants within the four blocks. When, in the second half of the sixteenth century, all Jews in the Papal States had to transfer to Ancona or Rome, the area was somewhat enlarged to accommodate between 6000–8000 people.

The original boundary of the ghetto, via del Portico d'Ottavia, has some houses with traces of Renaissance facades, but most of the area is scruffy apart from restaurants specializing in Roman Jewish cuisine. Stumps of classical columns of the Portico d'Ottavia rear from the pavement, giving an impression of an upsurge of buried memories. As elsewhere in Rome, visitors walk above earlier settlements. In the case of the ghetto, this is partly because there was extensive rebuilding in the first decade of the 20th century. Once the city's largest fishmarket was located beneath the remains of the Portico which was built in 161 BCE, twelve years after the first Jewish embassy came from Palestine to request Rome's protection. Jewish merchants probably came from Alexandria and elsewhere to live in Rome in the following century: in 59 BCE Cicero spoke of Jewish inhabitants. It was the earliest Jewish settlement in Europe. Julius Caesar favored the Jews of Rome by authorizing their yearly contribution to the Temple of Jerusalem and his successor Augustus was even more liberal.

When Paul of Tarsus arrived in Rome, there was a thriving Jewish community of perhaps 30,000 with 13 synagogues, mainly in the traders' district of Trastevere (which means: 'on the other side of the Tiber'). Their sites have not been identified but the oldest remains of a European synagogue are at Ostia on the Rome seafront. Some Roman Christians, who may have participated in the first Pentecost during a visit to Jerusalem, met Paul on his arrival. Soon there were clashes in the synagogues because, while Paul spoke of Christ, there was disagreement as to whether he represented a new strand in Judaism or was the founder of a different religion.

However, the distinction between Jews and the followers of Christ was clear enough to Emperor Nero when he sought scapegoats after Rome burnt in 64. He had Peter and Paul and other Christians killed but no followers of Judaism. Three years later the Jews of Palestine rebelled against Rome which eventually destroyed Jerusalem and then obliged Roman Jews to pay a yearly tribute to the Temple of the Capitoline Jupiter rather than to the devastated Temple of Jerusalem.

The Jewish prisoners of war paraded in the triumphal procession of the Emperor Titus bearing the seized vessels of the Temple such as the seven-branched candlestick, the golden table and the horns or trumpets used by the priests to announce, among other things, the Jubilee. The procession is represented in bas-relief on the Arch of Titus in the Forum. Two of the leaders of the resistance in Jerusalem were forced to participate and one of them, Simon bar Giora, was beheaded after it. Many of the prisoners were among the 15,000 workers who built over a period of ten months the Flavian amphi-theatre better known as the Colosseum; some Roman Jewish families claim to be their descendants.

Jerusalem was renamed Aelia Capitolina, but Jews in Rome retained their rights. A rabbinical school, a Yeshiva, functioned there and it became the spiritual center of Jewry in the western Mediterranean. Emperor Alexander Severus was so pro-Jewish that he was nicknamed the Chief Rabbi. After the Emperors became Christian, however, there was often hostility.

In 1215 the Fourth Lateran Council decreed that Jews had to wear identification, a yellow circle for men and for women two blue stripes on their veil. During Carnival, Jews were forced to race on their hands and knees after the horse race along the central Corso thoroughfare. Some Jews were prominent in the medical profession, the only one they were allowed to practice, and one became the first doctor for a pope.

For the Jewish community, the papal election was a lottery. In 1402 Benedict IV decreed that they were to have all the rights of Roman citizens, but within a few years, they were harshly treated again. Martin V (1417–31) gave protection but his successor Eugenius IV (1431–47) segregated them and excluded them from most trades and law studies. Humanist popes such as Nicholas V and Pius II were comparatively tolerant, but friction was generated within the community after Alexander VI (1492–1503) obliged it to accept some of the Jews expelled from Spain.

Leo X (1513–21), the second son of Lorenzo the Magnificent, was princely in all respects from encouragement of the arts to liberality in money matters. He employed Jewish physicians, established a university chair of Hebrew, introduced laws to protect Jewish bankers and permitted reprinting of the Talmud. During his pontificate Jewish art and scholarship flourished in Rome.

However, when the papacy began to combat the Reformation, Jews in Rome suffered. The Roman Inquisition and the Jesuit Order wanted to repress heresy and galvanize the church. At the Jewish New Year in 1553 copies of the Talmud were burnt in the Campo dei Fiori square. In 1555, under Paul IV, all Jews were ordered to live in an area of about seven acres, subject to occasional Tiber flooding, where only a portion of them had lived before. For just over 300 years the gates were shut on them daily at sundown.

The 'Iron Pope', Sixtus V (1585–1590), who was considered too severe by many Romans, exempted Jews from wearing distinctive clothes, allowed them to practice any trade and to build all the schools and synagogues they needed, and employed Jewish medical doctors. Some other popes were lenient but for most of three centuries the Jews were punitively taxed, their work opportunities were limited to money-lending, the rag trade or running second-hand shops, and they were obliged to attend sermons designed to bring about their conversion. Nobles often guided Jewish converts during their instruction and gave them their surnames when they were baptised. The church where they had to attend sermons stands in the Portico d'Ottavia. Many began to put wax in their ears to block out the preaching but then police inspected the congregation to ensure there were no earplugs. Towards the Tiber, another church, San Gregorio in Divina Pietà, has a facade inscription from Isaiah in Hebrew reproving Jews for ignoring the Lord's message.

Mutual aid societies helped the Jews to survive. These sodalities or confraternities not only provided for the needy but kept Jewish education and culture alive. A papal decree had specified that there be only one synagogue but there was discord between Jews of different rites such as the Sicilian and the Catalan whose adherents had been driven out of Spanish domains. A compromise was reached by allowing five different places of worship within the one building. But the restrictions on the Jews' activities and the cramped conditions of the dank ghetto tended to reinforce prejudice against its inhabitants.

Roman Jews achieved liberty and equality briefly when Napoleon's forces conquered Rome in 1798; discrimination returned with the election of Pius VII in 1800; conditions improved when the French ruled for five years from 1809 and worsened again with the return of Pius. But on the night of 17 April 1848, the Passover, the gates of the ghetto were thrown open by order of Pius IX. The walls were destroyed.

Shortly afterwards Pius IX fled from Rome and a republic was established which recognized the equal rights of the Jews. When, with the help of French forces, Pius returned in 1850, he had abandoned his liberal sympathies and Jews were again ordered to live in the ghetto, although its walls were not rebuilt. Once again Jews were not allowed to own property or run businesses with Christians.

The papal treatment of Jews received international attention because of the case of Edgardo Mortara, who was born in Bologna to Jewish parents but was raised as a Catholic in Rome. When Edgardo was six, papal police arrived at his home with orders to take him away because a former Mortara family maid had claimed that she baptised Edgardo shortly after his birth when he was in danger of dying. The police took Edgardo away because a Christian could not be raised by Jews: he was placed in a Rome institution which prepared Jews for conversion. He became a monk and died in a Belgian abbey in 1940, shortly before the Nazis arrived and rounded up those with Jewish blood.

The church did not permit baptisms without parental consent but nevertheless this had taken place. In church law it was illicit but still valid. Pius IX refused to surrender Edgardo. Cavour, the Prime Minister of the Kingdom of Sardinia who was angling to have the capital of a united Italy in Rome, successfully exploited the case to influence international public opinion against the papacy. As the Italians now controlled Bologna, previously part of the Papal States, Sardinian officials brought a charge against the Inquisitor who had ordered the seizure of Edgardo. There were various versions of the story of the housemaid at the time Edgardo was baptised, and various interpretations of her motives, but the Sardinians lost their case. Church laws had been applied correctly even if those of nature were flouted.

Discrimination against Jews in Rome ended when Italian forces occupied the city in 1870. In 1904 an imposing synagogue, which is a feature of the Rome skyline, was erected by the Tiber; John Paul II was to visit it in 1986 and to speak of Jews as 'elder brothers in the faith.'

Something worse than the papal regime was in store when the Fascist government introduced racist legislation: religious discrimination was replaced by racial persecution. Pius XI offset the growing racism of the Fascist regime by asserting that 'spiritually we are all Semites.' During World War II over 4000 Jews found refuge from Nazi-Fascists in the Vatican, in the papal villa at Castelgandolfo, and in 155 Roman religious institutions. Some Jews were given baptismal certificates or clerical clothing to save them. The first postwar congress of the delegates of Italy's Jewish communities expressed to Pius XII the 'profound sense of gratitude which animates all Jews for the proofs of human brotherhood furnished them by the church during the years of the persecutions.' The wartime rabbi of the Roman Jewish community, Rabbi Zolli, became a Catholic, changing his first name from Israele to Eugenio out of admiration for Pius XII (Eugenio Pacelli).

In September 1943 the German police chief in Rome, SS Colonel Herbert Kappler, had threatened deportations unless the Jewish community provided fifty kilograms of gold within 36 hours. The Vatican offered to help the Jews meet the demand but they managed to do so by themselves; all the same, in October the Nazis deported 2091 Jews in 18 sealed cattle trucks to German concentration camps. Very few were to return. In March the following year, 73 Jews were shot, along with 262 other Roman citizens, in reprisal for the killing of German military police by a Partisan bomb in central Rome. The Germans killed and buried the victims on the outskirts of Rome near Jewish catacombs of the first century: like the Christians they did not cremate their dead.

SUB-TEXT: THE CATACOMBS

The earliest Christians in Rome, such as Peter, were buried in pagan necropolises, 'cities of the dead'. Later some wealthy Romans let their Christian slaves be buried on their property or, if they themselves converted, opened their burial grounds to their Christian friends. This seems to have been the case of the family which owned the property where the catacombs of Domitilla are situated. Flavia Domitilla, niece of the Emperor Domitian, was a first century martyr whose family gave this property to Christians. Early in the third century, the church was given a burial ground, probably by the family of the martyr Cecilia, who was to become the patroness of music. 'Cemetery' meant 'dormitory': Christians believed their dead were simply sleeping in the Lord until the resurrection.

Initially burials took place in surface tombs, some of which had additional underground chambers for these were considered better protected. Tombs were not recycled; when more space was needed the underground chambers were extended into long galleries which were sometimes linked. As they could not go underground beyond the surface boundaries, they were excavated at ever deeper levels. Many-tiered galleries provided miles of shelf space within a small area. In some sites there are as many as eight levels from floor to roof, in which niches were cut according to the size of the corpse. The prevalent volcanic stone, compact tufa, lent itself to this because it can be hacked away in chunks like Parmesan cheese. The corpse, in a winding sheet, was laid in the niche and closed off hermetically with tiles or a marble slab. These catacombs had air vents and skylights, and fixtures beside the tombs to hold lamps or torches. Larger recesses were used for family tombs, while there were rooms which could take up to sixty people for the eucharist. Christians did not hide in the catacombs during persecution as the Roman authorities knew their location, but in at least one case Christians were trapped there during a eucharistic celebration.

The usual explanation of the word 'catacomb' is that it derives from a quarry site on the Appian Way, near where the St Sebastian basilica now stands, called *catacumbas*, or from the word for a dip in the road at that point. There are catacombs in other places such as Tunisia, Malta, Syracuse and Naples, but Rome has at least seventy Christian and six Jewish catacombs; some scholars say these latter were the models for the Christian ones. Four are listed in the telephone directory and one runs beneath the Saudi Arabian embassy.

Most pagans chose cremation but some were commemorated by mausoleums or tombs placed near a major road because they believed they would live as long as passers-by remembered them. The heaviest concentration of these was on the Appian Way which ran south to the port of Brindisi, gateway to the East.

Pagans commemorated the birthday of the deceased, but Christians commemorated the death day, since for them it was birth into eternal life. There seems to have been similarity, however, between the pagan and Christian commemorative meal which was a combination of wake and picnic. Since burial had to be outside city walls, those commemorating the dead had probably come a long way and would be hungry and thirsty. Structures at the St Sebastian catacomb suggest that a repast was sometimes taken on the terraces above the mausoleums. The amount of wine which flowed may have been a constant whether the ceremony was pagan or Christian; some catacomb frescoes suggest it was copious.

The Christian inscriptions reflect assurance about the afterlife. A husband pays tribute to his worthy wife Aurelia who had died at the age of 28: 'I loved her for nine years without her causing me any bitterness. Keep well, dear. Be in peace with the blessed souls. Stay serene in Christ!' Even the names reflect their beliefs: Hope (*Spes*), Reborn (*Renatus*), Resurrection (*Anastasia*) and Pentecost. For Christians the darkness of the catacombs was illuminated by an otherworldly light.

Their wall paintings, stucco reliefs and mosaics are poignant even if mediocre: bread and wine are depicted in a basket above a fish, symbol of the Christ they become; Lazarus responds uncertainly to the new life Christ has given; Moses is present, as well as Peter and Paul. The style is the same as that of pagan Rome but the subjects are new. The first depiction of Mary is in the catacomb of Priscilla on via Salaria. Perhaps because it is behind a high wall and is run by nuns, this catacomb gives the idea that it is still family land. A certain Priscilla, who is buried on the site, is believed to have made this former quarry available in the second half of the second century. She was of the prominent Acli family, one of whose members, Acilius Glabro, was exiled by the Emperor Domitian for what seems to have been his Christian faith. Several martyrs and two popes, Marcellinus (296–303) and Marcellus (308–309), are buried there.

Under the direction of Callistus, a former slave who had served a harsh prison sentence in Sardinia, a public cemetery for Christians was constructed early in the third century. At that time Callistus was a deacon, one of the bishop of Rome's main collaborators, but became pope himself in 217. He spent twenty years supervising the excavation of galleries which at their greatest depth are about fifty feet underground. Measuring 150 by 55 feet, they are in a grid pattern with seven parallel passageways and each has up to eight tiers. They constitute a unique archive of the early church: nine popes, nearly all martyrs, were buried there—Pontian, Anterus, Fabian, Lucius I, Stephen I, Sixtus II, Dionysius, Felix I and Eutychian.

Sixtus II was killed in a private cemetery off the Appian Way. Of Greek extraction, he was elected in 257 and, when not dodging the imperial police during a period of persecution, he improved relations with the churches of North Africa and Asia Minor. On 6 August 258, he was addressing Christians gathered in a private cemetery when police broke in and beheaded him. Blood drenched Stephen's episcopal chair. Later that day, two of the three deacons were executed, and the third, Lawrence, who was the church of Rome's treasurer, was grilled to death a few days later. At least that was the traditional version of the event, but it has been modified: it is claimed now that Lawrence was not grilled but decapitated for refusing to disclose the church's wealth with which it sustained in Rome about 1500 widows and orphans. This would justify the phrase attributed to him, 'The poor are my wealth.' It is thought that during this persecution, to protect them, the remains of Peter and Paul were transferred temporarily from their tombs to the catacombs now under the St Sebastian church, where many third century graffiti in honor of the two apostles are still visible.

After Christianity was recognized in 313, it was presumed that Roman culture and Christianity would meld and less attention was given to the catacombs. But an apostate emperor, Julian, emerged and, although Christian emperors succeeded him, Pope Damasus (366–384) felt the need to stress that Christians should be as proud of their early heroes, the martyrs, as pagan Romans were of Romulus, Remus, Julius Caesar and others. To draw attention to the martyrs, he had rubble cleared from the catacombs, authorized liturgical ceremonies there and labelled the tombs with marble slabs whose handsome lettering was invented for the purpose by a friend, Dionysis Philocalus. The rhyming texts were written by Damasus. One begins 'Here lie together a shoal of saints' and ends 'I, Damasus, confess that I would like to have been buried here but I did not want to disturb the saints' ashes.' With his mother and sister, he was buried nearby.

As a student in Rome, Jerome, who had not yet begun his translation of the Bible but was a gourmet interested in girls and a legal career, used to visit the catacombs on Sundays with fellow students: 'Often we could enter these crypts which have been hollowed out of the depths of the earth and which, along the passageway's walls, contain corpses,' he reported. 'Everything was so dark that the prophet's saying 'Let them go down living to hell' (a quote from Virgil's *Aeneid*) seemed almost to have been fulfilled. Here and there a ray of light from above relieved the horror of blackness, yet in a way you imagined it was not so much a window as a funnel pierced by the light itself as it descended. Then we would walk back gingerly, wrapped in unseeing night, with Virgil's line recurring to us, "Everywhere dread fills the heart, the very silence dismays."'

The catacombs were at the mercy of invaders. In the mid-seventh century many martyrs' remains were brought into the churches within the walls because beyond them invaders smashed funerary slabs, robbed the catacombs and left them filled with rubble. Their memory gradually faded until the beginning of the seventeenth century when a Maltese archaeologist, Antonio Bosio, located thirty catacombs in Rome. They aroused interest only for a limited time because the papacy was more interested in showing its continuity with imperial Rome.

However, in the nineteenth century, anti-papal movements found inspiration in ancient, republican Rome and the papacy turned to the city's Christian past as proof that it could survive persecution. The catacombs were rediscovered once again: the memory of some had been lost altogether while the location of others was known only imprecisely. The key figure was Giovanni Battista De Rossi, born in 1822, whose father collaborated with Cardinal Ercole Consalvi, the secretary of state. Educated by the Jesuits, De Rossi was intrigued by the writings of Antonio Bosio but his father forced him to study law as was the family tradition. Moreover his father prohibited Giovanni from visiting the catacombs because he shared contemporaries' fears that they were unsafe, unhealthy hideouts for brigands and lairs of dangerous animals. A Jesuit convinced the father to relent but De Rossi did risk his life several times: he was lost for a period in the labyrinthine corridors and was nearly buried twice when sections of the catacombs collapsed.

Before undertaking field work, De Rossi built up a reputation as a rigorous scholar, studying epigraphs, topography, early Christian writers and pre-seventh century pilgrim guidebooks which had not been available to Bosio. He was assisted by his brother Stefano, a geographer.

Since the Middle Ages, the received wisdom was that the catacombs of Callistus lay under the St Sebastian basilica, but De Rossi's studies had convinced him that they were under the adjacent vineyard. As the vineyard owners made more cellar space for their wine barrels, they threw out the marble fragments they encountered. De Rossi found among them a broken slab which read ... *nelius martyr*. He was certain it was part of the inscription on the tomb of Pope Cornelius (251–253). And early Christian sources specified that Cornelius had been buried in the Callistus catacombs.

His intuition confirmed, De Rossi went to Pius IX, who had been elected only three years earlier. He had encouraged De Rossi but also baited him frequently about the 'pipe dreams of archaeologists.' De Rossi tried desperately to convince Pius IX to buy the vineyard to allow excavations. But Pius, who enjoyed teasing, said that there was no way he could be persuaded to buy it. De Rossi was crestfallen. Pius told a collaborator that De Rossi left him 'like a whipped cat,' but before the young archaeologist departed from the papal palace the pope got word to him that he would buy the vineyard.

Four years later, after clearing away the detritus which blocked the stairs and corridors, De Rossi found the tomb of Cornelius and the remainder of the inscribed slab. That same year he discovered also fragments of an inscription by Pope Damasus in honor of Pope St Eusebius (310). In 1854, elsewhere in the Callistus complex, De Rossi found the crypt where no fewer than nine third century popes were buried.

Because of this momentous discovery, Pius IX visited the catacomb. As he held the marble fragments with his predecessors' names, his cheeks flushed and tears filled his eyes. He asked, 'Are these really the funerary slabs of my predecessors who lie here?'

'They're simply pipe dreams,' replied De Rossi, 'pipe dreams of an archaeologist.'

'Oh, you're really twisting the knife, De Rossi,' said Pius, realizing that sometimes the baiter is bit.

This discovery, plus identification of the nearby tomb of St Cecilia, the third century martyr who is the patron of music, were De Rossi's greatest coups. His work created international excitement; among other things it provided inspiration for the best-selling novel by Henryk Sienkiewicz, *Quo Vadis*. De Rossi continued working fruitfully at St Callistus and other catacombs and wrote a monumental work on underground Christian Rome. This explorer of the catacombs died at the age of 71 on 20 September 1894. Not the least of De Rossi's achievements was to create a special team of catacomb excavators. His first workmen were recruited from the agricultural laborers in the Appian Way zone but they were inexpert and often damaged the remains. Those they did not damage they were inclined to steal and sell to unscrupulous antique dealers. To avoid this, De Rossi created a squad of diggers, mostly recruited from the mountainous Abruzzo region, who became employees of the Holy See. There is still such a squad, which recalls the one which worked for Callistus and is depicted in the catacombs.

Moreover, De Rossi argued successfully for the permanent presence there of a religious community. The aim was to provide custodians but it also served as a reminder that this was a religious as well as an archaeological site. Again the liturgy was celebrated there as in the first centuries. For some years, Salesian Order priests have been installed at St Callistus.

De Rossi had an unexpected vindication in 1991 when a workman in the St Callistus complex noted a horseshoe-shaped pattern in a certain grassy zone. Soundings showed that the grass was shorter in the horseshoe-shaped portion because it was growing above brick walls. De Rossi had suggested that this was the site of one of the fourth century basilicas built with funds provided by Emperor Constantine and which was mentioned in early pilgrim guidebooks. However, after the seventh century invasions no one knew its exact location because the invaders had reduced it almost to its foundations, which were gradually interred. Twentieth century archaeologists had searched for it in another part of the St Callistus complex. In 1994 tests by the Pontifical Commission of Sacred Archaeology suggested that De Rossi had been right once more. The excavations may be completed in time for the Jubilee, which will highlight the catacombs at the same time as it draws attention to the martyrs of this century. Five catacombs are open to the public and an additional one will be opened for the first time in the year 2000. There is concern that too many visitors may damage the catacombs but alternative itineraries are being developed within them to reduce the wear and tear.

HALFWAY TO HEAVEN

Before imperial recognition of Christianity in 313, there were no Christian church buildings in Rome. Evidence of the Christian life at that time is found underground in the catacombs but it was not exactly an undergound church, even if not recognized. Except during the periods of persecution, Christians lived as other Romans and met to celebrate the eucharist in their houses. They did not want to be distinguished except by their more charitable behavior. They did not want temples because each of them considered him—or herself a temple of the Holy Spirit.

There was a startling change, therefore, when Constantine built imposing meeting places for Christians, oblong halls with a double colonnade and apse, an architectural form known as a basilica. He also provided, not only in Italy but elsewhere in the Mediterranean region and the Middle East, lands to supply revenue for their upkeep. Christians, who had not had any buildings set aside specifically for their meetings, suddenly found themselves with edifices which are huge even by today's standards.

A paradoxical aspect of this change was that, in the process, what had been in the open went underground. Roman law allowed friends to bury those who had been crucified. After Peter's crucifixion in Nero's chariot racecourse, he was buried in the nearby pagan necropolis on the slopes of the Vatican hill. Because of the high water level, no catacombs were possible there. Peter's open-air tomb was always tended with care and eventually was protected by a low wall. A shrine-like structure was built above it.

Constantine decided to honor Peter by building a basilica above this shrine, situated in a city of the dead, the houses of which had the names of the deceased affixed to the facades. Constantine had all the houses and monuments sliced through, except for that of Peter, and packed with earth to provide a base for the basilica, at the same time levelling part of the Vatican Hill because the building was to occupy more space than the former necropolis. The top of the shrine pierced the floor of the basilica and was its focal point.

It is still the focal point of the present basilica, which replaced the original one between the sixteenth and seventeenth centuries. Visitors look down towards it at the altar of the Confession and come still closer if they descend inside the basilica to the lower level or grottoes where the tombs of many popes are found. Better still is to enter the excavations at the side of the basilica, as is possible in small groups. The immediate area of St Peter's tomb is enclosed in transparent casing, but close to it are various tombs decorated with Christian motifs and streets of pagan house tombs, a few of which have Egyptian or Etruscan decorations. Here visitors come face to face with life and death in ancient Rome.

Admiration for the present basilica is tinged with regret for the indulgence scandal which raised funds for it. For those who expect intimacy it is a disappointment, but if a side chapel, such as that of the Blessed Sacrament, is closed off it has the feel of a small church. St Peter's power and glory is for public occasions, for the rolling applause as a pope proceeds down the central nave. It comes into its own when congregations top ten thousand.

The interior is so well proportioned that initially one is not aware of its size. Yet many architects worked on it for over a century and Michelangelo's design was altered by lengthening the nave. It is only from side-on that one can appreciate the poise of his cupola in all its serene beauty.

There are a few traces of the first St Peter's, including, above the central portal looking out to the square from the vestibule, a restored Giotto fresco of the barque of Peter dating from 1298, the central bronze doors made between 1433 and 1445, and the round porphyry marble slab on which Charlemagne knelt on Christmas Eve 800 to be crowned as the first Holy Roman Emperor. Then it was near the altar; now it is in the central nave close to the entrance.

Another memorial of the earliest years is the obelisk in St Peter's Square which was a marker in Nero's chariot racecourse. It is the only thing extant which Peter himself would have seen. At that time it stood to the left of the present basilica but in 1586 Sixtus V decided to make it, after appropriate exorcism, the centerpiece of the square. It was the first obelisk raised in modern times; 900 men with 140 horses and 46 windlasses were engaged in the task for over four months. All spectators were ordered under pain of death to maintain absolute silence when it was being pulled into position. However one of them, a sailor, who saw that the ropes were smoking and would soon snap, cried '*Aigua ae corde*', Genoese for 'Water on the ropes.' This shrank and taughtened them. As the sailor was from Bordighera, near Genoa, in gratitude Sixtus V commanded that henceforth the palms used in St Peter's on Palm Sunday should be bought in Bordighera—as is still done.

The basilica is a mine of such stories. For instance, one of the monuments in the left-hand nave is a magnificent bronze tomb of Innocent VIII (1485–1492) by Antonio Pollaiulo, the only monument transferred from the original St Peter's. The pope is shown holding the relic of a lance given to him by Sultan Bajazet, who alleged it had pierced Christ's side. Rome accepted the gift somewhat gingerly, both because of Bajazet's fearful reputation and because there were already two other lances in European cities for which the same claim had been made. However, the inscription on Innocent's tomb praised Bajazet for his gift, though after his death it was modified, as can still be seen, to describe him as *tyrannus*—tyrant. Truth will out, given enough time.

Close by is a monument with portraits of the last three members of the royal House of Stuart who lie in the grottoes below: the Old Pretender, Bonnie Prince Charlie and Cardinal Henry, who all spent many years in Rome. Near the entrance in the opposite nave is Michelangelo's *Pietà* statue protected now by a transparent casing in case anyone wants to emulate Lazlo Toth by taking a hammer to it. In the central nave is the dignified bronze statue of St Peter whose toe is worn smooth by the touch of countless pilgrims. There is a dispute whether it is a thirteenth century work by Arnolfo di Cambio or is a much earlier sculpture of a philosopher. For the Jubilee, St Peter's 6000 square meters facade was cleaned and repaired after damage by atmospheric pollution and acid rain. The first such cleaning since its completion in 1616 took place only in 1985–86 but, a pointer to the acceleration of atmospheric degeneration, it is foreseen that another will be needed after a further five years.

The layout of St Paul's Outside the Walls is like that of the first St Peter's. The original was destroyed by a fire in 1823 and, after an international subscription, was rebuilt by 1854. When the basilica was burnt, excavations were made around the tomb of St Paul, but they were not completed in the way those of St Peter's tomb were in 1949. Paul was beheaded nearby and his body was taken by Christians for burial on this site. The church which Constantine had built over his grave was enlarged by later emperors.

The present basilica, which is down-river from St Peter's in an unattractive zone, has a heavy, reconstructed air, but the original basilica's triumphal arch decorated by fine mosaics, and its beautiful cloister, have been preserved intact.

St John Lateran is not built above the tomb of an apostle but is an imperial foundation. Emperor Constantine had it built near the city wall over the remains of the barracks of the emperor's private guards. It is on the opposite side of Rome from St Peter's because Constantine was not ready to upset pagan sensibilities by having a Christian assembly hall in the center of Rome; he preferred to build a new Christian city in Constantinople (Istanbul).

St John's is the cathedral of Rome, whose bishop is the pope but, in fact, it is the seat of his cardinal vicar. The basilica had to be rebuilt after being ravaged by the Vandals, was then destroyed by an earthquake and twice burnt down. It was left unroofed while the papacy was in Avignon. Francesco Borromini restored it in the four years before the Jubilee of 1650 and, apart from the eighteenth century facade, it remains substantially unchanged. It is imposing but somewhat heavy as if to symbolise an august institution responding to the Reformation. More attractive are its thirteenth century cloister and the separate fifth century baptistry with intriguing mosaics. Close by is the Scala Santa, supposedly the Holy Stairs up which Jesus approached Pontius Pilate, which explains their alternative name of Pilate's Steps. Tradition held that St Helena brought them from the Holy Land but there is no evidence for this. They lead to a chapel with fine mosaics.

St Mary Major is the smallest and most beautiful of the four original Jubilee basilicas and the only one not related to Constantine. It was built to honor Mary after the Council of Ephesus (431) had pronounced that she was the Mother of God. Its fifth and thirteenth century mosaics are aesthetically and theologically noteworthy. Among its treasures are what was traditionally considered part of the manger in Bethlehem, and some relics of Thomas Becket which have received scientific verification. It has Rome's highest belltower (76 meters) and on the balcony it is possible to see the facade mosaics from close-up. Its tomb of Gian Lorenzo Bernini, covered by a simple stone slab inscribed 'Joannes Laurentius Bernini, Glory of Art and the City / Here humbly lies,' is touching in its simplicity compared to the showy monuments he created for others.

Philip Neri (1515–1594) embodied the joy which should characterize Jubilees. He combined pilgrimages with picnics and enjoyed them so much that he popularized the practice of visiting, in addition to the four original basilicas, three additional ones: St Sebastian, Holy Cross of Jerusalem and St Lawrence. Since his time, many pilgrimages embrace all seven. With his companions, Neri would go to St Peter's on the evening before visiting the other six churches. The following morning they would set out early along the via Ostia to St Paul's which was set among wheat fields. Then they went across country to the St Sebastian basilica, where Philip had often prayed alone and visited the catacombs. Those who needed to attend confession did so, then all took the eucharist during a Mass accompanied by polyphonic music, perhaps by Palestrina. The party went singing along the

Appian Way, enjoyed brunch in a vineyard, then reached the Lateran before the sun was at its hottest. On leaving the Lateran, they climbed the Holy Stairs on their knees. It was only a stone's throw to Holy Cross of Jerusalem with its reminders of the Passion, after which they followed the city wall to St Lawrence's, shaded by tall cypresses. When it was cooler they retraced their steps past Holy Cross and St John's to St Mary Major where the day closed with more Palestrina music and the hymn *Salve Regina.*

The St Sebastian basilica has been mentioned in connection with the catacombs beneath it. Sebastian was an officer of the Pretorian guard who was killed because of his faith; he became a favorite subject for Renaissance painters. What are believed to be his remains have been brought up from the catacombs to the baroque church which bears his name.

Holy Cross in Jerusalem was built within an imperial palace to house the objects which Emperor Constantine's mother, Helena, is supposed to have brought back from the Holy Land, including fragments of the cross on which Christ was crucified, two thorns of his crown, a nail and the bar of the good thief's cross. These are found in the finely decorated chapel of St Helena which is said to be built above earth she brought from Golgotha. St Lawrence Outside the Walls was originally built by Constantine to honor the deacon who was decapitated because he would not disclose information about the funds of the church and deny his faith. His headless body had been brought to the catacombs on this site in 258. The original church was rebuilt in the sixth century, as it was a drawcard for pilgrims, and in the thirteenth was extended so harmoniously that it is not easy to identify its seams.

RESHAPING ROME

Popes were wholly responsible for Jubilees before the twentieth century but now, although popes promulgate them, civil authorities have to pick up most of the bill and look bad if they flop. The Rome municipality, the Lazio regional assembly and the national government, which are all involved in Jubilee 2000, are accused of being at the service of the Vatican. Vatican officials, on the other hand, have complained about the civil authorities' sluggishness: two curial cardinals, Roger Etchegaray and Rosalio Castillo Lara, said that preparations began too late, while the first secretary-general of the Central Committee for the Jubilee, Archbishop Sergio Sebastiani, compared Italy unfavorably in this respect to Israel. Perhaps he was expected to ensure that more progress was made: in November 1997 he was replaced by Archbishop Crescenzio Sepe.

Francesco Rutelli, the handsome mayor responsible for coordinating the state's preparations, had a Radical-Green Party background but also a Jesuit education and realized that his political future was tied to a successful Jubilee. He promised that there would be no kickbacks from public works contracts but his good intentions did not resolve the organizational difficulties. The Jubilee made Rome more acutely aware of the problems of being a national capital enclosing an international capital.

Normally Rome is hard-pressed to handle about 15 million tourist presences annually. The figure is based on nights spent in a hotel; if a tourist spends three nights, it is counted as three presences. Official estimates were that the number would almost double in the year 2000.

Romans, mindful of the traffic snarls and other inconveniences during preparations for the World Soccer Cup in 1990, fear that they will be doing more penance than anyone else for the Jubilee. They complain of undergoing hellish problems to facilitate the entry of others to heaven. Critics of the Jubilee are legion. Alberto Ronchey, formerly Minister for Culture, says that he will leave Rome during it. He suggested that Rome follow the example of Saudi Arabia which sets a quota for pilgrims from each Muslim country so that the total does not exceed two million and has built a residential complex for them halfway between Jiddah and Mecca. In earlier centuries, he pointed out, some protection was provided by the difficulty of travel but now in 24 hours jets can deposit in Rome people from anywhere in the world and the city will be submerged. Already, Ronchey added, 220,000 cars crowd into the central city daily, although it was not built for automobiles and cannot be modified for them. It will certainly be damaged by the Jubilee, he concluded, but it is not clear who will benefit from it.

'The Vatican, a huge power which dominates Rome and its administrators, has decided to hold a Jubilee,' wrote Guido Ceronetti, a poet, translator of the Bible and curmudgeon. 'No one opposes it. No one is perplexed even though the [Catholic] Christian Democrat Party is no longer in power.' He called the Jubilee an 'inhuman project' and placed a curse upon it. Later he returned to the argument describing the Jubilee as a 'calendar hoax [because the third millennium begins from 2001] and a religious absurdity for if the Word became flesh how can a date be assigned to such an event?' Plans for re-evangelization triggered by such an event, said Ceronetti, are 'suitable only for tourist pamphlets.' It would make Gospel sense to emphasise the Messianic aspect 'but this requires acceptance of the abhorred tragic character of our existence.' He acknowledged a huge spiritual hunger in the West-which-eats, but only crooks, he charged, could talk of a spiritual event when the Jubilee means, in fact, an occasion to relaunch Rome as a tourist venue, a kind of Olympics of the holy card, of pizza from the papal stall, and warned that 'a fake spiritual event provokes [divine] punishment.' He forecast that it will be a banquet for bag snatchers, thieves, drug traffickers, as well as those who sell white and black flesh, and predicted that many who arrive as pilgrims will remain as illegal immigrants.

Mario Pirani, a journalist, suggested that the only way to prevent a new barbarian invasion would be to reach an agreement with the

106 national Jubilee committees on the numbers they can send and exact a tax from visitors to meet the additional expenses for police, health and garbage services.

The novelist Enzo Bettiza compared the Jubilee with the Parallel Action of Robert Musil's novel, *The Man without Qualities*. The Parallel Action was a kind of Austrian Jubilee to promote peace, which was to culminate in 1918 with the seventieth anniversary of the advent of Emperor Franz Joseph. It was a hot-air balloon of rhetoric, a black hole of banality which ended, ironically, not with peace but war. Bettiza warned that, despite its intentions, the Jubilee could have the same defects and by flooding Rome with visitors could likewise have disastrous results.

Instead of Martin Luther denouncing Rome's greed, this time Umberto Bossi, leader of the Northern League, protested against government support for the Jubilee. Why should northern Italian taxpayers bear its expenses, asked Bossi, when most of the money will be absorbed by what he calls 'robber Rome'.

Two of the critics cited, Ronchey and Ceronetti, were among the founders of a laicist Jubilee Observatory to check on the running of the occasion as a 'big business whose lack of transparency suggest it is a mixture of incapacity and illegality.' The Observatory committee asked how the organizers had decided on expenditure such as $US2.4 million for teaching English to bus drivers and city police involved in the Jubilee.

On 5 March 1987, the government allocated $US1878.5 million for the Jubilee but the funds became available only 15 months later. Many ambitious projects had been mooted but, given the lack of time, it was decided to concentrate on improving existing transport, health and reception structures. The opportunity for an imaginative reshaping of Rome had been missed. Among the projects which will not be completed in time was an underground railway line linking the Vatican to the Colosseum and St John Lateran. Plans to convert Rome's old prison, Regina Coeli (Queen of Heaven), for social use, which would have been a suitable gesture, have also been put on hold.

The most controversial project was the construction of a 2600-meter tunnel to avoid the traffic jams between the Tiber embankment and massive Castel Sant' Angelo, and, at the same time, allow establishment of an extensive pedestrian island from this point to St Peter's. However, after an expensive exploratory survey, doubts about the advisability of digging close to the foundations of Castel Sant' Angelo remained and the project was postponed until after the Jubilee. It was replaced by a 350-meter tunnel which begins beyond Castel Sant' Angelo. A second controversial project and daunting engineering task was construction of a car park and commercial center under Propaganda Fide College atop the Janiculum Hill. It is in Vatican territory but the expenses will be shared by the government and the Vatican. In the third millennium, it will provide parking for those who attend papal audiences: as it is, each Wednesday and many Sundays, traffic in the zone is congested because of tourist buses which park near St Peter's whereas local residents would like to see them accommodated in the Vatican Gardens. There are alarming previsions of 3000 tourists buses constantly in Rome during the Jubilee but organizers promise that they will not be allowed to approach closer than the ring road where shuttle buses will take over. But how many shuttles can Rome handle?

In 1875 there were plans for an underground railway in Rome but nothing was done until after World War II. By 1995 there were only two lines, compared to 17 in Paris, and the route of one had been determined by electoral considerations. For the Jubilee, one will be extended to near the entrance of the Vatican Museums while another overground train station will function on the other side of the Vatican. A pedestrian island is planned between St John Lateran and another major Jubilee church, Holy Cross of Jerusalem, and the roads to the airport will be widened.

Jubilee funds will be used to improve accessibility of sites, a large slice will go for urban upkeep, restoral and security, somewhat less for cultural initiatives and least of all for protection of the environment. The cleaning of smog-dirtied facades of historic buildings has already enhanced Rome, but, surprisingly, by April 1999 nothing had been done to refurbish the building complex which, apart from the basilicas, was most connected with Jubilees: the Archconfraternity of the Holy Trinity for Pilgrims and Convalescents. Many public lavatories will be built. The name for them, *vespasiano*, is a reminder that Emperor Vespasian, an old soldier who knew the importance of latrines, introduced them in ancient Rome, but they are rare today where coffee bar toilets are expected to meet the need.

There are various projects for the monuments of pagan Rome, including extensive refurbishing of the Colosseum where, among other things, a sector of the wooden stage will be rebuilt. Visitors will be able to inspect at close range archaeological excavations under way in the Forum.

The excavation and restoration of the mausoleum of St Helena, the mother of Emperor Constantine, is under way, while $6 million was designated for the Holy Spirit Hospital on the Tiber bank near St Peter's, founded by Innocent III in 1198. In 1473 Sixtus V enlarged it for the Jubilee of 1475—hospitals in Rome developed partly to look after pilgrims. In the seventeenth century, the Jesuits, who had learnt from Incas in Peru the use of quinine against malaria, made Holy Spirit Hospital the world center for its production. The hospital has instruments, three libraries and archives which document its 800-year history but they have not been put in order and are barely accessible in basement rooms which abut on excavations of the villa of Agrippina, mother of the Emperor Caligula.

Rome has always lived largely from pilgrimage, or tourism, governance and bureaucracy. It needs great events and recognizes that its international standing is tied to staging a worthy Jubilee. But because of too many cooks, bureaucratic complications and conflict of competencies, preparations started so late that it seemed Rome had in mind the Olympic Games of 2004, for which it was front-runner, rather than Jubilee 2000. But Athens was awarded the Games and the Jubilee remains Rome's best international showpiece. Those trying to complete the projects in time recommended prayers to St Jude, the saint of impossible causes. Even if the organization is inadequate, Italians improvise readily and are usually well-disposed towards visitors. The climate, the historic buildings and art, the cuisine and the pulse of life could work their customary charm in the year 2000.

Since the high Middle Ages, pickpockets and other petty crooks have made a beeline for Rome for major religious events and are expected to honor the tradition for the year 2000. There are already thefts of works of art from the churches and even from the vestibule of St Ignatius Loyola's restored quarters, while pickpockets are said to be refining their skills working in pairs on the less frequented and controlled bus routes. Gypsies who have come to Rome from Eastern Europe are notorious in this field but there are also locals with light fingers. The police registered a Mafia telephone conversation about tenders for construction of the fifty new churches planned but the cardinal vicar of Rome, Camillo Ruini, made light of it, saying he was more worried about the sluggish bureaucracy. Already in 1995 a bank (Banca Popolare Capitolina e del Lazio), situated close to the

Chamber of Deputies, was closed because, with the aid of a false *monsignore*, it was hoaxing people through promises of lucrative contracts for refurbishing Rome's historic churches for the Jubilee. So much money is involved it would be no surprise if there were scandals connected with sponsors and the Jubilee logo.

Between scams and forecasts of collapse of a city unprepared for millions of pilgrims, it seems Rome is due not for Jubilee 2000 but Apocalypse 2000. But perhaps chaotic cosmopolitanism is its vocation. It fared well towards the end of the preceding millenium: it was not fear-stricken as were some other parts of Europe but tried to renew itself and had some success, if only temporarily.

JUBILEES
1300–2000

CRUSADES AND INDULGENCES

Rome was not gripped by fear at the end of the first millennium. On the contrary: the advent of Gerbert of Aurillac, who as pope took the name Sylvester II, improved prospects for the papacy even though the Roman families who usually fought over it did not welcome the first French pope.

As control of the papacy meant control of a city without effective civic autonomy, it whetted the appetites of the most powerful Roman families. For over a century, the papacy had been close to chaos: John VIII (872–82) had been murdered; Stephen (896–9) was strangled in prison; John XII (955–64), 18 when elected, reportedly died while lovemaking; Benedict VI (973–4) was killed in Castel Sant' Angelo.

The papacy could only improve and Gerbert was the man to achieve this. A brilliant, versatile scholar and teacher, equally at home in mathematics and music, in astronomy, philosophy and literature, he was a pioneer with the abacus, terrestrial and celestial globes, and the organ. For a time he was abbot of the monastery of Bobbio in north Italy. Subsequently he became archbishop of Rheims and then Ravenna.

The Saxon emperor Otto III, who had studied under Gerbert, took up residence in Rome in 999 and ensured that he was elected.

Together the young Saxon and the French polymath, who had broken the brawling Romans' hold on the papacy, seemed destined to restore luster to the city. The name Gerbert chose as pope was a program in itself because Sylvester I had been pope at the time of the Emperor Constantine; it suggested that Otto was in the same mould and that there was to be a new beginning.

Rome probably had fewer than 30,000 inhabitants, compared to a million or more at the height of the Empire. The social welfare system had broken down and no church had been built for 150 years. As there was little trade, the city was largely dependent on its rural environs. Nevertheless a contemporary could still call it 'the capital of the world and the queen of cities.' For some, the memory of Rome's glories, and its imposing ruins overshadowed its desperate condition.

In the year 1000 there was neither fire nor plague nor terror in the city, merely frightening storms when Emperor Otto brought a relic of St Adalbert to the church of St Bartholomew on the Tiber island. Adalbert, who had lived many years in Rome, had been archbishop of his native Prague, had taken Christianity to the Poles and the Prussians and had been martyred by the latter.

The arrival of the relic was a reminder that, although for over a century the papacy had been a morass, the Christian message was spreading to Central/East Europe, to Hungary and Poland whose leaders, by accepting it, obtained papal recognition as kings. Conversion of the Hungarians opened a land passage to the Holy Land for pilgrims who previously had travelled the more dangerous sea route.

On the day after Christmas 1000, Sylvester assigned Terracina County, between Rome and Naples, to Daifer, the son-in-law of the Count of Tusculum, presumably to obtain an ally against a Roman aristocratic family, the Crescenti, who often controlled papal elections. Sylvester decreed that those to whom he assigned the county be obedient in peacetime and supply troops during wars. It was hardly the act of someone who believed that the end of the world was imminent.

What was imminent, in fact, was a revolt by the local aristocrats which induced both the emperor and the pope to leave for Ravenna. In 1002 Sylvester was allowed to return but he died the following year. Because he had established in the Lateran Palace, the papal residence, a rudimentary astronomical observatory, Romans said that he was a sorcerer; after his demise, the legend spread that the rattle of his bones in the Lateran foretold the death of his successors.

Fears of the millennium, of Satan being liberated after a thousand years as John the Evangelist had foretold, would have made more sense in the Rome of 1033, which was the thousandth year after the conventional date of Christ's death. At that time the pope was the violent and dissolute Benedict IX who had been installed by his uncle, Alberic III, head of one of the families which controlled papal elections. There is no evidence, however, of fear of an imminent end to the world in 1033 either. In fact, that year, for the first time, a bull or lead seal attached to an imperial document bore the inscription *Roma caput mundi, tenet frena orbis rotundi*: 'Rome, head of the world, holds the reins of the globe.'

Europe as a whole was slowly recovering from raids by Saracens and marauders from the north. The legend of widespread panic at the end of the first thousand years was largely fabricated later by writers anxious to show the ignorance of the Middle Ages and the unwarranted fears inculcated by religion. There were only isolated cases of panic.

Winds of changes were felt in the church as well as in society at large, partly because monastic congregations were rejuvenated and expanded, particularly in Burgundy and Lorraine. They enjoyed the backing of the emperor against local aristocrats and even against bishops.

Christian monarchs considered they had a divine ministry, a hallowed role in protection of the church from the time Emperor Constantine had accepted Christianity in 313. In the ninth century, Charlemagne had regarded himself as another Constantine, overlord of the church with the pope as his chaplain. Otto III, whose mother was a Byzantine princess, had modeled himself on both Constantine and Charlemagne.

Kings were anointed with the holy oil used in the consecration of bishops, their emblems of office such as the sceptre were blessed with formulas similar to those of ecclesiastical ceremonies; at coronation they wore vestments which were ecclesiastical in origin, as did the Queen of England for her coronation in 1953. For three centuries from 750 they believed they had a superior role to that of bishops in guiding the church.

John X had reaffirmed the king's role in 921, when the archbishop of Cologne consecrated a bishop of Liège appointed by a local duke. John reminded the bishop that he should have awaited a royal command because 'no bishop is to be consecrated in any diocese without the order of the king.' John expressed the outlook of a period of papacy-monarchy harmony in which the church counted on the protection of civil authority. The evolution of the papacy's relations with civil authorities from the mid-eleventh century provides part of the context for the Jubilee of 1300.

Medieval society was coterminous with the church, which was why heresy was considered a social crime. But as the papacy became more conscious of its strength the idea that popes and kings guided the church together was downplayed. Instead it was asserted that the pope was vicar of Christ who was both high priest and kings of kings. As vicar of Christ, the pope not only was superior to other bishops but could depose unworthy rulers, judging Christian kings according to Christian moral law. In theory, this exalted vision liberated the papacy from dependence on earthly powers but, in fact, it brought it into collision with secular rulers. A key test was who had the right to appoint bishops.

What has been called the monarchical theory of the papacy developed rapidly in the twelfth century, finding its summation in the phrase, 'the pope who can also be called the church.' At the same time, the papacy increased its disciplinary, juridical, financial and dogmatic control over the church throughout Europe.

But as a government it lacked effective coercive powers apart from the spiritual weapons of excommunication or interdict which could deprive a people of all ecclesial services except Christian burial. It could also release people from the obligation of obedience to a sovereign which was an invitation to revolt. The Catch-22 for the papacy, however, was that although it might influence politics by these methods, they often tarnished its image. Spiritual sanctions could be controversial and, moreover, obeyed the law of diminishing returns. At times the papacy's political and pastoral aims were at odds. Its role as a supranational arbiter, the representative of a moral and spiritual order above the political, was damaged by its role as a player. It was a player because the emperor of the Holy Roman or German Empire which extended into north Italy could only be rightly crowned in Rome; the emperor needed the pope's approval. It was a player also because of the Papal States, the wedge of land across central Italy which was supposed to ensure the papacy's autonomy. After southern Italy, it was the second largest Italian principality. Moreover, there were papal vassal states such as Hungary, Scotland and Aragon which involved it in international politics.

As rulers became more conscious of their national interests, they challenged the papacy by the claim that 'each king is emperor in his own land,' that is, there was no authority above him. There were all the conditions for a memorable papacy-emperor clash. The build-up to it can be dated from 1046 when the German Emperor Henry IV decided to break the hold of Roman families who were once again dominating the papacy. He ensured a succession of four German popes of whom the most significant was Leo IX (1049–1054), an Alsatian nobleman who was a relative of Henry and had been a rigorous bishop for twenty years. He agreed to be pope provided that the clergy and people of Rome accepted him. They did and he entered the city as a barefoot pilgrim.

Leo had a more exalted concept of his office than his immediate Italian predecessors. His pontificate was an attempt to harness the reform movement, with its expanding monastic support, to the broader vision of the papacy as the leader of Christendom. On arrival in Rome he held a reform synod, then constantly travelled to preside over similar synods in Germany and France: in five years he spent little more than six months in Rome. The synods condemned simony or the sale of ecclesiastical preferment, moral laxity and clerical marriage. During his travels, Leo also settled disputes which made the presence of the Church of Rome tangible beyond the Alps for the first time in over 200 years.

He brought to Rome some of the leaders of the monastic renewal movement such as Humbert, who became a cardinal. Previously cardinals had mainly liturgical duties, but now became, as one of them, Peter Damian, said, 'spiritual senators of the universal church.' Leo made them a college which, among other things, took over the discussion of matters of faith formerly handled by synods. But they did not yet have exclusive rights to elect the pope: lay people were still involved, which was another factor involving the papacy in politics.

Leo, the first to use the word 'curia' (court), remodelled the papal administration along the lines of the French and English courts. He also increased its financial efficiency which was essential for a more powerful papacy.

He rejuvenated the church, but a major breakdown occurred in 1054. As there was doctrinal-semantic-jurisdictional discord, he despatched Cardinal Humbert to negotiate with Constantinople but the reformed papacy's claims were so confident and its style so abrasive (dissenters from Rome, the patriarch was informed, were nothing but a 'confabulation of heretics, a conventicle of schismatics, a synagogue of Satan') that Christianity was sundered East from West.

The resulting mutual excommunication was the culmination of a long period of growing estrangement between Rome, the see of St Peter which had a spiritual primacy, and Constantinople, the new Rome and site of temporal power. The excommunications were rescinded only when Paul VI met Patriarch Athenagoras in December 1965: they both expressed regret for 'the offensive words, unfounded reproaches and unworthy actions' of 900 years earlier.

To push through reforms designed to make the church more evangelical, Gregory VII (1073–1085) radicalized papal claims: the means contradicted the end. To break the practice of secular rulers bestowing the insignia of authority on bishops, he exalted the papacy. The subsequent controversy was fierce not only because of Gregory's imperious temperament but also because it was a clash of principles. Born as Hildebrand to a Tuscan family, he had been raised in Rome but may have spent some time in one of the Cluniac reform monasteries. He had been summoned back to Rome by Leo IX. Gregory was concerned for the church in countries as diverse as Norway, Denmark, Hungary, Poland and Spain but wanted every church to be in harmony with Rome, not only in faith, as had always been demanded, but also in liturgy and organization. He clashed with many bishops and was abandoned by some cardinals because of his high-handed ways. Peter Damian called him a 'Holy Satan'.

In 1075 he published 27 of his radical ideas. One was that the pope was a universal pastor with worldwide authority over the church; others were that he alone could appoint bishops and that he had the power to depose emperors. Not surprisingly, this brought him into collision with Emperor Henry IV, who might otherwise have aided him in church reform. Indeed he clashed with almost all rulers except William the Conqueror who championed reform in his recently conquered territories.

Gregory deposed Henry who requested and obtained pardon at Canossa. But by the end of Gregory's reign, Henry was winning out against the pope. Part of the Gregory-Henry battle was fought in the streets of Rome.

A French noble and monk, Eudes, who had been Gregory VII's legate in Germany, was elected as Urban II in 1088. By using moderation, he achieved some of Gregory's aims. He favored a Concordat at Worms in 1122 which brought the church-state struggle over the investiture of bishops to an end, at least for fifty years. Urban was in a difficult situation both because the emperor was hostile and because there was a rival claimant to the papal throne, an antipope. It was not until six years after his election that Urban, who had been confined to southern Italy, entered Rome. There he launched a series of reform synods. One of these in Clermont, France, decreed that the Peace of God, the suspension of hostilities on days chosen by the church, should be observed weekly throughout Christendom. Christians were obliged to do penance for those they killed in war but still warlords and warriors threatened to tear Christendom apart.

From various reports of Urban's speech at Clermont it seems that, to recompose unity among warring Christians, he proposed a purifying and pacifying pilgrimage to the Holy Land. It seemed a brilliant stroke as it would not only remind Christians of their ideals but also foster rapprochement with the Eastern Church. But the pilgrimage became armed, a Crusade, which brought the church into conflict with Islam. Eventually there was a reaction against Crusades by St Francis of Assisi and others but initially they restored the papacy to its leading role in Christendom which had been challenged by the German emperor. The Crusades were to become 'the foreign policy of the reforming papacy' and were a major factor in the lead-up to the Jubilee of 1300. It was decreed that 'whoever from devotion alone, and not for the purpose of gaining honors and wealth, shall set out for the liberation of the Church of God at Jerusalem, that journey will be reckoned in the place of all penance.' This concession was extended later to all who supported the Crusades which took place not only in the Holy Lands but in the Iberian peninsula, in the Baltic region and against the Albigensians in southern France. Crusade preachers compared the indulgence for the Crusades to the Jewish Jubilee: in one, heavenly debts were cancelled; in the other, worldly debts. One consequence of the Crusades was the introduction of a Rome-administered income tax on all clergy which was later extended, inspiring much hostility.

The first record of an indulgence, in the sense of a relaxation of penance, dates from the eleventh century. Of course the grant was given only to those who had confessed their sins: confession removed their guilt but not the debt of temporal punishment incurred. Without the indulgence, those who confessed would still have been obliged to carry out penance. In earlier times, absolution, necessary for readmission to the church community, was granted only after completion of public penance. When absolution was granted immediately at the end of auricular confession, penance still had to be carried out, whether in this life or in purgatory. Remission of penance could be partial or total; this last was called a plenary indulgence, and it could be applied to the souls in purgatory.

Indulgence grants, which could be conceded by any bishop, were made from the church's treasury of merits accumulated by Christ and the saints. Granting of indulgences in exchange for alms led to abuses which were condemned as early as the Fourth Lateran Council in 1215.

Crusades accustomed Christians to gleaning indulgences about the same time that the concept of purgatory was being more exactly plotted. Traditionally there was belief in a state of purgation after death in which souls were purified of any vestiges of sin before entering heaven. By the eleventh century, the state of purgation became a place. Most agreed that purification was by fire but there were differences about details. The basic teaching endorsed by several councils was that prayer and good works by those on earth could help souls in purgatory. As Rome held the keys to the treasury of grace, its attraction was increased by the consolidation of the concepts of indulgence grants and purgatory.

The position of Rome was strengthened also by the continuing development of canon law. In the eleventh century Bologna became the center for the revived study of Roman law which, in turn, spurred interest in church law. In the mid-twelfth century a monk, Gratian, produced a compilation of church decrees from the earliest days, with a commentary which reconciled the contrasts between them. He elaborated also in great detail the necessity and methodology of auricular confession. His codification contributed to centralization which increased when, in 1234 and 1298, the first official collections of papal decretals appeared. A further development was that certain grave cases were reserved for the pope to decide the appropriate penance. An office of the papal administration, the Penitentiary, was established to handle such cases. This reinforced Rome's reputation as the place to obtain pardon and made it the preferred goal of many pilgrimages undertaken as a penance. Recourse to Rome was popular since it allowed escape from local social control.

Bernard of Clairvaux foresaw that emphasis on law would make popes judges between people rather than leaders of them. He also deplored the time consumed in endless legal issues: 'Don't you see where all this damnable business is leading you?' he asked Eugenius III (1145–1153) when the trend to legalism was in its early stages. 'You're wasting your time.' Rome became the court of ultimate appeal and, in many cases, of first instance for all Christendom, with a consequent growth of the administration and its income.

One of the more outstanding of a series of canonist-popes was Innocent III (1198–1216) whose 18–year pontificate meant a new splendor for Rome. Some of the hills where the wealthiest ancient Romans had built their mansions were uninhabited at the beginning of the thirteenth century and the Forum was a cow paddock. Romans lived mainly in the flat Field of Mars area within an ample bend of the Tiber, with only two settlements on the other side: that of Trastevere at one end of the Janiculum Hill and, at the other, the area around St Peter's which had been the first invaded by the original Romans when they crossed the river. St Peter's was outside the city walls as was St Paul's.

The area around St Peter's, in fact, was a separate city enclosed within walls which had been built in the mid-ninth century after Saracen marauders had looted the basilica and the apostle's tomb. It was known as the Leonine City as the walls had been built by Leo IV. They ran from fortified Castel Sant' Angelo, the mausoleum of the Emperor Hadrian on the Tiber bank, to the Vatican Hill, enclosed the basilica and returned to the river to embrace the various compounds where foreign communities lived.

Within the Leonine City Innocent built a fortified residence in 1208. It is the core of today's Vatican palaces around the Cortile del Pappagallo (the Courtyard of the Parrot). A compact, three-storey structure, it had a five-storey corner tower and contained accommodation for a chancellor, treasurer, almoner and their staff, a chapel and chaplain's apartment, a bakery, wine cellar, kitchen and smithy's workshop.

Before building the papal residence, indeed in the first year of his reign, Innocent had provided for his family's security by constructing a tower block and fortified compound near the Forum of Nerva, where it still bulks large. Although he claimed suzerainty over the whole terrestrial globe, he was in hostile territory if he crossed a bridge over the Tiber. He fully secured his home base only after seven years during which he had been forced for periods to leave the city. 'In height and width,' wrote a contemporary about the tower block, 'it surpasses any other tower.' There were scores of these in Rome which must have made its skyline like San Gimigniano's today, particularly as independent bell towers, on the model of those at the Monte Cassino abbey, began to rear alongside churches. The skyscrapers of their day, these towers were the redoubts of Roman families fighting for control of the city and the papacy.

On the Tiber bank, where it still stands, Innocent built the Holy Spirit hospital. Some contemporaries said it was to compensate for his pride in building Rome's biggest tower block but for that prudence may have been the motive.

Innocent, who had studied theology in Paris and law in Bologna, as cardinal had written popular devotional treatises, one of which was *The Misery of the Human Condition*. Only 37 on his election in 1198, small, handsome Innocent was forceful but also witty and humane. He was sensitive to criticism of Rome's handling of income: in 1212 he asked pilgrims to explain on their return home that all offerings to St Peter's were used for the thousands of candles which burnt there daily and to maintain those priests who were not canons with an income from ecclesiastical benefices.

Because the Curia had expanded but, with few exceptions, its members depended on fees rather than salaries, it was a hotbed of corruption, bribery and forgery denounced in many satires such as *The Gospel According to the Silver Mark*. Innocent clamped down on the abuses by introducing a regular scale of fees but did not establish a fully-salaried bureaucracy. The centralization of the church, which meant greater control over ecclesiastical benefices, the property which produced income for clergy and church institutions, contributed to the papacy's growing wealth, which was derived also from tithes and Peter's Pence, the yearly offering of faithful to the pope which had originated in England. Rome was becoming a banking center. Innocent encouraged provincial and national councils of bishops but also insisted on bishops making regular periodical visits to Rome, a practice which still persists. However he reserved major issues for himself.

He endorsed the ideals of evangelical poverty and supported some of its proponents who might otherwise have ended in conflict with the church as had the Waldensians. He approved the preaching of Francis of Assisi and commissioned that of the Spaniard Dominic Guzman, founder of the Dominican Order, against the heretics found near Albi in southern France. When the Albigensians killed a papal legate, a crusade was launched against them in which the inhabitants of Béziers were slaughtered to the infamous cry of 'Kill all, kill all. God will know his own.'

The fourth Crusade, which he launched, had as deplorable an incident as the Béziers slaughter when, in 1204 because of Venetian rapacity, the crusaders sacked Christian Constantinople. This damaged Catholic-Orthodox relations but perhaps more damaging was the creation of a Latin hierarchy in the Middle East, the Latin Patriarchate of Constantinople, Jerusalem and Antioch.

Whereas previous popes had been considered vicars of St Peter, Innocent made great use of the title 'Vicar of Christ' to whom, he claimed, 'was given not only the universal church but the whole world to govern.' Despite this statement of principle, he showed tact regarding the Romans' desire for a civil government. They had revolted for this in 1143. Innocent recognized a measure of sovereignty for the city and its senate. He said he would not interfere in temporal affairs except where he was owed allegiance as in the papal and vassal states, where moral or spiritual issues were at stake or where there was no arbiter, which gave him virtually an all-embracing brief.

When two rival candidates for the crown of the Holy Roman Empire applied to him, he first chose Otto IV, then switched his support to Frederick. He excommunicated King John of England for refusing to recognize Stephen Langton (Thomas Becket's successor) as Archbishop of Canterbury but when John submitted, and made his Anglo-Irish domain a papal fief, Innocent declared void the Magna Carta, which the barons had wrested from John in a moment of weakness. His policies produced increased anti-Roman sentiment among the English, including the clergy. In 1204 Innocent recognized Joannitza as king of the Bulgarians. He clashed unsuccessfully with Phillip II of France over his right to tax clergy. He had completed the development of what has been called the papal monarchy which claimed a plenitude of powers over the church. But the original aim of the reform movement, of which he was a representative, had been instead a simpler, more evangelical church.

After Innocent's death, papal politics became even more awkward: a protracted conflict pitted it against the Holy Roman Emperor Frederick II and, as a reaction, it sought aid from the House of Anjou on which it became dependent. Gregory X, a north Italian noble who was elected in 1271, had met Thomas Aquinas while studying in Paris and was on a crusade when elected pope. He seemed strong enough to curtail French influence, which had increased because of the papacy's need for Anjou protection, and also to make the church more pastoral. In 1274 he opened the Second Council of Lyons which aimed at reform, reunion with the Orthodox and, once again, recovery of the Holy Land.

It was an attempt to revive the reformism which had inspired the First Lateran Council of 1215. Participants at the council had been confident that the papacy could lead reform but Innocent III had chosen greater centralization as his means. Although the same reform aims had been professed at the First Council of Lyons in 1245, by this time there was much criticism of the effects of centralization: papal taxation on clergy and control over benefices were called 'extortion' in confirmation of the accusations made in the previous century by the English historian William of Malmesbury that Romans lived by 'selling justice for gold and by putting a price tag on every form of canon law.' For many who still wanted reform, the papacy had become part of the problem. Gregory solicited situation reports before the Council of 1274 and received much criticism of his curia, and also of papal support for friars such as the Franciscans and Dominicans from secular clergy who considered themselves discriminated against. But even the critics still hoped that the papacy would reform itself. The council achieved reunion with the Orthodox but it was not endorsed by the clergy or people when the Orthodox delegates returned home; no new crusade was launched although the pope wanted one, and Gregory's death two years later prevented him ensuring application of the reforms decided at Lyons.

Papal authority declined while cardinals remained in conclave for 27 months from April 1292. Finally one of them received a letter from a monk warning that there would be divine retribution unless they gave a leader to the church. The writer was an 85-year-old hermit, Pietro del Murrone, who lived in the mountains near Italy's Adriatic coast where, because of his reputation as a saintly ascetic and miraculous healer, he had attracted many disciples. The cardinals, either at their wits' end or convinced of the need for radical change, decided to make him pope.

It seemed the fulfilment of the dreams of those who wanted a more spiritual church detached from politics and wealth. Some believed that he was a predicted 'angel pope' who would usher in an age of the Holy Spirit. These expectations were influenced by the teaching of Joachim di Fiore (1130–1202) and others who predicted a new era. Joachim, a Calabrian monk, had foretold the imminent replacement of the papacy, mired in temporal affairs, by an age of the Spirit, of peace and liberty. He implied that the church was only a stage on the way to the Kingdom of God. In the fourteenth century this type of teaching would be taken to the extreme by certain Franciscans who identified the papacy with the anti-christ.

On a donkey escorted by his protector Charles II of Anjou, king of Sicily and Naples, Pietro reached the basilica of Santa Maria di Collemaggio at L'Aquila in the Abruzzo, which was the northernmost part of Charles' territory. There he was consecrated as Celestine V. He granted a plenary indulgence to those who attended the consecration and confessed their sins, as he did also to those who visited the basilica on 29 August, the feastday of John the Baptist as martyr. It was the first time that a plenary indulgence was granted for a visit to a church. By opening the church's treasury of grace he hoped to assist reconciliation between feuding mountain folk.

Celestine's pontificate was to show that you could select a pope without political ties but you could not take politics out of the papacy. He was easily manipulated by his protector Charles of Anjou, particularly as he resided in the Castel dell'Ovo, which still stands on the Naples seafront, rather than in Rome which he never saw. He appointed Charles' nominee to key positions in the church's central administration and, moreover, even tried to have his own disciples take over the important Benedictine abbey of Montecassino.

Although saintly, he was silly when it came to government but at least he recognized that he was inspiring dissatisfaction. He asked the college of cardinals if he could resign. Benedetto Caetani, a leading canonist, and the other cardinals responded promptly that he could. Caetani himself succeeded Celestine as Boniface VIII.

Boniface, who immediately transferred from Naples to Rome, resumed Innocent III's policy of commanding monarchs but with less success. He was an experienced diplomat but had an abrasive manner and, moreover, Rome had been losing power during the thirteenth century because of the growth of nationalist attitudes.

His attempt to support Scottish independence from England was unsuccessful, as was that to place his candidate on the Hungarian throne. He was damaged by a losing clash with Philip IV of France who had imposed taxes on the clergy without seeking prior papal consent. Boniface's loss was a severe blow to papal pretensions. He excommunicated the cardinals of the rival Colonna family who then fled to France, forming an ominous alliance with Philip.

In 1298 Boniface was asked to arbitrate in the dispute which had kept France and England at war for four years. He did so but said that he was acting 'as a private person, as Lord Benedict Caetani, as an arbiter and friendly umpire in restoring peace and concord.' It was surprisingly modest, an admission that the papacy's arbitration depended ultimately on the consent of the contending parties, but it was effective. However in its public declarations the papacy seemed trapped in rhetorical overkill.

Boniface cancelled Celestine's grant of a plenary indulgence for visits to the Collemaggio basilica on 29 August on the grounds that it could encourage moral laxness. The Franciscans accused him of having forced Celestine to resign. Celestine had wanted to return to his monastic community but, probably fearful of the possibility of a schism led by the ex-pope, Boniface had him confined to a castle where he died in 1296. His enemies claimed Boniface had killed Celestine.

Throughout the Papal States statues were erected in honor of Boniface as ruler, a cult of the personality previously unknown. In his bull *Unam sanctam* he asserted that for salvation every creature should be subject to the Roman pontiff. In 1302, he was about to excommunicate Philip IV of France when Philip's adviser Guillaume de Nogaret broke into Boniface's palace in his home town of Anagni, south of Rome, with mercenaries and a member of the Colonna family who wanted to kill Boniface; some historians maintain that he gave Boniface a resounding slap on the face. The French planned to take him to France to be judged by a Council but Boniface's fellow citizens saved him. Badly shaken by the humiliation, he died within a month. It was Boniface who invented the first Jubilee.

THE CITY OF
PARDON

B oniface was one of a series of popes from Rome or its environs who, towards the end of the thirteenth century, made the city a flourishing cultural capital which attracted artists such as Cimabue and encouraged its own such as Cavallini to work on its churches and palaces.

Innocent III had been more interested in political strategies than in church buildings which he barely subsidized. Boniface pursued similar political aims with less shrewdness but also continued the urban renovation of his immediate predecessors which reflected the new-found wealth of the papal administration. The city regained its elan.

The compact building Innocent had erected near St Peter's, the core of the Vatican today, was expanded and decorated and a large walled garden, which seems to have been a deer park, was added. The four great basilicas were remodelled and redecorated and a loggia for benedictions was added to St John Lateran.

These developments seemed to converge with others to prepare for the Jubilee of 1300. Although architecturally it ignored the Gothic style which shaped cathedrals such as Chartres and Salisbury, Rome was touched by the prosperity and quickening pace of life in much of Western Europe.

The orders of mendicant friars it had endorsed had responded to the changes with more flexibility than the longer-established monastic orders and became influential in the universities which, taking the place of monastic and cathedral schools, sprang up in Paris, Oxford, Bologna, Padua and elsewhere.

By the mid-thirteenth century Aristotle's metaphysics was exercizing an intellectual influence through translation and also because of the commentaries on it by the Arabic scholar Averroës. Some theologians combated this influence as a threat to the faith, but by about 1270 Thomas Aquinas showed that much of the new outlook was compatible with divine revelation. In the intellectual sphere, Christianity was responding with aplomb to a world which was demanding greater autonomy.

Some Franciscans provided an intellectual backing for the order's emphasis on an affective spirituality by maintaining that as well as Thomistic rational certainty there was also experimental certainty in which God was present through a spiritual encounter. This outlook was reinforced by diffusion of Franciscan-inspired art which depicted Christ not as serene Lord of the universe but as suffering on the cross. Ever more frequently he was presented not in his glory but in his pain. About the same time, theologians invented purgatory or, at least, made its pains more graphic.

The fall of Acre, the last Crusader stronghold, in 1291 made it difficult for Christians to visit the site of the Passion and walk in Christ's footsteps. However there was a vigorous response: more pilgrims went to Rome. If Christians could not reach Christ's tomb they would visit those of his apostles Peter and Paul. Rome became the new Jerusalem once again.

This reaction came after the Crusades had accustomed people to a link between pilgrimage and indulgence because crusades had become armed pilgrimage. And the indulgences could be applied to those in purgatory which was coming into sharper focus. Everything seemed to prepare for a Jubilee. But 1300 began without anyone having summoned a Jubilee or Holy Year; indeed it was an unknown concept.

On the first of January, people crowded into St Peter's because a preacher, probably a canon of the basilica, had promised an extraordinary indulgence to those who attended. It was rumored that a special indulgence had been granted on the same day in 1200. As the year began at Christmas, 1 January was a working day and the crowds arrived only after sunset. Their expectations were disappointed.

According to the contemporary account of Cardinal Gaetano Stefaneschi, the pope met a 107-year-old pilgrim being carried to St Peter's who told him that in 1200 his father, a laborer, had come from the Savoy region and, to gain an indulgence, lived as long as his means allowed in Rome. 'My father asked me to come at the beginning of the next century,' the pilgrim told Boniface.

He ordered archival research but it did not produce any evidence of a special indulgence at the beginning of the century. Nevertheless, after an unusually large number of pilgrims arrived for the annual procession of what was believed to be a relic of Christ's passion, Veronica's veil, on 17 January, he decided to go with the tide even though earlier he had cancelled Celestine's indulgence for a visit to a church in L'Aquila as conducive to laxness. From St Peter's he issued a bull on 22 February which deserves to be cited in full:

> 'Boniface, Bishop, Servant of the Servants of the Lord.
>
> 'For perpetual remembrance. The trustworthy tradition of our elders affirms that great remissions and indulgences for sins are granted to those who visit in this city the venerable basilica of the Prince of the Apostles. Wherefore We who, according to the dignity of our office, desire, and ought to procure, the salvation of each, holding all and each of these remissions and indulgences to be authentic, do, by Our apostolic authority, confirm and approve the same, and even grant afresh and sanction them by our present writing.
>
> 'In order that the blessed Apostles Peter and Paul may be the more honored as their basilicas in this city shall be the more devoutly frequented by the faithful, and that the faithful themselves may feel that they have been reinvigorated by an abundance of spiritual favors in approaching their tombs, We, confiding in the mercy of Almighty God, in the merits and powers of these His Apostles, in the counsel of our brethren, and in the plenitude of the apostolic authority, grant to all who, being truly penitent and confessing their sins, shall reverently visit these basilicas in the present year 1300, which commenced with the festival of the Nativity of our Lord Jesus Christ just celebrated, and to all who being

truly penitent, shall confess their sins, and shall approach these basilicas each succeeding hundredth year, not only an ample and copious, but the fullest pardon of all their sins.

'Whoever wishes to gain these indulgences must, if they be inhabitants of Rome, visit these same basilicas for thirty days, either successively or at intervals, at least once a day; if they are foreigners or strangers they must in like manner visit the basilicas for fifteen days. Nevertheless, each one will merit more, and will more effortlessly gain the indulgence as he visits the basilicas more frequently and more devoutly. Let no man, therefore, dare to infringe or impugn this Our rescript of confirmation, approval, renewal, grant and decree. And if anyone presume to assail it, let him know that he will incur the indignation of Almighty God and of the blessed Apostles Peter and Paul.'

This was a centennial celebration; there was no mention of the Old Testament Jubilee. However the Jesuit scholar Hubert Thurston claimed that an unnamed contemporary Roman canonist, commenting on the bull, referred to the Jubilee recommendation of a socio-economic clean slate.

Although no record had been found to confirm the 107-year-old's story, Boniface established a century as the interval between celebrations and granted a fuller indulgence on less onerous conditions than ever before. In the century to Nicholas IV's death in 1292, the indulgences offered to pilgrims spending Lent in Rome had multiplied ten times. But still Nicholas offered only seven years as the major indulgence at St Peter's. Boniface had made a once-in-a-century mega-offer which opened the way to an inflation of indulgences.

Boniface, who stood at the acme of the monarchical papacy, had revived an earlier style in which the pope was in the shadow of Peter the Gatekeeper. Endorsing a grassroots movement, he had found a way to show troublesome rulers such as Philip IV that Rome still had a universal relevance.

He spoilt matters somewhat by issuing another decree which, as well as threatening sanctions against anyone harming pilgrims, excluded from the Jubilee's benefits anyone trading with the Muslims and, unless they had a change of heart, his enemies King Frederick of Aragon reigning in Sicily and the Roman Colonna family who had sided with the French king.

Such was the flood of pilgrims, aided by peace in Italy and clement weather, that a new gate was opened in the city walls. By horse, by foot, by ship they came from the German lands, Hungary, France, the Iberian peninsula (the Jubilee is described in the prologue to the first Spanish novel *El libro del Caballero Cifar*) and, to a lesser degree, from the British Isles. Some arrived by ship at wharves on the Tiber but most came by road using shank's pony. Some young people carried the aged on their shoulders. Those who did not have enough money for the journey sold their possessions. Office holders, such as a notary of Orvieto municipality, had to find a subordinate as replacement before receiving permission for the trip.

Contemporaries spoke of two million visitors, which was about fifty times the city's population. The only VIPs were the brother of the French King Philip, Charles of Valois, who arrived with a retinue of 500 horsemen, and Charles Martel, son of the King of Naples, who hoped the pope would back his bid for the throne of Hungary. Democratic Florence, a growing economic power, sent a delegation dressed as monarchs, including the kings of England, France and Bohemia, and also the Great Cham of Tartary. Boniface commented that Florence would be a new world power.

A merchant from Asti in Piedmont spoke of two clerics standing day and night by the altar of St Paul's literally raking in the pilgrims' offerings, which led to charges that the papacy enriched itself and also used the pilgrims' offerings to finance wars. The offerings were voluntary and not a condition for gaining indulgences. About 50,000 gold florins were received at the two basilicas, which Cardinal Stefaneschi said was a little more than double the normal sum, adding that it was all spent either on maintaining the basilicas or providing for their clergy. A zone of Rome still called Castel Giubileo (Jubilee Castle) was probably bought with the offerings to provide clergy income.

Boniface seems to have been singularly unlikeable but even his critics had nothing but praise for the event. The most renowned of these was the Florentine Dante Alighieri, although some historians claim he was not in Rome until the following year. Dante detested Boniface, whom he considered a wolf rather than a shepherd, because, among other things, he believed the pope was partly responsible for his expulsion from Florence. Some scholars claim that an anonymous figure Dante placed in the Inferno and condemned as 'the coward spirit of the man who made the great refusal [of the papal office]' was Celestine whose retirement had opened the way for Boniface.

The idea that one could gain a remission equivalent to that obtained by a certain number of days of public penance must have appealed to Dante who made his own detailed map of the afterworld. *The Divine Comedy*, his account of the transfiguration of a pilgrim in hell, purgatory and heaven, was supposed to have taken place during Holy Week 1300. The opening of the poem, *Nel mezzo del camin di nostra vita* ('Midway this way of life we're bound upon'), accords with the fact that on 7 April 1300, Holy Thursday, he was 35, which is midpoint of the biblical span of three score years and ten.

In the eleventh canto of 'Inferno' he compares the one-way traffic instituted on each side of the Castel Sant' Angelo bridge for the Jubilee to a procession in the eighth circle of hell:

> *Just so the Romans, because of the great smother*
> *Of the Jubilee crowd, have thought of a good device*
> *For controlling the bridge, to make the traffic smoother,*
> *So that on one side all must have their eyes*
> *On the Castle, and go to St Peter's; while all the throng*
> *On the other, towards the Mount move contrariwise.*

In the thirty-first canto of 'Paradise' he describes a Croatian pilgrim in St Peter's venerating what was allegedly the veil Veronica had offered to Christ as he was carrying the cross and which bore the imprint of his face. In May 1999 a Jesuit scholar claimed to have rediscovered it in an out-of-the way Abruzzo church. It is not known exactly how it reached Rome, nor when, but it seems to have made almost as much impact as if Christ himself had come and the crowds flocking to it in January 1300 had influenced Boniface's decision to grant a centennial indulgence.

> *…one who, haply, from Croatia came*
> *To see the veil of St Veronica*
> *and held, unsated by its ancient fame,*
> *Looks all he may, musing the while with awe.*

But the most significant of Dante's references is in the second canto of 'Purgatory' where he describes new arrivals from a kind of waiting room at the outlet of the Tiber. To his surprise, a certain

Cascella, who had set some of his poems to music, arrives a long time after his death.

Dante asks him the reason for the delay. Cascella replies;

> 'I am not wronged, if he who may decide
> Both when he load his vessel, and with whom,
> hath oft refused me waftage,' he replied,
> 'For the just Will shapes his. But now for some
> Three months he hath received without demur
> Any and all of us who wish to come
> So, when I sought the shore where first the stir
> Of the salt water meets the Tiber, he anon
> Graciously took me as his passenger.'

'Purgatory' was a report from a roving correspondent in the next world who showed how Boniface's initiative had released Cascella from cold storage. It had enabled Cascella to reach purgatory, the realm of hope. The Jubilee was seen as a munificent gesture by the head of a church whose aspirations to dominate this world had met setbacks but whose claim to hold the keys to the next was not questioned. Boniface had thrown wide heaven's doors and to gain this benefit believers had to come to Rome, the city of the pope and also the city of pardon.

A FLOOD OF DIRTY
BARBARIANS

Boniface had shown that all roads still led to Rome, but within a few years of his death the Rome road led to Avignon. History gave a slap in the face to his grandiose ambitions as resounding as the one he allegedly received from a member of the Colonna family.

The French faction Boniface had opposed prevailed after his death. In June 1305 Bertrand de Got, archbishop of Bordeaux, was elected pope, and crowned as Clement V in Lyons. He intended to take up residence in Rome but eventually succumbed to French pressure to reside in Avignon even though he considered it only a temporary arrangement. After all, previous popes had also lived out of Rome for years at a time.

Avignon, which had 5000 inhabitants, belonged to the Angevin dynasty of Naples, vassals of King Philip of France. Within a month of his election, Clement appointed ten cardinals, nine of whom were French and two of them his nephews. In all he appointed 23 cardinals from within the borders of what is now France and they constituted an overwhelming majority. Clement resisted royal pressure to condemn Boniface and revoke all his rulings; he also canonized Celestine V, although not as a martyr of Boniface as King Philip had wanted.

The transfer of the papal court to Avignon deprived Rome of its major source of business as well as of prestige. Now bishops and ambassadors went instead to Avignon. Pilgrimages to the tombs of the apostles and martyrs were fewer. Rome was becoming a backwater.

Yet papal correspondence from Avignon still called its administration the 'Roman curia'; in a letter of 1335 Benedict XII referred to Rome as 'the only capital of Christianity' and when it was proposed to the French Pope John XXII that he transfer the papacy permanently from Rome he objected that then he and his successors would only be bishops of a little town: 'Like it or not, Rome is the world's capital.' Nevertheless there was no sign that the papacy would return to Rome and, in fact, by 1340 an imposing and sombre papal palace was built in Avignon. The 'Avignon captivity' lasted seventy years as if exemplifying the Italian adage that there is nothing as permanent as the provisional.

Rome had an exceptional advocate at the papal court, the poet and humanist Petrarch. On 8 April 1341, on the Capitoline Hill, he was crowned with symbolic laurel, the first poet laureate since ancient Rome. Subsequently this honorary citizen wrote a verse letter to Clement in which Rome itself asked for the pope's return. All of Rome's nobility, shopkeepers, craftsmen and plebeians sent representatives to Avignon to plead his return. In the party was a thirty-year-old notary, Cola di Rienzo, who impressed both the pope and Petrarch with an impassioned speech contrasting Rome's misery with its ancient glories.

The Romans wanted another Jubilee. Not in 1400, as Boniface had decreed, but in 1350; otherwise, the delegation pointed out, many would not participate in a Jubilee in their lifetime. Few could count on a 107-year span like the man who, in 1300, had claimed to remember the year 1200. In any case, the Old Testament Jubilee was held at fifty year intervals, the year after seven times seven years.

Clement, who said that 'a pontiff should make his subjects happy,' agreed without deciding to return to Rome; the pope's presence there was not necessary, all that was required was to visit the tombs of the apostles and also St John Lateran. Clement added an obligatory visit there for two reasons: the mosaic of Christ behind the high altar and the font where Emperor Constantine had been baptised. He shared the mistaken popular beliefs that the image of Christ had simply appeared on the wall rather than being executed by an artist and that the emperor had been baptised at the font by Pope

Sylvester though, in fact, he had been baptised only on his deathbed in Constantinople. The addition of St John Lateran meant the pilgrims had to walk eight miles daily.

Clement did not publish the promulgation immediately and two events put the Jubilee in doubt. In 1347 Cola di Rienzo, who in Avignon had been so eloquent about Rome's past glories, seized power in Rome, presenting himself as the people's tribune against the clergy and nobles. There was no real municipal autonomy: the absent pope was a senator and head of the civic community. Clement threatened that if the citizens did not abandon Cola, he would not hold a Jubilee. Subsequently Cola was overthrown but Clement was still uncertain whether he could trust the Romans.

Then in 1348 the Black Death, bubonic plague, swept through Europe and in some Italian towns killed more than half the population. Because of the danger of infection, collective pilgrimages and large meetings were inadvisable and, moreover, travelers were in danger from those survivors who became marauders. Rome itself was barely touched by the Black Death. In gratitude, Romans built a still extant steep marble staircase to the Ara Coeli church beside the Capitol. A statue of Cola, who was assassinated on the spot in 1354, stands beside it.

Despite his unease about the Romans and the Black Death, on 18 August 1349 Clement promulgated the Jubilee. He may have regretted it when, three weeks later, Rome suffered its severest earthquake ever. Petrarch described the almost total destruction of St Paul's while the roof of St John's fell, several of the nobles' tower blocks tumbled and the ancient ruins were further damaged.

In his bull, Clement referred to the Old Testament practice of a Jubilee held every fifty years as well as mentioning the request of the Roman delegation. Clement remained in Avignon during the Jubilee but convinced the English king, Edward III, to interrupt hostilities with France, so that English pilgrims would have safe passage, and interceded also with the French. The armistice was respected.

There was one VIP, Ludwig, the king of Hungary, who visited the basilicas barefooted and left as a gift at St Peter's 4000 gold coins. On the way to Rome, some pilgrims were robbed and some raped. Summer, when malaria threatened, was the low season, the peaks were Easter and Christmas. In Orvieto, law courts were suspended as were payments of promissory notes and other financial obligations so that people could go to Rome. The hostels en route and the inns in Rome were inadequate for the perhaps two million pilgrims at a time when the population of Western Europe was an estimated 53 million. Everyone in Rome was renting rooms. If promised beds for four, one pilgrim wrote, that night the visitors could find they were sharing with another quartet, but they had learnt that it was better not to complain. Of course, prices skyrocketed. Buccio di Ranallo from the Abruzzo region complained that veal, salt pork and fish were all dear, adding that 'Roman butchers subtly and deceitfully mixed and sold bad meat with good.' A hospice for German-language pilgrims, the Anima, was founded at this time; now it is a residence for German priests studying in Rome.

One report tells of Iberians walking with Cumbrians (Bavarians), Britishers, Greeks and red-haired Swabians. The reporter, a handsome, tall Tuscan whose reddish hair, at the age of 46, had already turned grey, had to convalesce for two weeks before reaching Rome because he had been kicked by a horse. He loved the city both for its Christian present, its pagan past and because it had satisfied his hunger for fame by making him poet laureate. 'Frvunceys Petrarch', as Chaucer called him, has been described as the first tourist because of his pleasure in travelling for travel's sake, though he wrote that he was glad to have missed an appointment with a friend because visiting all the sites 'with the curiosity of poets' could have distracted him from his religious round. As well as a sonnet on an aged pilgrim, he left a description of the city's attractions: 'The pilgrim will visit the tombs of the Apostles, walk the soil reddened by the blood of the martyrs, see the Savior's face either conserved on Veronica's veil or in the mother of all churches [St John's] ... enter the Sancta Sanctorum, a small place full of heavenly grace, visit the Vatican and the tombs of Callistus full of the bones of the blessed, see the cradle of the Savior [in St Mary Major], the decapitated head of John the Baptist, the grate of St Lawrence, where Peter was crucified and where, as Paul's blood flowed, springs of water gushed forth, and the place where, indicated by summer snow, a beautiful temple [St Mary Major] was built.' The first modern literary figure, with a keen critical sense as regards ancient texts, Petrarch in his list accepted the dubious along with the authentic without reserve.

Seventeen years later he wrote to a fellow writer, Giovanni Boccaccio, 'I went there [Rome for the Jubilee] because I wished to end my sinfulness which overwhelmed me with shame.' In the same letter he told Boccaccio that since the Jubilee he had been free of some of the temptations of his youth. 'I am so free of that plague that I now loathe and detest it a thousand times more than I ever found satisfaction in it.'

One pilgrim went after hearing a command which she believed came from God. The Swedish royal widow, Brigid, obeyed a voice which told her to go to Rome: 'Where the streets are paved with gold … and where the way to salvation is briefer, and wait there until you have spoken to the pope and the king.'

When she arrived, Rome fell so far short of her expectations that she turned to her spiritual director and asked, 'Is this all?' She complained that Rome's streets were not paved with gold but clogged with mud, its fields full of weeds, its clergy ignorant, immoral and greedy. In fact, some canons of St Peter's pocketed the faithful's offerings and, when reproved, attacked their superior. Some confessors, who had extracted payments from penitents, were imprisoned.

Brigid denounced conditions in Rome in a vain attempt to make the pope return. She lodged in the palace of the pope's brother, a cardinal, and prophesied disasters for the Romans. Her daughter came to live with her and participated in the *dolce vita* of young aristocrats while her mother continued dire prophecies about a city whose clergy and laity thought only of 'the joys of the flesh and turning a profit.' The Romans had more than enough of Brigid and her giddy daughter and tried to break into their residence to the cry of 'Burn the witch' [Brigid].

Having perfected her Latin in Rome, Brigid wrote to the papal legate, Cardinal Annabaldo Gaetani Ceccano, an ugly man whom she nicknamed 'monkey'. The nickname was taken up by the populace, which so annoyed Annabaldo that he placed an interdict on the city. He had arrived from the papal court in Avignon accompanied by hundreds of richly-accoutred horsemen, which Petrarch rebuked as inappropriate. Annabaldo announced that, to garner a plenary indulgence, Romans had to visit St Peter's, St Paul's and St John's in thirty days, as far possible consecutively: Italians on 15 days while for non-Italians the number of days was calculated on a sliding scale according to the distance they had travelled.

Romans were peeved. They would have liked a reverse order: the briefer the pilgrims' stay, the less they could make from them. Their ire was directed at Annabaldo. One day, as he rode from St Peter's to St Paul's, a stone hurled from a window hit his head. After that, he took up residence in Naples but died there in midsummer.

In a letter, Clement VI spelt out the moral of the story: 'It's better to be a small priest in Avignon than a great prelate in Rome.'

Without the pope, Rome had held a well-attended Jubilee, but, in the long run, if the papacy remained in Avignon, both would suffer.

English successes in the Hundred Years War against France made Avignon less safe and a Spanish cardinal-soldier, Albornoz, reconquered the Papal States. This encouraged Urban V, a French nobleman, to bring the papacy back to Rome. As the Lateran Palace had been burnt down in 1360, he decided to live at the Vatican rather than go there only for ceremonies. A major motive for Urban's return was his desire for reunion with the Orthodox whose headquarters were in Constantinople. He knew that only from Old Rome could he negotiate with the New Rome, as Constantinople considered itself. But he did not accept the Orthodox request for an ecumenical Council, preferring to strengthen the Latin Church in the Greek empire. In 1370, ignoring Brigid of Sweden's warning that it would mean an early death, he returned to Avignon. He died 52 days later.

A learned French cardinal was elected as his successor, Gregory XI. Through her letters, Catherine of Siena was one of the most pressing in urging him to come back to Rome: 'Above all, delay no longer in returning …' In 1377 Gregory left Avignon to take up residence in the Vatican but died the following year. When 16 cardinals met to elect his successor, Romans rioted and broke into the Vatican to insist that they choose not a Frenchman but a Roman or at least an Italian. The cardinals chose a scrupulous canonist, Bartolomeo Prignano, who was archbishop of Bari. He took the name Urban VI. He ordered cardinals and curialists to live more simply and began to detach the church from state affairs. But he proved to be cranky and had a violent temper, and the pro-French cardinals, whose lifestyle he threatened, took these defects as an excuse to elect one of their number, Clement VII, as rival pope. He resided in Avignon. There were now two popes, each with his own cardinals.

Romans revolted against Urban who, partly to win their sympathy, promulgated another Jubilee, adding St Mary Major to the list of basilicas to be visited. Urban believed that Jubilees should be held at intervals of 33 years which was Christ's lifespan. He also knew that Jubilees were an attraction his rival could not use and promulgated one for 1390. By that time a Neapolitan aristocrat, Pietro Tomacelli, had succeeded him as Boniface IX (1389–1404). The arrival of pilgrims from Germany, Poland, Hungary and England as well as Italy helped the parlous Roman economy, both ecclesiastical and civil. But Clement in Avignon prohibited his supporters, found mainly in France and Spain, from attending, providing further evidence of a scandalous division, contrary to the Jubilee spirit.

As the fourteenth century drew to a close, pilgrims converged on Rome from north Italy. Called the Whites from the color of their capes, they flagellated themselves and invoked mercy from God who they hoped would heal the divided church. Nobles such as Carlo Malatesta of Rimini and churchmen such as Archbishop Fieschi of Genoa were among them and in Rome they were joined by some barefoot cardinals.

Boniface IX was wary of this pilgrimage: the participants were convinced that among them was the new pope who would heal the schism and that they should stay at St Peter's until the fulfilment of the prophecies which inspired them. Boniface placated them by displaying Veronica's veil to an estimated 120,000 pilgrims and proclaimed an indulgence for those who performed penance for nine days.

Some participants complained that Rome itself was a jungle, 'without justice, love, reasonableness or unity.' In summer, an outbreak of plague compounded Rome's problems. As the pope had not promulgated a Jubilee for 1400, the status of the event is uncertain. A letter of 28 March 1400 indicated that a practice later identified with Jubilees had already begun: the opening of a Jubilee door, in St John's, to signify the passage from sin to grace, through Jesus who said 'I am the door' leading to the Father. It suggests that the door may have been walled up in 1390 or even 1350.

Probably because of the Holy See's financial needs, Boniface IX accelerated the trend towards an inflation of indulgences. Roman churches were offering greater indulgences than any others, some of them advertised in fake papal bulls designed to attract pilgrims. The mechanism of indulgences seemed to have less to do with spirituality than with statistics. And with finances.

Clement VI had granted indulgences to those who could not attend the Jubilee of 1350 but fulfilled its conditions and offered alms. Boniface did the same but in a more business-like fashion. In this way he gained popularity as well as income but some contemporaries saw that he was devaluing the currency of indulgences, as he did also by permitting Jubilees in Munich, Prague, Meissen, Magdeburg and

Constance. Unlike his predecessors, he had reserved half the takings in Roman basilicas for the papal administration.

Because two claimants to the papal throne weakened the papacy, there was an attempt to bring them together in 1407 but nothing came of it. Two years later, in Pisa, cardinals of both claimants met. They elected yet another claimant as Alexander V: now there were three, and three colleges of cardinals.

At the university of Paris it was said that it would not matter if there were a dozen popes; the office had become irrelevant. A contemporary, Nicholas de Clemenges, commented that Rome had exhausted people's sympathy by 'arrogating to itself the disposition over benefices of all ranks throughout the universal church and had despoiled all other churches, throttling their rights with its own.'

Emperor Sigismund, however, was concerned at the plethora of popes for he wanted a united church to ensure social cohesion. He forced John XXIII to hold a council in Constance for which the reformer John Hus was promised safe conduct, then arrested and burnt as a heretic. Because of the council, one of the papal claimants abdicated, the other two were deposed and in 1417 a member of a prominent Roman family, Oddone Colonna, was elected pope, taking the name Martin V.

There was pressure on him to remain in Germany or in Avignon but he decided to return to Rome where he would be freer from Sigismund's pressure. As Rome was under a warlord, he stayed in Mantua and more lengthily in Florence where street urchins taunted him with 'Martino is not worth a florino.' Eventually, after two years, he was able to take possession of Rome, which by then was in a bad way: 'Once full of princes and palaces,' a curialist wrote, 'now the abode of thieves, wolves and worms.' In 1408 not even the Mass for the feast of St Peter had been celebrated.

Now that the papacy was no longer contested, Martin was able to re-establish authority in the Papal States, which had become chaotic. He assigned portions of them to his relatives, a nepotism that enraged rival Roman families. He also wrote reproving the archbishop of Canterbury for damaging Rome by granting plenary indulgences to those who visited Canterbury cathedral but his letter was ignored.

He consolidated the papacy firmly in Rome for the first time since it had transferred to Avignon over a century before. He repaired roads, bridges and buildings. An important proof of the return to normality was the decision to hold the Jubilee in 1423, 33 years after that of 1390. Lorenzo Ghiberti made a golden tiara for Martin and other artists, such as Pisanello and Gentile da Fabriano, worked in the city which was regaining its confidence. More non-Italians than Italians arrived for the Jubilee. Some humanist cardinals, scornful of popular devotions, thought the Jubilee an obsolete institution and were embarrassed by what one of them called a 'flood of dirty barbarians.'

A PETRARCHAN POPE

'So many people came to Rome [for the Jubilee of 1450] that the city could not contain the strangers, even though every house became a hotel,' wrote a Roman, Paolo del Mastro. 'Pilgrims begged, for the love of God, to be taken in but it was not possible. They had to spend the night in the open. Many perished from cold; it was terrible to see them. Still such multitudes thronged together that the city was actually starving.'

The Jubilee of 1450 drew bigger crowds than any before. Paolo del Mastro continued his eyewitness account: 'In Holy Week the throngs coming from St Peter's, or going there, were so enormous that they were crossing the bridge over the Tiber until two or three am. The crowd there was so huge that often guards had to clear a passage through it with batons to prevent serious accidents. At night many of the poor pilgrims slept under the porticos while others wandered in search of missing fathers, sons or companions ...'

Christoforo a Soldo, of Brescia, claimed, 'A greater crowd of Christians was never known to hasten to any Jubilee: kings, dukes, marquises, counts and knights.' Among these were Duke Albert of Austria, the brother of the German emperor, and William, Earl of Douglas.

It was a triumph for Nicholas V, a celebration of his success in absorbing the Council of Basel which had lasted for 18 years (1431–49). The council conducted negotiations with the Hussite movement which began in Bohemia, inspired partly by John Wycliffe's teaching on the priority of Scripture. The council was disappointed, however, that the Eastern church ignored it, preferring to attend a council convoked by Rome which achieved reunion temporarily.

The Council of Basel had been outmanoeuvred by the papacy and the reform aspirations it represented were denied if they contradicted the papal system. Rome had a diplomatic victory: sovereigns found it easier to reach agreements with the papacy than with the amorphous council. The agreements strengthened the tendency towards national churches still in communion with Rome; popes and princes divided the tax income which had previously gone entirely to Rome. In 1449 Nicholas tactfully convinced the rival pope Felix V, elected by the Basel Council, to abdicate and the council to dissolve itself.

Nicholas later encouraged a treaty between the five major powers in the Italian peninsula (Venice, Milan, Florence, Naples-Sicily and the Papal States) to preserve the balance of power. The Papal States were a substantial principality which gave the Holy See a voice in all Italian affairs. The papacy wanted both to protect its autonomy through the Papal States and prevent a foreign power dominating the peninsula. The balance of power it encouraged would be upset by the formation of an Italian nation-state, like that of France.

Nicholas had been born in 1397 as Tomasso Parentucelli, the son of a Tuscan doctor. To earn money while studying he tutored in wealthy Florentine families such as the Medici, where his taste in art and learning was refined.

He was a pope after Petrarch's own heart, convinced that classical authors and learning could be welcomed by Christian humanists rather than shunned because pagan. His passion for ancient manuscripts enabled him to bequeath 1200 in Latin and Greek which became the basis of the Vatican Library. He paid well for translations of classical and patristic texts from Greek. He sponsored works by artists such as Fra Angelico and his pupil Benozzo Gozzolo, who decorated his still extant-chapel near the Vatican Library, and had grandiose plans to beautify Rome, particularly the Vatican area, with palaces and churches. He surrounded himself with humanist cardinals such as Aeneas Silvio Piccolomini, Nicholas of Cusa and the Byzantine scholar John Bessarion who had accepted the pope's authority.

Nicholas contributed to the confusion over the timing of Jubilees. Boniface had decreed that they be celebrated each century. Clement had sensibly reduced the interval to fifty years in accordance with the Old Testament recommendation, and Roman shopkeepers' requests, while Urban VI had further reduced it to 33 years. Nicholas had rescinded Urban's ruling but promulgated a Jubilee for 1450, only 27 years after its predecessor.

Some pilgrims shared Nicholas V's Christian humanism. Giovanni Rucellai, who came to the Jubilee from Perugia with his brother, brother-in-law and his servant, recorded: 'In Rome we visited the four basilicas on horseback in the mornings but in the afternoons we visited the ancient walls and other things of note.' In earlier pilgrimages, many had been interested only in Christian monuments.

The most spectacular event of the Jubilee was the canonization in May of the Franciscan Bernardino of Siena. During the Jubilee of 1400 he had nursed plague-afflicted pilgrims at the Scala Hospital in Siena. He had been a popular but controversial preacher, incisively castigating immorality, including that of the clergy. Twice he was tried for heresy in Rome, the last time only 19 years before the grandiose canonization ceremony in St Peter's at which Nicholas praised him.

Accommodation had been overstrained in 1350 but this time there was not even enough food. Each Saturday at St John's what were believed to be the heads of Peter and Paul were displayed and each Sunday, at St Peter's, Veronica's veil. As the congregations departed, Nicholas V blessed them. But even if all the pilgrims had left by Monday, 'by the following Saturday, there were so many of them it was impossible to understand anything.'

In summer, plague reduced their numbers. 'The houses, churches and hospitals were full of the sick and the dead,' Paolo del Mastro recorded, 'and in the streets people dropped dead like dogs ... so many died it was an abyss and, on the Tuscan and Lombard roads, only corpses were to be seen.'

Some of Nicholas' relatives died from the plague and he took refuge at Fabriano in Umbria, threatening excommunication of anyone who came there from Rome. By autumn the plague ceased and again Rome was overrun. The worst traffic snarls were on and around the Sant' Angelo bridge which took pilgrims to Castel Sant' Angelo and the Vatican side of the river. On arrival pilgrims were funnelled along a street to the bridge; there was little space at its entrance. At its other end was the St Angelo gateway which gave on to a portico running to

St Peter's. The bridge itself was crammed with shops, wandering vendors and animals.

At dusk on 19 September the bridge was packed with people who had received Nicholas' blessing (the papal blessing was the culmination of every pilgrim's visit) and thousands more were trying to get on to it. On the bridge, four horses and a mule shied. Those nearest backed away. The crowd advancing, unaware why those ahead were backing on to them, pushed them under the horses' hooves. Many were trampled underfoot and others fell into the Tiber. An eyewitness, without reference to Dante, said 'Really, it seemed an inferno.' The death toll was 172. Nicholas had the shops and huts on the bridge removed.

Repaying the favors he had received as a student, Nicholas entrusted banking services for the Jubilee to the Medici. It was a profitable year for Roman innkeepers and craftsmen, particularly those who made reproductions of Veronica's veil. Nicholas devoted some of the takings to the poor but also used them to buy volumes in Greek and Latin, as a contemporary noted: 'wherever they could be found without worrying about the expense ... he convinced learned men to write new works or translate, providing huge allowances for them.'

Subsequently he sent representatives elsewhere in Europe to extend the Jubilee benefits to those who had not been able to come to Rome. One of his legates was the austere and learned Cardinal Nicholas of Cusa, author of a study of various religions, pagan, Judaic, Muslim and Hindu as well as Christian, which emphasized their similarities.

Although the Jubilee had been a striking reaffirmation of the papacy's leadership of Christendom, like that of 1300 its success was quickly followed by major problems.

In 1453, it was discovered that some Romans had plotted to kill Nicholas and establish a republic. Nicholas had the conspirators executed. The plot was a reminder that republican aspirations persisted despite the triumphs of the bishop-sovereign.

The following June he learnt that Constantinople had been sacked by the Turks the previous month. He tried to organize a crusade but was not heeded because the new nation states gave priority to their national interests. Christendom was no longer responsive to Rome's summons: instead it was giving way to a series of nations which were more or less Christian.

ORBIS IN URBE

There could not be another tragedy, Sixtus IV decided, like that of the Sant' Angelo bridge during the Jubilee of 1450. A bridge further downstream had to be ready for the Jubilee of 1475 and it was (the Ponte Sisto).

In preparing for the Jubilee Sixtus had the services of the great Florentine architect Leon Battista Alberti, who transformed much of medieval Rome into a Renaissance city by widening and paving streets as well as opening new ones. Sixtus rose early to supervise construction work. The city was spreading into the vineyards and vegetable plots in what is now the Piazza del Popolo area where the church of Santa Maria del Popolo took its present form shortly afterwards. During Sixtus' reign, the chapel in the Vatican named after him, the Sistine, was built and its choir established. He founded the Vatican archives, expanded its library and hired the best artists to decorate the papal palaces. No expense was spared, but his plan to turn the Colosseum into a wool factory was not carried out.

Born in 1414 to a poor Ligurian family, Francesco della Rovere became a Franciscan and rose to be head of the order. He was a popular preacher, a perceptive theologian and a respected scholar. Personally austere, after his election as Sixtus IV he proved to be ruthless. He seemed to aspire to be neither Christ nor St Francis but a Renaissance prince.

His predecessor, Paul II (1464–1471), had reduced the interval between Jubilees to 25 years, which has remained the rule, but his unexpected death at the age of 54 prevented him presiding over that of 1475. Sixtus' fear that there would be too many pilgrims for the Sant' Angelo bridge might prove inadequate was unfounded as there were fewer visitors than in 1450. One reason was that in the preceding decade an indulgence craze had developed and they were dispensed throughout Europe. For 1475 they were restricted to Rome but this did not attract huge numbers, particularly as wars threatened some pilgrim routes. Moreover towards Christmas the Tiber flooded, then disease broke out.

Sixtus decided to prolong the Jubilee until Easter 1476 and allowed indulgences to be granted also in Bologna. A goodly proportion of pilgrims went there instead. Among those who did come to Rome were King Ferdinand of Naples, Queen Dorothy of Denmark, King Mattia Corvino of Hungary and Charlotte, the former Queen of Cyprus. The pilgrims' offerings, which were generous, were used for the papal-led struggle against the Turks who by now were threatening Italy.

Responding to an appeal from Spanish civil and religious authorities, Sixtus established the Spanish Inquisition. He also appointed two young nephews cardinals and favored them in every way. Nepotism was to prove a persistent defect of the papacy. Beset by factions, threatened by plots, several popes trusted only their relatives. Moreover, as the papacy was not a hereditary dynasty but an elective monarchy, some incumbents, as if mindful that charity begins at home, set up their relatives for ever by giving them titles and wealth. Pillaging the church's coffers was bad enough but it was worse still when papal policy was determined by the interests of the reigning pope's family. Dante, who upheld the dignity of the papacy, had realized how damaging was a policy shaped by a papal family's interests. The majestic Cancelleria palace, site now of the Vatican marriage tribunal the Sacred Rota, has been called a monument to nepotism. It was financed with 60,000 scudi which Sixtus IV's cardinal nephew Riario Sforza, in one night's gambling, won from Franceschetto Cibo, whose uncle was to be Innocent VIII (1484–1492).

A Medici, Pope Leo X (1513–21), confiscated the palace from the Riario family for plotting against him. In fact, Sixtus' nephews had involved him in the killing of one of the Medicis and, consequently, in a futile war against Florence. This and similar adventures, along with Sixtus' grandiose plans for Rome, indebted the papacy. He tried to raise money by decreeing that the first year's income from all benefices, less expenses, be sent to Rome and by boosting the offerings of alms for indulgences. A Bosnian archbishop wanted a council to judge Sixtus but the pope banned appeals to councils.

Alexander VI (1490–1503) prepared for the Jubilee of 1500 with at least as much care as Sixtus IV had for that of 1450. He decided that a Holy Door should be opened in each of the Jubilee basilicas in memory of Christ describing himself as the door of salvation. In St Peter's a new door-space was hacked out then filled with a thin layer of bricks which, to inaugurate the Jubilee on Christmas Eve, Alexander knocked down with an ordinary hammer. It had been done at St John Lateran from 1400 but Alexander gave it new importance by creating a ceremony which in most respects is still in force. While the pope opened the door at St Peter's, cardinals he delegated did likewise at the other three jubilee basilicas.

Adequate supplies were ensured for the pilgrims and prices blocked. A new straight street was opened from Castel Sant' Angelo to St Peter's. Fighting in the Milan area and brigands infesting one of the main consular roads to the north, the via Cassia, discouraged pilgrims but 100,000 were estimated to have received the pope's blessing on Holy Thursday. The crush was such, one participant wrote, that there was *Orbis in Urbe*, the world in the city. Among the notable visitors were an astronomer from Cracow, Nicholas Copernicus, who may have wanted to ascertain whether the earth still turned around Rome. While in the city he taught a course for scientists.

During Easter Week, Alexander VI, on horseback and accompanied by ambassadors and court prelates, visited the four basilicas. He was devout, a reformer of slack religious orders, politically shrewd and a promoter of missions but he certainly needed to ask pardon. Born Rodrigo de Borja e Borja near Valencia in 1431, he was the nephew of Callistus III (1455–8) who gave him benefices from the time he was a youth, then made him a cardinal and, at the age of 26, vice chancellor of the Holy See. He fathered several children and accumulated vast wealth which was as illegitimate as his offspring. In Italy, his name was spelt Borgia and he did his best to make it notorious.

Bribery helped him win the papal election in 1493. He was a competent administrator and a patron of the arts: during his reign, Pinturrichio decorated the Borgia apartments in the Vatican and Michelangelo prepared plans for a new St Peter's because the foundations of the original basilica were insecure.

Shortly before Alexander's election, a Genoese-born seaman Christopher Columbus, desiring glory, gold and the spread of the faith, had reached the Americas. It seems that the Holy See, as well as the Castilian and Aragonese royal houses, had backed his adventure; Columbus sought a cardinalate for his son but nothing came of it, perhaps because the Genoese pope Innocent VIII had been replaced by Alexander. At the time of Alexander, the first gold from the Americas was used to decorate the ceiling of St Mary Major. At the request of the Spanish sovereigns he divided the world, for the purposes of exploration, between Spain and Portugal, which is why Portuguese is the language of Brazil.

Alexander used the papacy to enrich his family and even tried to put the Papal States in their hands. The Borgias raised money by assassinations followed by appropriation of the victims' property and also by sale of the cardinalate which was then open to the laity.

Even before the corrupt Borgia family emerged, some considered that the church was too compliant with a worldly culture. A Dominican friar, Girolamo Savonarola, felt that Christian humanism had given way to a paganism in which aestheticism was sometimes mixed with necromancy. Machiavelli expressed something of the new spirit: 'To act, without considering whether the action be good or evil, to love, without worrying if it be right or wrong.' Savonarola denounced the excesses of Medicean Florence but also those of Rome. For him, Alexander was neither pope nor true Christian. Alexander wanted Savonarola to come to Rome but he did not go, perhaps fearful of the Borgia's poisoned sweets. Eventually Savonarola was condemned as a heretic, hanged in the Piazza della Signoria in front of the Florence Town Hall, then burned.

On 29 June in the Jubilee year, Alexander was giving an audience to two cardinals in his apartment when a chimney stack, toppled by a storm, crashed through the roof. Three people were killed but Alexander escaped with some injuries and fright. He resolved to mend his ways as he had many times, for instance after a son Giovanni had been killed three years before. But when, shortly afterwards, his favorite son Cesare killed the husband of his sister Lucrezia, Alexander protected him.

Although the pilgrim offerings in St Peter's were kept in a strongbox with three locks, a contemporary chronicler, Sigismondo de' Conti, claimed that notorious Cesare got to the strongbox and used the pilgrims' offerings to pay for his wars and vices. The Jubilee opened the church's treasure of grace but it was altogether too much that a pope's son got his hands on the Jubilee treasury. Alexander's inability to control his children or amend his life made a parody of the Jubilee and the papacy.

Some popes of the period were Medici or acted like Medici; others seemed Masters of Revels more than Vicars of Christ; Alexander was a slave to his passions and family. The contemporary Florentine historian, Francesco Guicciardini, deplored Alexander's 'most wicked customs, without sincerity, without shame, without truth, without faith, without religion; insatiable avarice, immoderate ambition, cruelty more than barbarous.' A Roman was more concise in a couplet left at an ancient torso called Pasquino (hence pasquinade) which stands near Piazza Navona:

> *Alexander sold altars, the Keys and Christ,*
> *As well he might, for he knew their price.*

Savonarola's prophetic powers had not been overstrained when he foretold that, with the papacy at such a low point, a scourge would follow.

JUBILEE OR COUNCIL?

There were cogent reasons for not holding a Jubilee in 1525 but Clement VII (I525–34) ignored them. One was the war in course between Francis I of France and Charles V of the Habsburgs of Spain and Flanders. Much of the war was fought in Italy. Some hoped that a Jubilee would lead to a year-long truce. It did not but at least that possibility provided some justification for going ahead with the project.

The other argument for not holding the Jubilee was stronger: the Lutheran revolt was under way and it seemed provocative to promulgate a Jubilee when indulgences were such a sore point. The protest against indulgences was not only caused by Jubilees but they were a conspicuous occasion for their abuse. They had got out of hand. The fight against the Turks as well as the nepotism and ambitious building projects of some popes had brought an ever-growing need for funds. Rome seemed to know the price of indulgences but not their value. In the worst cases of offering indulgences for alms, the church was accused of selling salvation. In less deplorable cases, indulgences seemed an accounting operation rather than part of a process of reconciliation and amendment of life.

On his arrival in Rome in 1511, Martin Luther, according to his own account, fell on his knees, held up his hands to heaven and cried,

'Hail, holy Rome, sanctified by the holy martyrs and by the blood they shed here.' Later, ascending the Holy Stairs near St John Lateran on his knees, he heard a voice which directed him to seek another path to grace. And he was incensed when spendthrift Leo X (1510–1521) sold indulgences to cover his debts and the expenses of the new St Peter's. 'The pope does well when he obtains indulgences for poor souls with his prayers,' Luther commented, 'but whoever says that, "as soon as coin in coffer rings, a soul from purgatory springs" is spreading damned and sinful human doctrine.' (Johann Tetzel and other indulgence preachers had claimed that payments brought instant release of souls from purgatory.) His attacks on indulgence abuse became a criticism of the theology underlying them and of the papacy, which suited the German princes whose primary interests were often not religious. If Clement had summoned a general council, as many who wanted a reform of 'head and members' requested, the breach with Luther's followers may have been healed, but instead he held a Jubilee.

Though the illegitimate son of Giuliano de' Medici, Giulio de Medici was nevertheless made archbishop of Florence and a cardinal by his cousin Leo X. As Clement VII he was to commission Michelangelo Buonarotti's *Last Judgement* and support other artists such as Benvenuto Cellini and Raphael, as well as Niccolo Machiavelli, Francesco Guicciardini and other men of letters. However, despite his conversations with leading cultural figures, he did not recognize that a spiritual revolution was under way. His rigidity, or refusal to sacrifice principle to expediency over Henry VIII's divorce from Catherine of Aragon, meant alienation of much of the church in England, just as Lutheranism was spreading from Germany to Scandinavia.

As the polemic against indulgences followed shortly after the invention of printing, attacks on the Jubilee were made in printed tracts. A book of satirical verse published in Germany in 1525 contrasted the Roman Jubilee with that of Christ:

> *One is that of Christ the Lord*
> *The other what the Popes accord.*
> *Who wisely reads this book at home*
> *Will not for pardon run to Rome.*

In other publications, Rome was attacked as 'the Whore of Babylon', the pope as 'Antichrist', and it was argued that, as Christ's grace had saved humankind, there was no need to pay money to win heaven. Of course, indulgences never pretended to forgive sin but were granted only to those who had confessed, but the point of the argument was that there was no need for Rome's mediation.

About this time John Calvin, in Geneva, made a scathing attack on relics, pointing out that many were fake or dubious and argued that, even when authentic, they were not useful. The crusaders had brought back many relics from the Holy Land and Constantinople which only seemed to increase the demand for them. Remains of saints were divided into ever-smaller pieces. The church tried to check their authenticity but many hoaxes were perpetrated which discredited all relics: it was easy to make fun of the several heads of John the Baptist, countless nails or splinters said to have come from the true cross and various shrouds of Christ. Guidebooks promised that in the basilica of St John Lateran pilgrims would find the heads of Peter and Paul, the Ark of the Covenant, Moses' tablets, Aaron's rod, manna in a gold urn, the two fish and five loaves which nourished multitudes and the table on which the Last Supper was served.

When the church was being criticised for its lavishness, Clement's adoption of a gold hammer, or more exactly a pick with a hammer head on one side, to open the Jubilee door in St Peter's indicated that he misjudged the mood of the times. There were comparatively few pilgrims in 1525 and a plague for many months in Rome was not the only reason.

The atmosphere had changed dramatically by 1550. In 1527, the Lanzichenecchi, the emperors' troops, had sacked Rome, stabling their horses and bivouacking in St Peter's. The papal court, valiantly defended by the Swiss Guards who had been established two decades earlier, had taken refuge in fortified Castel Sant' Angelo. Michelangelo Buonarotti painted his 'Last Judgement' in the Sistine Chapel after the sack of Rome, and the stark terror many figures express, in contrast to the ceiling scenes painted there much earlier, is attributed by some to the shock caused by the onslaught. Another consequence was apocalyptic preaching on the Sant' Angelo bridge with threats such as, 'Hell for sinners! Hell for adulterers!'

Renovation of the papacy and the church was being fostered by Alessandro Farnese whose sister had been one of Alexander VI's mistresses. Alessandro himself had fathered four illegitimate children and was made cardinal (nicknamed 'Cardinal Petticoat' because of his sister's relation with the pope) before ordination as a priest in 1519. As Paul III, he continued papal patronage of art, revived Carnival and favored his own family outrageously. In his *Memoirs*, Benvenuto Cellini, the Florentine goldsmith who designed coins for both Clement VII and Paul III, describes a Rome in which plagues were frequent and popes could do anything they liked. Cellini reports Paul III explaining why he gave him (Cellini) safe conduct although he had killed: 'Geniuses like Benvenuto are not subject to the law.'

But Paul recognized the need for church reform. He encouraged new religious orders such as the Society of Jesus (the Jesuits), Barnabites, Ursulines, Theatines and Somaschi, instituted the Roman Inquisition and launched the Council of Trent.

He died towards the end of 1549 without promulgating a Jubilee. The subsequent papal election lasted ten weeks before, on 8 February 1550, a Roman canonist, Giovanni Maria Ciocchi del Monte, was chosen and took the name Julius III. He was in the tradition of pleasure-loving Renaissance popes but honored his election oath to ensure resumption of the Council of Trent.

Julius immediately promulgated a Jubilee; the Holy Year door of St Peter's was opened in February. Emperor Charles V, the French king Henry II and the Duke of Florence sent ambassadors while the dukes of Ferrara and Urbino attended in person. Perhaps more interesting figures present were the former Spanish soldier, Ignatius Loyola, who was living in Rome with his first Jesuit companions, and Philip Neri, a Rome-resident Florentine layman, a prankster and mystic who two years earlier had founded the Holy Trinity Confraternity devoted to welcoming pilgrims in a hospice where they had free accommodation.

Such hospices, like those built along the pilgrim routes, were evidence of the Jubilees' social effects. They also had a cultural aspect: some of the earliest oratorios were composed for them and, since the late fifteenth century, during Jubilees the Confraternity of the Gonfalone (Banner) had presented sacred dramas in the Colosseum and elsewhere as part of them.

SCRIMMAGE AT THE HOLY DOOR

Gregory XIII took the silver hammer-pick in both hands and smashed it against the brick screen before the Jubilee door of St Peter's on Christmas Eve 1575. The handle broke, cutting his fingers, but he hammered with determination until a hole appeared in the brickwork. Officials who had stood on either side of the door then continued the onslaught with mallets. The screen fell with a crash.

Pandemonium ensued. The front ranks of the crowd, workmen who had previously loosened the mortar of the screen, and even guards threw themselves on the rubble. It was not only because the bricks had a pontifical imprint but because gold and silver coins and medals minted for the previous Jubilee were always enclosed in the screen as if it were a Christmas pudding.

Francesco Mucanzio, the papal master of ceremonies who recorded the episode in his diary, shouted at the souvenir seekers to desist but his voice could not be heard above the din. Gregory was to enter St Peter's first, promising a new reign of peace and justice, but some of the crowd, estimated at 300,000, rushed in ahead of him. This prevented clerics sweeping the threshold and washing the lintels with holy water. The pope said some of the prescribed prayers but in the uproar not even the choir's responses could be heard.

After half an hour, a way was cleared for the pope's entry, a *Te Deum* was intoned and the guns of Castel Sant' Angelo fired to celebrate the inauguration of yet another Jubilee. At the end of vespers, the pope learnt that in the crazed scrimmage at the door six people had been killed.

It was a disconcerting start to a Jubilee which had been prepared carefully by Gregory XIII who, among other things, intended it as a plea for God's help against the Turks. Born on 1 January 1502, the son of a Bolognese merchant, Ugo Boncompagni had been a law professor for eight years during which, although unmarried, he fathered a son. Cardinal Charles Borromeo, Archbishop of Milan, convinced the future pope to take his faith seriously and later he helped draft many of the decrees of the Council of Trent which concluded, after a span of 18 years, in 1563.

Although 70 when elected in 1572 he was still a hard worker who ensured application of the Tridentine decrees, partly through support for the rapidly expanding Jesuits who trained clergy rigorously. He established the Jesuit College named after him, the Gregorian University, and also many residential colleges for priests in Rome including those for the English, Greeks, Armenians and Maronites. As well as encouraging missions in India, China, Japan and Brazil, he used the nunciatures, which previously had exclusively diplomatic functions, to push through church reform. He would stop at nothing to win back Protestants: he had almost complete success in Poland and some in Germany. During his reign, the calendar introduced by Julius Caesar was replaced by the Gregorian calendar which dropped ten days and established a new rule for leap years. It was not adopted immediately in Protestant countries; England introduced it only in the mid-eighteenth century. He started construction of a summer residence on one of Rome's hills, the Quirinal, which is now used by the Italian President, and also built major churches such as the Gesù and Sant' Andrea della Valle.

The new St Peter's was under construction. Pilgrims saw the facade of the basilica built by Emperor Constantine, similar to the present St Paul's Outside the Walls, but thrusting up behind it was the 'drum' of the new St Peter's which was not yet crowned by its dome. Michelangelo had died eleven years before the Jubilee. The original St Peter's continued to function while construction of the current basilica went ahead. For critics, the new St Peter's represented Rome's appetite for money and power, but for others it represented new energy and, when the dome was finally in place, new confidence and centrality.

It can be seen as a proud response to the Reformation, an affirmation not only of God but of humanity, of its works and glories. But it may also have been a response to the loss of Constantinople and Hagia Sophia, the 'Great Church', where the last Mass, on 2 May 1453, was concelebrated by Orthodox and Catholics because reunion had taken place temporarily.

Perhaps it was partly to compensate for those losses, and for the shock of the transformation of Hagia Sophia into a mosque, that a new church was built. Constantinople had been the second Rome; Rome would be the second Constantinople while remaining itself. The decision to replace the original St Peter's had been taken before the Jubilee of 1575. It was a surprising decision because probably the original St Peter's could have been buttressed. It was also carried out with a certain callousness because, at a time when relics were sought far and wide, the bones of all the early popes, such as Gregory the Great, seem to have been thrown away or into a heap now under the new St Peter's. Moreover, precious works of art were destroyed.

The building of a new St Peter's was an indication of a titanic energy which was at work also in the cultural ferment. Many catacombs had just been rediscovered; scrupulous, stubborn Cardinal Cesare Baronio was at work on his painstaking 12-volume *Ecclesiastical Annals*, which responded effectively to Lutheran versions of church history; and the gifted composer Giovanni Pierluigi da Palestrina became director of the pontifical choir.

Important for the resurgence of the city was the repair and reconnection of the first aqueduct since Gothic besiegers had cut them all in 537. For over a thousand years Romans had depended on the Tiber for their drinking water. Another effect of the cutting of the aqueducts had been the installation of floating grain mills on the river. Soon other aqueducts were reconnected and spectacular fountains erected at their terminals to celebrate the return of water, with its connotations of pardon, baptism, passing time, abundance and playfulness, to the city of stone.

Gregory's thoroughness was evident in the Jubilee preparations which included fixing stable rent, inn and food prices, and construction of the broad via Merulana which joins St John Lateran to St Mary Major, an amenity praised by the French visitor Michel de Montaigne who had noted that Roman roads were poor 'because of defects in the terrain and because hardly anyone lives by manual work.'

Gregory advised curialists to avoid ostentation. New-fangled coaches were all the rage among cardinals and aristocrats: Charles

Borromeo, the archbishop of Milan, commented that in Rome two things were necessary: 'to love God and keep a coach.' There were at least 2000 coaches in a city which now had about 80,000 inhabitants, but the pope wanted cardinals to revert to horseback for ceremonial occasions. A contemporary print shows a cardinal's coach built on the lines of a brewery dray. Under a covering, probably of red velvet and gilt, the cardinal is seated in a raised look-out at the rear, his attendants can be seen in the middle of the coach and there is another figure behind the horses and driver. The coach looks large enough for journeys along the consular roads. When cardinals moved they were accompanied by other coaches so that, as Mucanzio wrote, 'the roads are obstructed for all other passengers … if there is a ceremony it becomes impossible for people on foot to move along.'

Some cardinals had more than one coach, but Gregory's recommendation was heeded, for many of them visited the Jubilee basilicas on foot. Gregory himself, who was 73, was taken to them on a litter but walked the last stretch. His zeal, that of his predecessor Pius V and the influence of the Council of Trent were felt in the 'fervor and devotion' contemporaries noted.

'It is fortunate,' the Venetian ambassador Tiepolo reported to his government, 'that two pontiffs of such irreproachable lives should have succeeded one another, for by their example every one has become, or appears to have become, better … the whole town leads a better and incomparably more Christian existence.'

Eight years before the Jubilee, Pius V had finally introduced an effective measure against indulgence abuses by abrogating 'every indulgence … for which a helping hand must be offered, and which contains in any way whatsoever permission to make collections.' It reduced revenue for many churches, monasteries and hospitals but also drastically reduced indulgence 'traffic'.

Charles Borromeo embodied post-Tridentine seriousness. He realized that thorough preparation was needed to benefit spiritually from a Jubilee and also that his whole diocese of Milan could benefit by extending the Jubilee there for a year after it concluded in Rome. He took 13 days to come from Milan as a pilgrim, visiting on the way sanctuaries at Camaldoli, La Verna, Vallombrosa and Monte Oliveto. During the month he spent in Rome he made the prescribed visits by foot, and sometimes barefooted, not only to the four basilicas but to the three more which by now had been added to many pilgrims' itineraries: St Lawrence Outside the Walls, St Sebastian and Holy

Cross of Jerusalem. He also gave hospitality to Milanese pilgrims in his residence at the church of St Prassede and frequently climbed the Holy Stairs

Confraternities had been encouraged by the Council of Trent and were prominent during the Jubilee. They were associations of laity for a religious or philanthropic purpose. Their members wore colorful habits which had a hood to ensure anonymity while doing good; the garb was to be adopted by the Ku Klux Klan—to ensure anonymity while doing evil. They came from all over Italy and beyond and often were met on arrival by members of Rome's corresponding confraternities. In the city streets they held processions of as many as 7000 people at a time, carrying crosses or other religious symbols and singing haunting hymns. Montaigne described one such procession: 'The most notable and surprising thing I have ever seen anywhere was the extraordinary number of people in the streets ... once night fell, lights appeared everywhere because all the confraternity members held a torch as they converged towards St Peter's. I believe 12,000 torches passed in front of me because from 8.00 pm the road was always full of this procession which, although the participants came from various directions, was so orderly that there was never a gap or an interruption.'

Most involved in the Jubilee was the Confraternity of the Holy Trinity for Pilgrims and Convalescents established by the layman Philip Neri who, by 1575, had become a priest and had founded a religious congregation which held meetings where the Bible was read and commented upon, prayers were said, psalms sung and music played. The meetings were held not in a church but in a hall known as the Oratory. A development of the music used there took the name Oratorio, while in some countries the religious congregation itself became known as the Oratory.

An innkeeper, Rocco Marsini, described his experience of the confraternity on arrival in 1575 with a group of sixty pilgrims from Viterbo. They were resting near the Milvian bridge, which brings travellers from the north across the Tiber, when six confraternity members arrived, entertained them with music and invited them to lodge at their hospice near the Ponte Sisto bridge a few miles downstream.

On arrival, they were met by forty men wearing the red habit of the confraternity who took them to pray in the church attached to their hospice, a huge, extant building near the Ponte Sisto. After a copious dinner, they were taken to a room where confraternity members washed their feet in tepid water and dried them with fragrant towels before sending them by pairs to double beds with fresh linen. Confraternity members also accompanied Marsini and his companions when they fulfilled the Jubilee obligations.

The majority of the guests were Italian. Many non-Italians, such as Germans, Spanish, French and English, found accommodation in their own national hospices or colleges. For the 1575 Jubilee, Armenians, Ethiopians and Arabic-speaking Christians arrived providing a reminder that the church was not simply European.

Certification by a bishop was necessary for entry to the Trinity hospice because, as accommodation was free, some pretended to be pilgrims. Three hundred and sixty-five meals could be provided at the same time in the refectory. Nobles and prelates competed to raise money for it, serve at its tables or wash pilgrims' feet. The Trinity hospice was also to house Europe's first convalescent hospital.

About 400,000 people attended, which was less than for some previous Jubilees but in many European countries Catholics were in difficulties. Mindful of the troubles of English Catholics, Gregory decreed that they could benefit from the Jubilee indulgence by reciting 15 rosaries.

A new motif in this Jubilee was rejoicing at the return of those who had become Protestant. There was an underlying sadness connected with this, however, for it was a reminder that, although more authentically religious, Rome was no longer recognized as the center of Christianity by all Western Christians.

INCENSE AND
BURNING FLESH

Devout Clement VIII (1592–1605) ensured meticulous preparation for the Jubilee of 1600 during which he walked barefoot to the Jubilee churches each month. He had been born Ippolito Aldobrandini, the son of a Florentine lawyer driven from the city by the Medici, had graduated in law and served the papacy for years before becoming a priest. Sixtus V (1583–90) made him a cardinal and appointed him as his legate for a successful diplomatic mission in Poland

Sixtus, an imperious Franciscan, provided both a model and a cautionary tale for the future Clement VIII. He epitomized the energy coursing through Rome as a result of the Council of Trent but also because of economic and demographic growth. It has been said that in this period each pope tried to cover with gold and marble whatever had been left bare in Roman churches by his predecessors. A contemporary compared the new St Peter's to the celestial Jerusalem as described by John the Evangelist and Rome's fountains to the water of life which rises there. Its martyrs were the secret source of repeated rebirths. Their relics had been brought from the catacombs into the city churches when it was threatened by Goth and Lombard invaders. Other relics had been brought from Jerusalem both at the time of St Helena and during the Crusades. Crusaders had also brought relics from Constantinople as had centuries earlier many refugees from the iconoclastic controversy. Rome was a huge reliquary and church art was created to honor the saints' remains.

Behind the defences erected by the Council of Trent and the policing of thought by the Inquisition, Rome was to serve as a model for doctrine, devotion and also church building: new structures such as St Andrea della Valle, begun in 1591, were copied as far away as Cracow.

Sixtus had wiped out banditry in the Papal States by executing thousands of bandits, then displaying their heads on the Sant' Angelo bridge and in other public places. He made Rome a splendid baroque city, opening up roads to link the seven pilgrim churches (one of them, which runs from the top of the Spanish steps towards St Mary Major still bears his name—the via Sistina); at important sites he erected cross-crowned Egyptian obelisks which still stand like exclamation marks in the text of Rome. The dome of St Peter's was completed during his reign; the Lateran palace was rebuilt and the Vatican printing press established.

By a vigorous economic policy he made the papacy financially independent. He reorganized the papal administration and raised the number of cardinals to a maximum of seventy, two measures which lasted until the Second Vatican Council and helped him enforce the decrees of the Council of Trent. He encouraged missionaries in Japan, China, the Philippines and Latin America.

Sixtus had been a towering figure but was hated by many Romans who, on his death, tore down his statue on the Capitoline Hill. His nickname, the Iron Pope, and his motto 'Don't suffer fools gladly,' reflect a man who cared only about getting the job done.

Clement was more likeable and more obviously pious than Sixtus. He too was a hard worker but lacked Sixtus' decisiveness and also his tight financial control. Both were austere, but still appointed teenage relatives as cardinals.

Clement continued Sixtus' policy of applying the Council of Trent although the momentum of renewal was decreasing. He recognized the former Huguenot Henry IV as King of France even though this entailed recognition of the Huguenots' religious freedom and civil rights. Henry's subsequent support helped Clement reduce Spanish influence both in European politics and in the college of cardinals.

He endorsed proposals to allow millions of Christians in what is now eastern Poland and western Ukraine to retain their Eastern liturgy provided they recognized the papacy's jurisdiction. It was intended as a first step toward eventual reunion of the Eastern and Western churches but instead it was considered, as today, an offence by the Orthodox.

The Jewish community in Rome offered 500 straw mattresses and an equal number of bedspreads for Jubilee visitors. Clement prohibited the raising of swine within the city walls during 1600 and ordered that stones obstructing carriages be cleared from roads. Plaques from this time, carrying threats of punishment for those dirtying the roads, are still visible in central Rome where, at the time of Clement, people often tossed garbage into the streets, horses added their contribution and fountains were obstructed by fruit and vegetables cooling in their waters.

For the Jubilee, Carnival was suspended. Visitors found that Rome was not the Babylon condemned by Protestant polemicists: some converted, including the son of a German pastor who was related to John Calvin. Such well-publicized conversions kept alive hopes that Protestantism might eventually be absorbed.

Although Clement was in poor health, during the Jubilee he visited the basilicas sixty times, double the number prescribed for Rome residents, and climbed the Holy Stairs seventy times. He attended talks by cardinals such as the historian Cesare Baronio and the Jesuit theologian Robert Bellarmine, whom he had made a cardinal the previous year. Bellarmine's *Disputations concerning the Controversies of the Christian Faith against Heretics of this Age*, which marshaled the Catholic response to Lutheranism, was to go through a hundred editions in the next 150 years.

Clement had a soft spot for pilgrims from his family's city, Florence, and invited them to eat with him. During Easter week, he heard the confession of pilgrims in St Peter's and daily during Lent invited a dozen poor people to lunch. He washed pilgrims' feet and served them at table. Some cardinals followed his example: Cardinal Andrea, nephew of Emperor Maximilian II of Austria, lodged incognito at the Trinity hospice before the pope discovered his presence and brought him to the Vatican. Within a few weeks he died there.

Other cardinals, however, continued to behave like princes: on his visits to the basilicas, Cardinal Farnese had a retinue of 120 horses. Some aristocrats had as many as 800. Among the VIPs were the duke of Bavaria, the viceroy of Naples, the ambassador of Henry IV of France and the naval commander of the Knights of Malta. The

Knights' fleet had been crucial in the battle of Lepanto of 1571 which saved Europe from the Turkish threat.

Romans rushed from one part of the city to another to see the arrival of the confraternities. On the evening of 9 May, that from Foligno arrived: first children dressed as angels, then adults as Old Testament figures, followed by scenes of Christ's passion. Seen in the flickering light of the pilgrims' torches and with their musical accompaniment, the Foligno show was much admired by Romans. The pilgrimage from L'Aquila, in the mountainous Abruzzo region, consisted of 1200 people who walked in total silence while that from Apulia, in the heel of the peninsula, entered barefoot as the pilgrims whipped themselves with chains. Pilgrims from the wine-producing hill towns near Rome acquired a reputation as brawlers, noisy and bibulous. For the following year, Clement conceded the Jubilee indulgence beyond Rome on fulfillment of certain conditions.

At times confraternities clashed. Some members of the Trinity Confraternity squabbled with those of the Gonfalone over precedence in crossing a bridge. However they joined forces against members of a Neapolitan Confraternity which arrived at that moment. Their leader threw away the crucifix he was carrying and drew his sword.

The Trinity hospice, subsidized by the pope, took additional quarters in buildings along the Tiber bank to handle the influx and some of its wealthier members invited pilgrims to their own homes. Altogether it accommodated 210,000 pilgrims out of an estimated total of half a million in a city whose population was by now over 100,000. One participant recorded in his diary the number of foreign priests who attended: 2545 from Gaul and Brittany, 126 Greek-speakers and Dalmatians, 109 from Poland, 83 from Germany, two each from Moscow, Spain and Portugal, and one from England.

Two episodes in 1600 mirror the chiaroscuro of the era. For the church of San Luigi dei Francesi, completed only twenty years earlier, an artist who was just thirty had finished his first great religious painting. Caravaggio had come to Rome from Lombardy about 1589, at the age of 16, and later Cardinal Francesco del Monte had taken him into his residence. Initially the priests of San Luigi declined his work but, in 1600, hung his depictions of St Matthew's Calling and Martyrdom. Probably the priests were shocked by the paintings' hyperrealism emphasized by light shafting into the gloom of a torrid world and even more by Caravaggio's reputation as a violent brawler quick to use his sword. Six years later he killed an opponent after an argument at the end of a ball game and had to flee Rome. The Jubilee should have resounded for Caravaggio, some of whose paintings capture the drama of conversion and who personally needed pardon frequently, but he may have been wholly absorbed by his first major success.

A second episode reflected the darker side of the Counter-Reformation. This was both a Catholic reform movement, which had begun before Luther and was now supported by popes such as Sixtus V and Clement VIII, and also a battle against the Protestant Reformation and doctrinal error in general. At the Campo dei Fiori in central Rome on 17 February 1600 Giordano Bruno was burnt to death as a heretic. A metal gag used on those who insulted God was applied to Bruno at the stake. It had two blades, one against the tongue, the other against the palate.

Bruno, 52, a noble from Nola near Naples, became a Dominican but his philosophical studies gradually brought him to advocate a kind of pantheism and despise not only Catholicism but also Lutheranism and Calvanism as superstition. Arrested in Venice and tried by the Inquisition in Rome in 1593, he spent seven years in prison where he retracted several but not all of his opinions. In such cases, priests were laicized and civil authorities applied to them the law against heretics as a social danger. Bruno is the best-known of the thirty heretics put to death after trial by the Roman Inquisition during Clement's reign. Combating the Reformation had made it zealous in stamping out heresy. During the Jubilee of 1600 the aroma of incense was tinged by the smell of burning flesh.

NO ORDINARY POPE

A nother Jubilee was held in 1617 but it was Lutheran, held in Saxony to celebrate the first centenary of the Reformation. In Rome, Jubilees were recurring in a regular 25 year rhythm. The Jubilee of 1625 was virtually the inauguration of the pontificate of Urban VIII, which promised to be exceptional: Urban himself said, 'I am no ordinary Pope.' There was no hint that, before his time was out, his friend Galileo Galilei would be threatened with torture and forced to abjure the Copernican system; that Urban would plunge into a losing conflict over the small fiefdom of Castro which wrecked papal finances and made him remorseful about squandering revenue; and that his death in midsummer 1644 would be greeted by Romans as a liberation.

Maffeo Barberini, born into a wealthy Florentine merchant family in 1568, was educated by the Jesuits. After graduation in law at Pisa, an uncle who was a pronotary apostolic launched him on a curial career in which he carried out several successful diplomatic missions. When elected Urban VIII, he was 57, a handsome man with a moustache and goatee, a Latin versifier with a fine library who, to a Belgian observer, seemed 'more prince than pope, more governor than pastor.' He was a throwback to the Medici popes and, indeed, his family had become one of the Florentine new rich at the same time as the Medici and the Chigi families.

Urban inaugurated the new St Peter's and embellished Rome immensely through patronage of Gian Lorenzo Bernini, whose self-portrait as a young man shows him with a long, dark rat's-tail moustache and a goatee. He had a thin, Don Quixote-type face, brimming with energy. Gian Lorenzo, who was to put his imprint on Rome, was born in Naples in 1598 to a sculptor-father, Pietro, who took him to the papal city as a boy. Art historians argue whether the beached boat fountain in Piazza di Spagna should be attributed to father or son. Gian Lorenzo was an architect, painter, scenographer and medalist, as well as one of the greatest sculptors, and each skill fed the others. Rome was the stage which gave full play to his virtuosity, dynamism and theatrical instincts.

He was charming, the favorite of Pope Urban and the fashionable world, which made some artists suspect he was a lackey; they also resented that occasionally he took credit for the work of others. His religious fervor was praised, but this was most evident towards the end of his life. Earlier he was notorious for his rages: when he discovered his brother was sleeping with his mistress he tried to murder him and have his mistress disfigured.

Among other works Bernini carried out under Urban VIII were completion of the palace of the pope's family, which is now the National Gallery of Art, and the Triton fountain in front of it; the facade of the missionary headquarters, Propaganda Fide, on Piazza di Spagna; the statue of St Longinus holding a lance in St Peter's; and the baldacchino there, which was begun in the year before the Jubilee. This canopy over the main altar, with its writhing columns, is decorated with the Barberini bee emblem. The marble plinths on which it stands have a series of bas-reliefs of the Barberini escutcheon which seem to show a woman's expression as she gives birth. It is believed to be in thanksgiving for the successful completion of a difficult pregnancy by Urban VIII's favorite niece.

Although a patron of the arts, Urban cared little for ancient monuments, stripping bronze from the Pantheon which, according to some, was used for the Bernini canopy but, according to others, to cast cannons for Castel Sant' Angelo as part of his strengthening of defences. The spoliation of the Pantheon provoked a withering pasquinade: *Quod non fecerunt barbari, fecerunt Barberini*—The Barberini have done what the barbarians dared not.

He intended to make a resplendent Rome and a stronger Papal States the basis for a decisive role in Europe where the fate of the Reformation was still in the balance and the Thirty Years War was being fought. But little came of his plans and Protestantism consolidated its hold on north-west Europe.

Urban had diplomatic skills but also genuine religious concerns. He wrote many hymns for the revised breviary; to combat the proliferation of saints, which was one cause of the Reformation, he put control of canonization totally in Roman hands, establishing procedures which persisted until 1983; he strongly supported the missions and founded the Urban College which still trains missionaries. He approved new religious orders such as the Vincentians founded by St Vincent de Paul.

However, he shared a weakness of several predecessors in a court where, as one observer said, 'no one is so low that he cannot aim at the highest post and no one is so well-positioned that he can be sure of not falling.' Except, of course, the pope, and Urban gave a high priority to ensuring that his family would have no monetary worries even after his death. He made cardinals of a brother and two nephews, arranged careers for other brothers and lined the pockets of many relatives.

On 6 August 1624, a year to the day from his election, when a mood of confidence still prevailed, he promulgated the bull of the Jubilee. He shifted emphasis away from Old Testament origins, emphasizing that Christ was the Jubilee. Because of the threat of plague, he replaced St Paul's Outside the Walls with Santa Maria in Trastevere where he consecrated a Holy Year door. The governor of Rome prohibited anyone carrying arms during the Jubilee.

Urban established a new plenary indulgence, gained by praying in certain churches to bring about the end both of the Thirty Years War (it was to continue for another 23 years) and the conflict which erupted that year between Genoa and Milan. Accompanied by cardinals, clergy and magistrates, he himself went in procession to several churches in addition to the Jubilee basilicas and to the Trinity hospice where he washed pilgrims' feet as well as making donations. Debt prisoners at the Cardinal Borghese penitentiary were released after their debts were met from prison funds.

The pope's nephew, Cardinal Francesco, provided lodging for Greek, Scottish and English pilgrims. Each cardinal had a responsibility for certain national groups of pilgrims and these were his. Urban's sister-in-law Costanza organized a successful collection of money and goods for the pilgrims.

Among the VIPs were saintly Leopold, brother of the German Emperor Ferdinand II, who lodged modestly at the Trinity

Confraternity hospice rather than more comfortably in the Vatican; Ladislaw, the son of King Sigismund of Poland, and the Duke of Alcalà, a special envoy of Philip IV of Spain.

A Roman complained that pilgrims who were nothing in their place of origin acquired airs once they lodged with the Trinity or Gonfalone Confraternities. Their processions, he continued, left no space for others and, if two of them intersected, they fought over the right of way. The commentator might have been consoled to learn that the number of pilgrims was a little lower than for the previous Jubilee.

INNOCENT BUT FOR OLIMPIA

The year 1650 should have been particularly propitious for a Jubilee because the peace of Westphalia, which closed the Thirty Years War, had been concluded in 1648. However the Westphalia agreement was not to Pope Innocent X's liking: he damned it as 'perpetually null, worthless, invalid, iniquitous, condemned, frivolous and without authority.' But he was ignored. The papacy was no longer an arbiter of international politics but a small-time player, increasingly peripheral when rulers determined even religious issues according to the dictum 'one king, one law, one faith.' This was true not only of Protestant rulers but of Catholics such as Louis XIV of France, the Sun King. The religious divisions of Europe were recognized by the peace of Westphalia with Protestantism confirmed in much of north-western Europe, where lay the growing maritime powers England and Holland whose colonies, consequently, were not Catholic: the 'Mayflower' had reached America thirty years before.

Reduced papal political clout seemed to spur Rome to more triumphalist display; it became the European capital of festivities. Among celebration of saint's feast days, spectacular canonization ceremonies and processions by confraternities there were countless occasions for ostentation. For major feasts, huge intricate contraptions with moving parts, called *macchine*, were built. Sometimes they were as tall as a palace and not much less expensive. The fact that they took months to plan and build but were used for only a day testified to their sponsor's wealth. The ephemeral was exalted, even if sometimes these cardboard and plywood contraptions were trial runs for permanent structures. The craftsmen who worked on them have contemporary equivalents in those who worked on the films of Federico Fellini.

Innocent X (1644–1655) was pope during an arid period for papal politics but was fortunate in the artists on hand: Francesco Borromini who restored St John Lateran, and Antonio Algardi who prepared for the Jubilee the bas-relief in St Peter's showing St Leo the Great stopping Attila the Hun and was also to make a huge bronze statue of Innocent to rival that of Urban VIII on the Capitoline Hill.

Both Algardi and Borromini were rivals of Bernini but he had gone out of favor as had all those associated with Urban VIII. There was little time for Algardi and Borromini to rejoice, however, because Bernini's design for the fountain of the rivers in Piazza Navona proved irresistible. Bernini was back in town. He provoked a shock by his sculpture of St Teresa in mystic ecstasy which some said looked to have earthier origins.

Baroque architecture and sculpture were exuberant, confident gestures to an imaginary public which made Rome a city-theatre.

Innocent asked Cardinal Antonio Barberini to account for his handling of the church's wealth under Urban VIII. Antonio and his brother Cardinal Francesco fled to France, declaring themselves French citizens. The powerful French Minister Mazarin threatened Innocent, who pardoned the Barberini. Although indignant about his predecessor's favoritism, Innocent enriched his own family and established for them the magnificent Villa Doria Pamphili near the Vatican but in more extensive grounds. He fell under the influence of his widowed sister-in-law Donna Olimpia Maidalchini, boundlessly ambitious and 'a revolting glutton'. When one of her three sons, a cardinal, decided to marry, she had the youngest, Francesco, made a cardinal although he was only 17.

Giambattista Pamphili, born in Rome in 1574, graduated in law and began a legal career in the curia. After diplomatic missions, Urban VIII made him a cardinal. Velasquez's renowned portrait of him after his election as Innocent X shows a moustached man with a goatee who has a punctilious, guarded expression. At the time of his election he was seventy, taciturn, diffident and dilatory, but the authoritarian, energetic Donna Olimpia was on hand to help him with decisions: in her he had found the right man for the job.

Innocent backed missions, made the Dominican College in Manila a university and approved a decree against adoption in China of local customs in the liturgy. He condemned the Jansenist teaching on grace and free will. Under him a humane prison was constructed and Piazza Navona, where the family palace was situated, assumed its present form.

At the opening of the Jubilee door in St Peter's, the papal guards had difficulty controlling the large crowd. Simultaneously Cardinal Francesco Maidalchini opened the door at St Mary Major and tried to take the coins and medals which had been walled-up there at the end of the previous Jubilee but the cathedral canons claimed them for themselves. The canons of St John Lateran were more diplomatic, offering the treasure in their Jubilee door to Donna Olimpia.

She headed a committee which organized collections for pilgrims in each of Rome's 14 districts. In the Monti district, 45 napkins, 22 pairs of sheets, 11 handkerchiefs, nine towels, eight pillow cases, three barrels of wine, two tablecloths, two used shirts, linen to be woven, plates and candles were collected.

They would not have been needed by the ambassador of Philip IV of Spain who arrived with 300 coaches. Two brothers of Duke Ferdinand II Medici of Florence wanted to lodge incognito but the pope invited them to the Vatican. Fifty-year-old, deaf Margherita of the ruling family of Savoy stayed at a monastery because she was a lay Franciscan. She received Donna Olimpia austerely but Olimpia tried unsuccessfully to impress Margherita by holding an elaborate reception when she returned the courtesy.

On Easter morning a Spanish confraternity held a procession to Piazza Navona entirely transformed for the occasion by a row of columns decorated with vegetation and 1600 lamps. In the middle, choirs sang and, at the two extremes, were pavilions donated by the Castilians and Aragonese containing statues of the resurrected Christ and the Madonna. One visitor said the spectacle by itself was worth the trip from Spain. During the Jubilee, Spain's remaining imperial splendor was on display because it had favored Innocent's election.

Despite the Peace of Westphalia, war continued between France and Spain and on certain days it was fought between pilgrims of these nations on Roman streets. A warning was left at the statue of Pasquin,

'Masianiellos are born in Rome too.' Three years before, in Naples, a certain Masaniello had led a revolt against Spanish rule there. For a time, Spaniards were advised to remain indoors in Rome.

Innocent did not concede reduction of the prescribed thirty visits to gain the indulgence; even in bad weather the 76-year-old pontiff made the visits himself. Cardinals walked barefooted to the basilicas. An estimated 700,000 pilgrims attended the Jubilee, of whom over 300,000 lodged at the Trinity hospice. Innocent established a hospice for poor bishops. 'If the innovators', wrote a contemporary, 'could see the devotion of the crowds at the sanctuaries and the number of cultured people among them, they would not attack the Jubilee as an institution.'

Johann Frederick, Duke of Braunschweig, with some other Protestants, submitted to Rome because of their experience of the Jubilee. In 1651, as by now was customary, Innocent X extended the Jubilee worldwide. That same year, the protests of Romans but also of other governments forced him to exile Olimpia from his court. However she was back again two years later and remained until his death in 1655. The Vatican coffers had been emptied for his relatives but they were too stingy to pay for his funeral. For some days his corpse lay in a rat-infested room until a canon of St Peter's paid five scudi to have it put in a coffin and interred. A Roman legend claims that on some full moon nights, near the Pamphili Palace on Piazza Navona, Donna Olimpia's coach flashes past with her grasping a strongbox containing the treasure of the Vatican.

SPECIAL EFFECTS

A broadside issued in England described 1675 as THE POPE'S GREAT YEAR OF JUBILEE: 'a Mart or Fair...where all sorts of Indulgences, Pardons, Remissions, Relicks, Trash and Trumperies are to be exposed to sale, and may be had for ready money at any time of the day; with the usual ceremonies thereunto appertaining.'

It carried doggerel of the same tone:

> *For now with you I shall be free*
> *This is the year of Jubilee,*
> *When all are welcome to their charge,*
> *For we our coffers shall enlarge ...*
>
> *Pardons, and indulgences,*
> *Relicks and such rarities,*
> *If you but ready money bring,*
> *You shall not want for any thing.*

The Jubilee took place towards the end of Clement X's six-year reign. Emilio Altieri, of a well-known Roman family, had been elected in 1670 after a conclave lasting five months. A curial lawyer before ordination at the age of 34, he had been a diplomat, residential bishop and head of a curial Ministry. He had been made a cardinal

only a month before his predecessor's death, which may have facilitated his election in a conclave blocked for five months because of
mutual vetos imposed by France and Spain. Throughout his pontificate he had difficult relations with Louis XIV of France. He had
served in Poland as a diplomat and his policy towards it was a success:
he financed John Sobieski who defeated the Turks and was elected
King of Poland the year before the Jubilee. Clement canonized several saints, including South America's first, Rose of Lima, and beatified the Spanish mystic John of the Cross.

He ensured scrupulous preparation for the Jubilee including, as
customary, an order to prostitutes not to scandalize the pilgrims. The
opening ceremonies were preceded by church bells tolling for days.
On Christmas Eve Clement was accompanied to the Sistine Chapel
where he mounted the *sedia gestatoria*, the portable chair in use until
the 1960s, whose projecting supports were shouldered by ambassadors
and curial officials. It enabled the pope to be seen by members of the
crowd and bless them, but was also useful because Clement, like
Innocent at the previous Jubilee, was old (84) and feeble.

He managed, nevertheless, to knock down the brick screen to
open the Jubilee door of St Peter's as a choir sang motets, the cannons
of Castel Sant' Angelo boomed and fireworks went off all over Rome.
Aristocrats watched the ceremony from special stands. Among them
were some English Protestants and Christina, the former ruler of
Sweden, who had settled in Rome after her conversion from
Lutheranism; she now lies in St Peter's. Also present were the Prince
of Baden, the Duchess of Modena and other German and Italian
nobles.

Christina had been influential in the election of the preceding
pope, Clement IX, whose secretary of state, Cardinal Decio Azzolini,
was her close friend. The daughter of the paladin of Protestantism,
King Gustav Adolph of Sweden, she had succeeded him at the age of
six. As an adult, she handled the affairs of state directly and also called
to her court figures such as the French philosopher Descartes. She was
courted at a distance by Oliver Cromwell as a Protestant hero and virgin Queen, the new Elizabeth. Curious, volatile, a keen hunter and a
lover of opulence, in 1654 she abdicated in favor of her cousin Carl
Gustav, then left for the Netherlands where she announced her conversion to Catholicism. On arrival in Rome the following year she
was welcomed by the college of cardinals at the Porta del Popolo,
whose inner face had been redecorated by Bernini and which bore, as

it still does, an inscription prepared by the pope: *Felici faustoque ingressui* (For a happy and blessed entrance).

She sought unsuccessfully the throne of Naples, then to return as Queen of Sweden. The secretary of state tried to obtain for her the Polish throne. When this attempt failed too she had to be satisfied with her palace in Rome being the center of the city's literary and artistic life and the nucleus of the Arcadia academy.

Christina also participated in the Easter ceremonies: accompanied by other aristocratic *grandes dames*, she washed the feet of 12 pilgrims at the Trinity hospice and left there money and her decorated apron and towel.

During a confraternity procession on Easter Tuesday, 44 men carried a *macchina* designed by Carlo Fontana which represented a temple with four columns at each corner and four angels. Inside were scenes of Christ's Passion. On Easter Thursday evening, a different confraternity carried another *macchina* by Fontana, illuminated by torch light, to St Peter's. On Good Friday it was the turn of the Trinity Confraternity: its procession was led by its chief official, Prince Gaspare Altieri, a relative of the pope, who carried a sceptre inset with gold, silver and precious stones. That evening Cardinal Paluzzo Altieri, Donna Caterina Altieri and Prince Angelo Altieri gave a dinner for 1300 pilgrims. Christina of Sweden, with her love for the luxurious, for theatre and the big gesture, had chosen the right city.

She was present in Piazza Navona on Easter Sunday when the Spaniards put on their show: two huge mausoleum-like *macchine* on which statues of Christ and the Virgin stood. Other *macchine* shaped like pyramids or towers filled the elliptical piazza and all were burnt to ashes at the end of the day.

They were seventeenth century special effects; no limits were placed on the attempts to inspire wonder. The master of all this, Gian Lorenzo Bernini, had survived longer than any pope to see his third Jubilee. Since the Jubilee of 1650 he had planned and supervised the installation on the Sant' Angelo bridge of eight sculpted angels each of which held an instrument of Jesus' passion. He inserted the elevated *cattedra* or chair of Peter in St Peter's under a window which refracted the setting sun into an explosion of golden light. It could have been one of the extravagant *macchine* which Bernini designed. He joined the basilica to the city and the world by constructing the out-reaching colonnade in the square before it. He was responsible for the stairway leading into the Vatican from the Bronze Door where the columns of decreasing size provide a *trompe l'oeil* impression of depth, and also the tabernacle of the Blessed Sacrament chapel in St Peter's. He died five years after the Jubilee, in the city he had reshaped, at the age of 82.

Poor health reduced Clement X's participation. He visited the basilicas only five times and it was September before he went to the Trinity hospice which had hired many other nearby buildings for the year: it accommodated about 300,000 of the estimated 500,000 pilgrims. He was to survive the Jubilee by only seven months. Nepotism had undermined his prestige. Clement made his adopted nephew, Cardinal Paluzzo Altieri, his secretary of state. Not only was Cardinal Altieri heavy-handed in this role but he took advantage of Innocent to obtain offices and wealth for his family. Romans were so angry at the extensions to the Altieri palace opposite the Gesù church that Clement decided not to visit it. That was prize grist for the mill of English doggerel writers and other critics.

A GOLDEN AUTUMN

The Jubilees of the eighteenth century took place while the church's political importance in Europe declined further, but in Rome itself life continued as in a golden autumn, 'at one remove from the present day.' It had not greatly changed from two centuries earlier and something of its atmosphere still survives.

The city occupied only about a fifth of the area within the Aurelian walls and was 'surrounded by solitude.' Buildings stretched from the Porta del Popolo to the Baths of Diocletian opposite the present railway station, from the Quirinal Hill to Trastevere on the other side of the Tiber, with the heaviest settlement in the large crook of the river opposite St Peter's. Grain mills were moored on the Tiber; there was no protection against its periodic flooding. In 1735 funds were available at last to build quays along the Tiber, but it was decided instead to restore the facade of the basilica of St John Lateran.

Goats grazed amid ruins, oxen wandered by obelisks, vines climbed ancient columns, hens and pigs were kept in historic courtyards. It seemed that the only interest in Rome's monuments, often half buried in rubbish, was as a quarry for limekilns. Use by the church ensured the preservation of such monuments as the Pantheon, which had been made a church in the seventh century; the column of Marcus Aurelius crowned with a cross; Castel Sant' Angelo which had become a fortress-prison; and the Colosseum, saved from pillaging by consecration to the martyrs who it was believed had died there.

Largely because of the Jubilees, Rome had some fine thorough-fares but most streets were dirty and narrow, which is why Romans called them 'bowels'. A visitor commented 'Heavy rains are Rome's brooms.' Streets were not named nor houses numbered until 1744. There was no domestic sewerage nor public lavatories. People relieved themselves in the street in broad daylight avoiding only those places whose owners, to protect themselves, had affixed a cross with the word *Rispetto*. At important receptions, princes and prelates had no qualms about relieving themselves into the pot plants before climbing stairways manned by liveried servants. There was no public cemetery; the dead were buried within the churches, which may have been one cause of the recurrent plagues. Malaria threatened in summer.

Rome was one of the last European cities to introduce public lighting. There was opposition to newfangled methods such as gas lighting which reduced natural darkness. The lamps before countless street images of the Madonna were considered sufficient. Carriages drove lampless. In December nights were enlivened by peasants who descended from the Abruzzi mountains to serenade the Madonna; to their hymns they added salacious suggestions about the locals who, nevertheless, paid them generously.

In the new baroque churches the gilt glittered, the colored mar-ble dazzled, the lines of the sculptures curved amply; others, which would have been better left untouched, had been baroquely refur-bished. The palaces of the aristocrats, for their dimensions and state rooms, rivalled the churches in grandeur, though their private apart-ments were often spare, small and desperately uncomfortable. Magnificence mattered, not comfort. Often the palaces were cheek by jowl with humble dwellings: the noble and the plebeian cohab-ited as did the lordly and the sordid.

Beside the palaces, fishmongers fried fish in huge pans, cabbages were cooked in Piazza Colonna, where their odor competed with that of the coffee which everyone, both private people as well as shop owners, roasted in stoves by the Aurelian column. Further down the Corso, in front of the Church of San Marcello, tripe was boiled in enormous cauldrons and quickly delivered throughout the city.

It has been said that papal despotism resulted in anarchy. The Treasury was a lucky dip, the judicial system a farce, the police cor-rupt. There was no check on the pope's powers but usually they were exercised benevolently and there were virtually no taxes nor military service. The postal system was lamentable.

A prelate was governor of Rome. He was supposed to work in accord with a senator and city magistrates. An ambassador reported, 'In Rome everyone gives orders, nobody obeys them and really things work well enough.'

Officials thronged the city. The Dataria, the papal chancery, alone employed 4000. Estimates of the employees in the Holy See's congregations, or ministries, run as high as 30,000 while the papal palaces also had huge staffs. Each pope brought his own entourage and once positions were created they remained. Officials comprised almost a quarter of the city's residents and together with their families numbered over half the population of 150,000. Those who were lucky enough to find a niche within the system of government tried to keep on the right side of their superiors as there were few alternatives; outsiders tried to ingratiate themselves with those who had found a niche.

There was only one, tightly-controlled daily paper or gazette, *Crakas*, but, as Giacomo Casanova noted, public grumbling was rife while Pasquin and other 'talking statues' allowed jibes at the government, as did the popular puppet shows.

Although in Milan and elsewhere there was capitalist development, in Rome there was little capital and also a distrust of profit. The malarial Pontine marshes which began only a little south of Rome inhibited agriculture and there was no industry. But there were excellent craftsmen for all kinds of building and decorative work. They preferred to work in the streets and in their own time which meant no interruption of their siesta. The city clock was on the facade of the Aracoeli church until someone remarked that elsewhere in Europe it was on the Town Hall. In fact, the Town Hall flanked the Aracoeli church and it was transferred there but for much of the century was inaccurate. The gap where it had been remained on the Aracoeli facade until restoral work for Jubilee 2000 began.

A consuming passion of the Romans was the lottery. They did not relish work but they still dreamt of becoming rich. There were countless lotteries, with no checks against fraud until, in 1731, all were abolished by the severe Clement XII. Six months later he introduced a state lottery because Romans were spending their money on lotteries outside the Papal States. A popular book linked dreams to lucky numbers on which gamblers betted. If this was not enough, they sought help from the Madonna or the beloved Bambinello, a tubby statue of the Baby Jesus in the Aracoeli church. Charles Dickens was to find it 'very like General Tom Thumb, the American dwarf; gorgeously dressed in satin and gold lace; and actually blazing with rich jewels.'

Tributes came from the church worldwide, with the largest share from France. Coins carried warnings against Mammon, for instance, 'I am the root of all evil.' One visitor remarked with relief that 'life does not revolve around money.'

Law courts abounded but the law was an uncodified jungle and cases dragged on endlessly. There was no penal code, only contradictory decrees from the Secretariat of State. Few stole but murders, usually with knives, were frequent: 18,000 in the last five years of the century. Romans were quick to quarrel and slow to forget grudges. Although pickpockets or thieves of any kind aroused indignation, assassins were often considered to have rightly taken justice into their own hands. A killer who grabbed a monk in the street and claimed sanctuary could not be touched by police. Asylum was offered not only in churches but also in cardinals' residences and any clerical establishment. Visitors to churches sometimes found that the delinquents enjoying asylum cooled their wine bottles in the holy water stoop.

Justice was administered by clergy, who tended to be lenient. Prison cells were first used in Rome, whose prison system was the best in Europe. For the occasional executions scaffolds were erected at one time or another near the Sant' Angelo bridge, Campo dei Fiori, the Pantheon, the Forum, Piazza Santi Apostoli, Piazza Del Popolo and St Peter's Square. The spectators often shouted to the victims that they would pray for them and look after their families.

Regulations about prostitution became stricter than those about courtesans during the Renaissance. However they plied their trade freely in the Piazza di Spagna area as the Spanish embassy there ensured exemption from normal policing. Premarital sex was frowned upon but, once married, women could live very free lives. 'The freedom of the women passes all belief,' wrote one observer even though he knew Paris. There were five women to every eligible male. It was socially accepted that married women take a lover, although not that they change them frequently. 'Chastity,' said Abbé Benedetti, 'is not the favorite Roman virtue nor gambling the worst vice.' It seemed an anticipation of what Byron was to write: 'What men call gallantry, and gods adultery,/Is much more common when the climate's sultry.' But some foreigners ran into the garlic barrier which, Shelley was to write, affected even countesses who 'smell so of garlic that an ordinary Englishman cannot approach them.'

Popes preferred to build churches rather than theatres. In 1745 Benedict XIV visited the newly-opened Tor di Nona theatre on the Tiber bank opposite Castel Sant' Angelo. The owner tried to take advantage of this by putting the words *Indulgentia Plenaria* over the entrance but had to apologize publicly. Although Clement XIII forbade clerics to attend plays, cardinals continued to do so and the order was repealed, but women were not allowed to act, sing or dance. Their roles were taken by *castrati*. St Alphonsus Ligouri defended 'euphonious castration'. The church's opposition to the practice was inneffectual as shown by a shop near the Vatican which proudly displayed a signboard: 'Pope's Chapel Singers Castrated Here.'

Montesquieu wrote that these ambiguous creatures would have set the least likely of men on the road to Gomorrah. Some dressed as clerics, some were entertained by cardinals. One made improper suggestions to Casanova in the Cafè Greco which still functions on Via Condotti.

The visual arts were less vigorous than in the previous century. Baroque still predominated but it had lost its divine spark, sculptured figures repeated gestures without spontaneity, painting kept to the tried and true. Towards the end of the century, the architect Wincklemann from Brandenburg spread the gospel of ideal forms stripped of all inessentials and found a supporter in rich Cardinal Alessandro Albani. The sculptor Antonio Canova was considered Michelangelo's heir. Rome was more popular than ever as a place for artistic study, largely because of its monuments.

Although energy was diminishing in the visual arts there were still noteworthy achievements. One was the Spanish Steps. The 137 steps, which should really be called the French Steps as they were paid for by the French, replaced dusty paths through palm trees, and have three flights and landings because they climb to the Trinity church. The stairway was nearly completed by the end of the 1725 Jubilee and, in the same period, its architect Francesco De Sanctis completed the facade of the church at the Trinity hospice. In that same year an equestrian statue of Charlemagne was installed at the far left of the portico of St Peter's to balance Bernini's statue of Constantine on the far right.

Another achievement was the exuberant Trevi fountain, a playful inland sea, completed in 1760; most of Rome's fountains were built in this century. A third noteworthy endeavor was that of the

Venetian Giovanni Battista Piranesi, who was born in 1720, studied in Rome and worked there until his death in 1778. His engravings are both a portrait of Rome and imaginative tribute to the potency of its ruins. The Knights of Malta church on the Aventine Hill is the only one on which he worked.

Unlike the visual arts, music flourished. In 1703 Clement XI had forbidden the study of music in convent schools as it could tempt girls from 'the modest ways that become their sex so well,' but with time the ban was ignored. As Jérome Lefrançais de Lalande reported, music was everywhere: 'it is quite usual to hear concerts, singers and chorus in the streets, with tambourines and mandolins, so that one's evening walks are very gay.'

Montesquieu remarked on the strong demand for new music, not matched in France. Cimarosa and other composers worked to satisfy it. Every church was a concert hall, some nobles and cardinals had theatres in their palaces. In that of Cardinal Pietro Ottoboni, Handel and Scarlatti competed on the organ and harpsichord; it was a dead heat on the harpsichord but Handel won out on the organ.

To protect its repertoire, none of the audience was allowed to take notes during performances in the Sistine Chapel. But in 1770 a 14-year-old, who was so small that he had been held up to kiss the foot of the statue of St Peter in the basilica, recalled all Gregorio Allegri's *Miserere* after one hearing. It was predicted that more would be heard of the adolescent from Salzburg, Wolfgang Amadeus Mozart. Pope Clement XIV asked to see the musical spy and, rather than reprove him for breaking the rules, loaded him with 'graces and favors'.

It was said that in Rome one third of the inhabitants were priests, one third did little work and one third nothing at all. Begging was tolerated as a spur to charity. Observers noted that Romans gave alms with good grace and they were accepted with dignity. Charitable institutions were second in number only to churches, hospitals were excellent and numerous. Santo Spirito, the largest, could accommodate 1600 patients and attached to it was Europe's first foundling hospital. At the lying-in hospital of San Rocco, pregnant women who wanted to conceal their pregnancy found a refuge well before their time. If anyone violated its rule of discretion, they were judged by the Inquisition. There were 200 centers for orphans and the aged as well as hundreds of refuges for the needy. Yearly the popes provided dowries for 1200 girls of marriageable age.

No prestige attached to the liberal professions; practically the only career was in the church. Primary schools were free for all but, as there was little incentive for schooling, attendance was slack.

At the beginning of the second millennium, the Roman aristocracy made the popes, but for centuries the popes had been making the aristocracy: because a family member became pope, the Aldobrandini, Borghese, Ludovisi, Barberini, Chigi, Odescalchi and Rospigliosi, among others, entered the Roman nobility. Election as pope was the biggest lottery win of all.

As Rome was the culmination of the Grand Tour, its aristocrats did not see why they should travel. In many cases, their curiosity did not extend beyond the latest fashions in Paris. Florentines said that knowledge never kept anyone awake in Rome. But the Roman aristocrats had an appealing quality: lack of affectation. Few lost the common touch, there were scant barriers between them and the working class—although that term is hardly appropriate for eighteenth century Rome.

Several aristocratic families had retinues which would be appropriate for kings. Coaches remained a major status symbol. Luigi Braschi, thanks to his uncle Pius VI, had twenty but pretended to own a hundred. After showing a French diplomat his stables, he asked what he thought of his hundred coaches. 'These twenty are splendid,' was the reply, 'we can see the rest another time.'

Aristocrats did not waste money on throwing dinner parties but often held afternoon or evening *conversazione* in their salons where gossip was exchanged and, less frequently, serious subjects broached. Sometimes musicians played in the background, little food was offered but great quantities of ices were consumed. Claire Clairmont, like her companion Shelley, found such soirees mind-numbing. After one she wrote, 'there is a certain Cardinal and many unfortunate Englishmen who, after having crossed their legs and said nothing the whole evening, rose up all at once, made their bows, and filed off.'

Montaigne had been surprised to find in Rome a society whose tone was set not by its women but by its clergy. Of the city's 36,000 dwellings, they held 20,000 on unbreakable tenure. In 1709 there were 2646 priests, 3556 monks and other male religious, 1814 nuns. There were 83 parish churches and over 300 others, 23 seminaries, 73 convents and 240 monasteries. Of the thirty religious orders, the barefooted, bearded Capuchins were the most popular. To earn their living they were prepared to carry candles at funerals, pull teeth or even model for painters.

Many who were not clergy donned clerical attire, a soutane and a distinctive three-cornered headpiece; there was no law against it. Lay employees of the papal government dressed this way as did apothecaries. So did others who hoped to become priests or wanted to give this impression. 'Rags or soutanes are the only wear,' wrote the Frenchman Jean Baptiste Dupratty. When Casanova arrived in Rome dressed to seduce, a priest advised him to change his attire and 'appear as a simple Abbé when you take your letters to Cardinal Acquaviva.'

'Here in this ancient capital of the world', Casanova later wrote, 'the man with his way to make has to be a chameleon ... he must be supple, insinuating, false and deep, stooping often, full of treachery and candid in appearance. He should always seem to know less than he does, and be patient, and never raise his voice. He must control his expression and be icy cold when everybody else would be on fire; and if at times, in this state, his heart is empty of religion, he needs religion in his head. He will know himself a hypocrite but, if he is honest, bear the mortification in silence.'

It would be a chilling description of any court but this court was in the capital of Catholicism. No other Catholic city, Casanova wrote, pestered one less about religion than Rome. But Casanova may have been better at seeing through other impostors like himself than in recognizing those with faith.

Romans were still steeped in their religion, even if it required purification. They wanted to hear, see and touch it in their drawing-room churches and opera-like ceremonies. A visitor spoke of the opera called Vespers and of the lighting display of Benediction. Romans were particularly devoted to the Madonna, a phalanx of saints and the Bambinello statue which was supposed to heal all ills and on request was brought to the homes of the sick.

The Counter-Reformation had corrected many abuses but Rome was still distant from the severity of Protestantism or the tensions of Jansenism. Romans would have considered such approaches took all the fun out of religion. The mood was accommodating.

Religion provided the Romans' entertainment. At the beginning of the century, including Sundays there were 150 feast days or religious holidays a year, and it was 1770 before the number was reduced to 120. Feast days were celebrated colorfully.

Inclusion among the prelacy or members of the papal court was the career fast-lane. 'Cardinals have tickets marked "Pope",' wrote

Dupratty, 'prelates tickets marked "Cardinal", priests have prelate tickets and the nobility tickets for extended credit.' Monsignors had the right to don violet stockings and hope eventually for a cardinalate, although aware that they were many hundreds whereas at most there were seventy cardinals. One who made it to the cardinalate explained, 'I know neither theology nor church history but I do know how to live in a court.'

Cardinals were part of the papal court but each cardinal also had his own court. By now, with some exceptions, they were worthy men but they conformed to the duty of display. Even a frugal cardinal who wore the same robe bestowed on him by the pope for twenty years had a retinue of fifty gentlemen-in-waiting. The cardinals' palaces rivaled those of the aristocrats because anything else would have seemed a betrayal of their office.

The poorest cardinal had at least three coaches. When Cardinal De Bernis drove from one part of Rome to another, he had a retinue of 38 footmen, ten Swiss guards, eight each of couriers and valets, four gentleman, two chaplains, as well as coachmen, grooms and equerries. As French ambassador, he was laying it on thick but when the seventy cardinals participated in a ceremony the traffic was paralysed.

As well as being princes of the church, the cardinals were a death-watch squad. They came into their own when a pope died, often selecting a successor in contrast with the pontiff who had appointed them. An interregnum was a dramatic time of indefinite duration, full of rumors and intrigue. European rulers often tried to exert influence, the approximately 700 Roman police and the army of secret police were on the alert, and householders had to put a light in their windows at night although usually the city was pitch black.

Of course only one cardinal became pope at each election but there were consolation prizes, in the shape of prestigious appointments, for those who ensured his election. Romans stripped the palace of the winning cardinal of its furnishings, jewels and plate. They were acting in advance on his words at the coronation: 'Silver and gold are nothing to me: what I have I give you.' The new pope would then throw three handfuls of gold, silver and bronze coins to the crowd beneath his window at the Lateran.

A visitor said that a cardinal's funeral caused as much excitement as a Carnival-time horse race along the Corso. But a description of the funeral of Cardinal Cavalchini indicates a slow pace: confraternity members, bearing candles and banners, led the procession which took almost an hour to pass the French embassy on its way from the Dataria to the church of the Holy Apostles. They were followed by various orders of monks each singing different hymns. After a break of 15 minutes in the poorly-organized event, the corpse, face uncovered, arrived in a hearse bearing his coat of arms. Civic and ecclesiastical dignitaries, some on horseback, followed. The 200 guests of Cardinal De Bernis, who watched from the windows of the French embassy, eased the tedium of the occasion by eating a 'prodigious quantity' of ices.

In the eighteenth century, the papal court resided at the Quirinal palace on the hill of the same name. Indeed the transfer there had begun at the end of the sixteenth century because the hill was considered healthier than the low-lying Vatican. Originally the site was chosen by Cardinal Ippolito d'Este for his town palace, with gardens which resemble those of his villa at Tivoli, but it was then made into a summer residence by Sixtus V. It is now occupied by the Italian president. The handsome building opposite the main entrance was built as the papal stables, while in 1734 the rococo Consulta building on the same square was completed to house papal offices. After the arrival of the papal court, urban development immediately quickened in the zone whose streets were planned by Sixtus V: from the nearby Quattro Fontane crossroads two of his obelisks are visible.

The papal court followed a complicated, Versailles-like ceremonial code but, in its daily life, distinction of rank meant little and prelates mixed constantly with hordes of victuallers, retainers, and even their relatives. With the exception of Clement XI, eighteenth century popes enjoyed a jape. In the superb Quirinal gardens looking across the city to St Peter's, underground pipes fed sudden jets which, to the pope's delight, drenched the skirts of women or prelates. One pope enjoyed tripping cardinals into the fountains, Clement XIV amused himself by sitting at his window and, with a mirror, deflecting the sun's rays into the eyes of passers by. Benedict XIV would leave processions to linger outside wine taverns. When strolling through the city streets, often along the avenue which ran straight to Porta Pia, the popes, accompanied by a few of their household, would converse with other pedestrians.

HIGGLEDY-PIGGLEDY
TO THE GREAT
PAW-WAW

Rome in the eighteenth century was an indulgent society but could it still draw people to obtain indulgences? There was unprecedented interest from England in the Jubilee of the year 1700. In London a comedy by George Farquhar, *A Trip to the Jubilee*, was performed with success at Drury Lane. Despite the title and a few references, it had little to do with the Jubilee except for the lines of the epilogue:

> *But from side-box we dread a dreadful doom,*
> *All the good-natured beaux are gone to Rome.*

One of the good-natured beaux was J. Jackson who, on 25 December, 1699, wrote a letter about the opening ceremony to his uncle Samuel Pepys. A priest at the English College managed to find Jackson a position close to the Holy Door of St Peter's and to the seats of distinguished foreigners such as Maria Casimira, the former Queen of Poland and widow of John Sobieski. As Pope Innocent XII was too sick to attend, his place was taken by Cardinal de Bouillon, who had a reputation as an inveterate gambler.

'The morning,' Jackson wrote, 'being yesterday the 24th, was ushered in by the jangling of bells I have mentioned; soldiers, like those of our Trained-Band, were placed in different quarters of the town to prevent disorders, and chiefly in the Piazza of St Peter's, where were the Swiss Halberdiers, in red and yellow, and a troop of horses, in armor, drawn up.'

About 4.00 pm, he continued, 'began the processions from the Vatican, through the corridor into the Piazza, and so into the Portico, drums beating, etc, all the while. First came the Choristers and the officiating Priests, with tapers in their hands, singing; then the Bishops; and last of all, the Cardinals in their Pontificalibus ... After a short office with some singing, which could not be well distinguished, the Cardinal de Bouillon advanced to the Holy Door, the guns of Castel St Angelo were discharged, and he knocked thrice with a silver hammer on a small cross of brass, fixed in the mortar of the door, pausing a few minutes between each stroke while some words were repeated. Having given the last stroke, he retired a little, and down fell the door, which made no small dust, being of brick, plastered on both sides, and kept together by a frame of wood round, and supported on the inside with props, which, being taken away, it fell into a case set to receive it, for its more ready removal; the Cardinals, etc, entering afterwards to sing vespers, and the people by degrees following in most astonishing crowds ...

'I afterwards saw the Cardinals' supper, in the Vatican Palace, which both for form and substance was very singular, and from hence went to the midnight devotions at St Lorenzo, where I heard most ravishing music suited to the occasion ... The crowd still continues at St Peter's so great with pilgrims going in at the Holy Gate upon their knees that I have not yet been able to make my way through it; but I have got a piece of the ruin of it, which will serve in the meantime to support my devotion.'

A Pilgrimage to the Grand Jubilee, published in London in 1700, gave a lively if somewhat hostile report, suggested by the title page's promise of 'A diverting account of ... the debauched Lives and Intrigues of Lustful Priests and Nuns.' It described the pilgrims en route: '... the roads were filled with numerous crowds of travellers, pilgrims, poor priests, and a continuous trail of sunburnt, sad, weatherbeaten sinners of both sexes, crawling along the highways in such despicable apparel that nothing, sure, but the mercy of an Infinite Being could think such a parcel of contemptible wretches worth notice. Had

I not known the occasion that called them together in these numbers, instead of believing 'em to be Christians going to a Jubilee, I should have took 'em by their looks and garb to have been infidel Indians moving towards grand Paw-Waw. All ranks and qualities were so promiscuously mingled, that they seemed to me like the original of Michael Angelo's "Resurrection", and that the whole world was jogging on in disorder towards a general tribunal—bishops in coaches, poor priests on foot, gentlemen on horses, beaus upon mules, pilgrims on asses; and thus they moved on higgle-de-piggle-de, like Don Quevedo's revel rout when they were running headlong to the Devil.'

On arrival he found that 'the innumerable concourse of strangers that are come hither on account of the Jubilee is ... so incredibly great that the country adjacent is scarce able to supply 'em with provisions ... The pilgrims that flock the city are so very numerous that from the opening of the Holy Gate until the 5th January it is computed that over 100,000 have visited the four churches appointed for gaining the indulgences of the Holy Year, besides other strangers, whose number is not much less, so that the whole town is thronged like a Bartholomew Fair in the height of their revels.'

True to style, Innocent XII prepared for the Jubilee painstakingly. Among other things, in 1698 four bandits of Spoleto were hanged and quartered in Piazza del Popolo because they had killed many travellers. It was an attempt to ensure safe passage for pilgrims.

A Neapolitan aristocrat, Antonio Pignatelli, born in Apulia in 1615, had been a governor, diplomat (Poland and Austria) and bishop before becoming pope. Austere and devout, on election as Innocent XI he decided to put an end to ravenous papal relatives ripping all they could from the church. He decreed that popes should never grant estates, offices or revenues to relatives and that only one relative, if suitable, could be eligible for the cardinalate and that with a low income-ceiling. The poor, he said, were his nephews, and he opened the Lateran palace to the handicapped and needy. He reduced the sale of ecclesiastical offices.

Despite his seriousness, offerings were less in 1700 than in previous Jubilees. He died, at the age of 83, while it was in course. Romans did not warm to him probably because they liked popes who were obviously enjoying life. They claimed that he was 'always crying'.

Benedict XII, who was pope during the 1725 Jubilee, was also zealously religious. The eldest son of a duke, Pietro Francesco Orsini was born in Apulia in 1649 into the same family which had produced Celestine II and Nicholas III. He upset his relatives by renouncing his inheritance to become a Dominican. He lectured in philosophy before reluctantly accepting the cardinalate. As a bishop in various towns, he continued to live as a simple friar, devoting himself to pastoral tasks but also writing theological texts.

He transmitted a similar seriousness to the Jubilee of 1725, prohibiting Carnival and other non-religious feasts, making the prescribed visits to basilicas himself in a modest coach with a small retinue and singing hymns on the way. He encouraged preachers to prepare people for the occasion and also fostered the new practice of forty continuous hours of adoration of the eucharist. As was customary for Jubilees, some churches were refurbished and embellished. For instance, the baroque chapel of the Monte di Pietà, the state pawnshop which took its social obligations seriously, had been built by Carlo Maderna less than a century before but for the Jubilee was renovated and high relief sculptures added, not only representing Faith, Hope and Charity but a fourth virtue, Alms-giving. During the Jubilee, Benedict went to the Trinity hospice to welcome 370 slaves who had been freed by religious. But his most important innovation was the holding of a local synod from 15 April to 29 May at St John Lateran to reinvigorate the church in Rome and the Papal States.

Benedict was an assiduous pastor, visiting prisoners, personally administering the last rites to the dying, passing entire days in the Santa Maria sopra Minerva friary living the life of a Dominican. But such activities were more suitable for a smaller city such as Benevento where he had been archbishop before the papal election. A pope had to think of the church worldwide as well as be sovereign of the Papal States, head of an extensive court and a large administration. Needing help and diffident of the cardinals, Benedict placed total trust in a collaborator from his time in Benevento, Niccolò Coscia. Despite the protests of other members of the college, the scoundrel Coscia was made a cardinal during the Jubilee. Cardinal Coscia placed friends from Benevento in key positions in the administration and eventually had one of his proteges, Niccolo Maria Lercari, made secretary of state.

Nepotism had been abolished, at least temporarily, but Benedict had unwittingly created another avid gang intent on emptying the Holy See's coffers. Coscia's ascendancy had political consequences also: his men were open to bribes from Vittorio Amedeo II of Savoy who obtained recognition as a king. The Holy See was further weakened in international politics.

Romans hated the boys from Benevento, who bankrupted the papacy, and also Benedict for giving them a free hand. After Benedict's death in 1730, they tried to kill Coscia and his henchmen. In 1731, Coscia was tried and then imprisoned for ten years for abuse of power.

Although Benedict wanted to concentrate solely on pastoral care, international political problems were on the papacy's doorstep in the shape of His British Majesty, as he was known, Charles III Stuart, the Old Pretender, and his court. They lived in the Muti (now Balestra) palace on Holy Apostles' square. The Old Pretender used his kingly prerogatives to ensure that his son Henry was made a cardinal.

Romans had antiques and the English the money to buy them. The city was a center for art connoisseurs, dealers and collectors but also for spies. There were legions of police informers: it seemed that where two or three were gathered together in anyone's name, a spy was among them. They kept detailed records on everyone and sometimes collaborated with spies of foreign powers such as those of the British government who were keeping an eye on the Stuarts.

The presence of the Pretender was considered bad for trade as it discouraged loyal British visitors. At times he was also a diplomatic embarrassment: several diplomats prudently called him king but without specifying 'of Great Britain'. He had some support from the papacy and the notorious Coscia but Cardinal Alessandro Albani, who pretended to be a friend, was spying for the British.

The Old Pretender had arrived in Rome with his court in 1719 and was still there, still hopeful of an opportunity to take the British throne, and still spied upon, during the 1750 Jubilee of Benedict XIV. Perhaps he was irritated at the praise of Benedict by the British diplomat Horace Walpole: 'a priest without insolence or interest, a prince without favorites, a pope without nephews.'

Politically astute, Benedict concluded a series of concordats with Spain, Sardinia, Naples and Austria and improved relations with Portugal and Prussia. Some consider that he conceded too much to secular rulers, others that he showed realism as the Holy See was negotiating from a weak position.

Born in Bologna in 1675 of impoverished nobility, Prospero Lorenzo Lambertini became secretary of the curial Congregation for the Council and wrote a masterly historical-juridical study of canonization which is still of interest. At the time of his election in 1740 he was the popular cardinal-archbishop of Bologna.

He was affable, witty and tolerant. A zealot warned him that Antichrist had been born. Benedict asked Antichrist's age and, when the zealot responded that he was three, the pope said he would let his successors worry about him. He was appreciated by Voltaire, by Protestants such as Walpole and by Muslims, which aroused the suspicions of some Catholics. He restored and embellished the Holy Cross of Jerusalem basilica and opened an avenue between it and St John Lateran. He also embellished another important early church, San Martino a Monte, and Santa Maria degli Angeli into which Michelangelo had incorporated the remains of the Baths of Diocletian.

Simpatico and generous, Benedict was also a dedicated pastor. There was growing realization that a Jubilee required preparation and not simply visits to basilicas if it was to produce its maximum spiritual benefits. From early in 1749 Benedict issued a series of documents and decrees which deepened the Jubilees' background; one underlined the victory that Christianity had achieved over pagan Rome whose monuments, it said, served to glorify God. One decree enabled enclosed religious, the sick and prisoners to benefit from the Jubilee; another reduced the operatic character of church music.

Benedict personally advised preachers how to conduct spiritual preparation courses in Roman churches. He himself undertook ten days of Ignatian Spiritual Exercises under a Jesuit immediately before inaugurating the Jubilee.

The superstar of the Jubilee was an Italian Franciscan preacher, Lorenzo da Porto Maurizio, who from July 1749 gave cycles of sermons in Piazza Navona. He drew crowds which overflowed the piazza and, after preaching, he spent hours hearing confessions. Sometimes Benedict himself attended, as did many nobles. Drawing on a long tradition, Lorenzo moved listeners with tales of Christians dying for their faith at the Colosseum which, in fact, were inaccurate; although gladiators had fought wild beasts there, Western Christians were put to death only in other places such as the Circus Maximus. During the Jubilee, largely because of Lorenzo's preaching and shortly before his death, a cross was erected in the Colosseum and Stations of the Cross, a practice he had made popular, were held there. The previous year Benedict had dedicated it to the Passion of Jesus. Claiming the Colosseum for Christianity saved it from being further exploited as a quarry.

The preparations paid off. There were more pilgrims than at the two previous Jubilees and more confessions. Among them were people from Egypt, Armenia and the West Indies: the church was meeting increasing difficulties in Europe but was not confined to it. In 1751 Benedict made the pardon available to all Catholics worldwide who fulfilled the Jubilee conditions in a designated church in their own diocese.

The Jubilee year of 1775 began with the cardinals closed in conclave to elect a successor to Clement XIV (1769–74). Finally, after 135 days, on 15 February they chose Giovanni Angelo Braschi of Cesena in Emilia who took the name Pius VI. Tall and lordly, known as *il papa bello* (the handsome pope) because of his looks but also because of his vanity, he had studied law, was an experienced diplomat, had been private secretary to Benedict XIV and, in 1773, had been made a cardinal. Perhaps compensating for the fact that his parents were impoverished aristocrats, he revived the opulent style of Renaissance popes and even their nepotism, building the huge Braschi palace at the end of Piazza Navona for his nephew Luigi and providing large allowances for other relatives. Michelangelo had said that it would be a sacrilege to touch the temple of Venus beside St Peter's but Pius VI had no qualms about knocking it down to build a huge sacristy. He added the big bell to St Peter's and two clocks which are still on its facade, enlarged the Vatican's Pio Clementine archaeological museum, installed obelisks at the top of the Spanish Steps and before what is now the Chamber of Deputies, and dedicated himself to reclaiming the Pontine Marshes south of Rome. He gave much of the reclaimed land to his relatives.

During his reign, for the first time Naples refused to offer a donkey as sign of its feudal homage in a colorful ceremony known as the Chinea. This peeved Pius, but there were countless other occasions for spectacular fetes in which piazzas became theatres, the fountains ran with wine, *macchine* were burnt or Castel Sant' Angelo erupted like Vesuvius with fireworks including mortars; for the final explosion, called the Girandola or Catherine Wheel, 5000 rockets were ignited, flooding the night sky above St Peter's with color. Charles Dickens, who saw the same ceremony at Castel Sant' Angelo seventy years later, left this description: 'The show began with a tremendous discharge of cannon: and then, for twenty minutes or half an hour, the whole castle was one incessant sheet of flame, and a labyrinth of blazing wheels of every color, size and speed: while rockets streamed into the sky, not by ones or twos, or scores, but hundreds at a time. The concluding burst—the Girandola—was like the blowing up into the air of the whole massive castle, without smoke or dust.'

The illumination of St Peter's for the apostle's feast day on 29 June was visible all over the city. As dusk deepened, 1400 lamps outlined details of the building up to the top of the dome. Then, when it was dark and bells rang out, there was a surge of light from the almost simultaneous ignition of 6000 jars packed with wood shavings and turpentine. The whole square was lit as if it were daytime. All this was stage-managed by 365 men hanging from ropes who guarded their trade secrets jealously. Dickens said they managed to make St Peter's dome a 'transparent egg shell.'

Pius spared no expense to ensure that the city's ceremonial occasions had panache in 1775, and was protagonist of a unique event for a Jubilee year: as the newly elected bishop of Rome, in late November, he took possession of his diocese. This was done by pope, cardinals, prelates, ambassadors, clergy and people, in carriages, on horseback or on foot, winding their way across Rome from St Peter's to 'the mother of all churches', St John Lateran, on the other side of the city. The procession passed through the Forum which signified possession of pagan as well as of Christian Rome.

It was one of the major events of a comparatively quiet Jubilee year, during which the Trinity hospice welcomed 130,000 pilgrims, something less than half the estimated attendance.

An English visitor, Dr John Moore, made an acid comment after observing Pius VI in St Peter's. Pius kissed the foot of the statue of St Peter and then 'rubbed his brow and his whole head with every mark of humility, fervor, and adoration, upon the sacred stump ... This uncommon appearance of zeal in the Pope is not imputed to hypocrisy or to policy but is supposed to proceed entirely from a conviction of the efficacy of those holy frictions, an opinion which has given people a much higher idea of the strength of his faith than of his understanding.'

There were notable absences from the Jubilee: the Jesuits. Some were in Rome, but in Castel Sant' Angelo prison: the Superior-General Lorenzo Ricci, his secretary and his chief assistants, about twenty in all. The 25,000-strong Jesuits had been under attack by Protestants and the proponents of the Enlightenment but also had clashed with their fellow Catholics, the Jansenists. Then the Catholic absolute monarchies brought pressure on the papacy to suppress them. Portugal, followed by the Bourbon kingdoms of Spain, France, Naples and Parma acted in concert. The Jesuits were expelled from these countries and from Mexico, Chile, Peru and the Philippines.

Finally Pius' predecessor Clement XIV, a Franciscan, had succumbed to the pressure and suppressed the Jesuits' extensive educational and missionary work. They survived only in Lutheran Prussia, thanks to Frederick II, and in Orthodox Russia, thanks to Catherine II. No doctrinal or disciplinary charges were brought against the Jesuits but it was felt that they were politically inexpedient. The pope had dismantled his crack troops.

Lorenzo Ricci and his advisers were confined first to the English College and then transferred to Castel Sant' Angelo. The curial congregation which examined their case did not condemn them and Ricci requested release. But Clement died before a response was given, then the conclave dragged on for over four months. In November 1775, while taking a walk in Castel Sant' Angelo on a cold day, Ricci caught a chill which was to prove fatal. He was buried in the church Michelangelo designed for his fellow Florentines, San Giovanni dei Fiorentini, situated on the Tiber bank diagonally across from Castel Sant' Angelo only a few days before Pius VI, with pomp and ceremony, took possession of his diocese.

During the Jubilee, pardon was available to everyone but the Jesuits, perhaps because their sin had not been identified. It was one of the many unhappy episodes of Pius VI's reign. Another was a trip to Vienna in the belief that his presence would dissuade Emperor Joseph II from measures to reduce papal influence and subject the church to the state, This personal diplomacy proved ineffective.

Although Rome's population had reached 165,000 and it was still the goal of travellers with a classical education as well as of pilgrims, the conditions for a Jubilee were far from ideal. No longer could the papacy count on rulers heeding the promulgation of a Jubilee and facilitating pilgrimages, even if they were from nations they were fighting. Many rulers were no longer Catholic and even those who were did not automatically support Roman initiatives. Moreover irreligion was spreading. The Reformation had been a tragic sundering but now there were not only Christians who did not look to Rome but people who derided all religion as superstition and a bar to human freedom. The *philosophes* had seized the intellectual initiative, opening up new fields of knowledge for a new audience in a way hostile to religion, tradition and authority. Catholicism was vulnerable not only because of its doctrines but because it was identified with a social order which was questioned. It seemed that liberty, equality and fraternity could only be achieved against the church. Rome was not well-equipped to respond to the seismic shifts in France; it could hardly affirm its centrality because it was becoming an enclave.

There were ominous forewarnings of the Revolution. While the Estates-General were meeting in Versailles in 1789 the magician Giuseppe Balsamo, known as the Count of Cagliostro, who had been expelled from France three years earlier, created a stir in Rome by experiments in his residence in Piazza Farnese. The French ambassador Cardinal De Bernis was present and Cagliostro made the stone in his ring increase in size. Then, in the reflections of a carafe of water, he claimed to see Louis XVI besieged in his own palace and the monarchy in peril. The cardinal had a strained smile. That same year Cagliostro was arrested for trying to introduce abhorred Freemasonry to Rome and, in 1791, was imprisoned for life at San Leo near San Marino.

After Louis XVI fled to Varennes, it was rumoured that the king was on the way to Rome and a huge crowd gathered outside the French embassy. Some of them replaced the horses in de Bernis' carriage and dragged him through the streets. Rome rejoiced but Louis did not arrive. Two years later the royal sisters, Madame Adelaide and Madame Victoire, were received with ceremony on their arrival at Porta del Popolo and accompanied in an almost triumphal procession through Rome. Many others had fled from Versailles to hospitable Rome where they were able to enjoy virtually a continuation of court life as they waited for the storm in France to blow over. Other European aristocrats, uneasy about the madness in France, in 1789 came to Rome for a sparkling social season. Pius had protested against the Revolution, he condemned the Declaration of the Rights of Man and the state reorganization of the French church. When Louis XVI was executed, Pius declared, 'I see terrible misfortunes coming but I shall have nothing to say.'

It was Pius' time to suffer and he did so with a dignity which surprised some who had known him as a vain, newly-elected pope. Napoleon's forces occupied Rome in 1798. Pius VI, who was 81 and had had the longest reign, 24 years, since that of St Peter, asked to die near the apostle's tomb but a French officer responded, 'People die anywhere.' He was taken to Tuscany, then Valence in France where, on 29 August the following year, he died as a prisoner.

As the Revolution gathered momentum, the papal nuncio in Paris had been advised to take good care of the pope because he would be the last. But Pius VI had left instructions on how to hold a conclave in emergency conditions.

MISERERE, MISERERE

S everal ambassadors and cardinals advised Leo XII against holding a Jubilee in 1825 but he went ahead with it. Even some Catholic rulers were not disposed to encourage pilgrims and there were curial warnings against the possible infiltration of subversives. Leo wanted to reassert Rome's relevance after the damage done by the French Revolution and Napoleon.

In 1800 there had been no Jubilee. The conclave held in Venice after Pius VI's death in exile elected a Benedictine, Luigi Barnabà Chiaramonte, on 14 March 1800. Two years earlier he had upset conservatives by declaring there was no necessary conflict between Christianity and democracy. He took the name Pius VII and, in July, was able to come to Rome which had been occupied by Austrian and Neapolitan troops after the departure of the French. It was late to organize a Jubilee and, in any case, conditions were troubled, but the ceremony to mark his arrival was as spectacular as any which could have been staged during the Jubilee. In a certain sense, it was the occasion for Pius VII to take possession of both the city and the diocese which usually entailed a solemn procession from St Peter's, through the Campidoglio and Forum area to the seat of the bishop of Rome, St John Lateran, and return by another route. This was held the following year but with curtailed itinerary and display 'because of the disastrous state of the Holy See's finances.'

But no expense was spared by the nobility who arranged the welcome for Pius. Three streets converge on Porta del Popolo, the main gateway for those approaching Rome from the north. On either side at the end of the central street, the Corso, are twin churches. For the occasion, the nobility erected a triumphal arch spanning these symmetrical churches, with other arches framing the entrance to the lateral streets. Above the central arch was a colossal statue of Religion triumphing over error and falsehood. A contemporary spelled out its significance: religion was reasserting its guiding role for society after the anarchic period of the satanic, Freemasonic Revolution which, under the pretext of fraternal union and help for neighbours, deluded minds and perverted hearts: 'pretending to perfect society they undermined it, pretending to restore humankind's rights they betrayed them and spread ferocity, oppression and crime while preaching virtue, meekness, humanity and brotherhood as if these virtues were not preached already by the Gospel.'

Pius entered Rome amid an acclaiming crowd and accompanied by the music of several orchestras, the tolling of church bells and the salute of the artillery, all rejoicing that the church had triumphed again over the Devil, that right order and hierarchy were restored. He proceeded along the Corso, then to St Peter's and on to his residence, the Quirinal Palace.

The success of the Revolution, following on the suppression of the Jesuits, inspired about this time apocalyptic convictions. Some feared the events foreshadowed the reign of the Antichrist but there were also Catholics, particularly among Jansenists, opposed to the Roman Curia and the church's temporal power, who welcomed them as preconditions for a more evangelical church and an approaching new era. However these Catholics had little weight in Rome.

Pius VII made brilliant Enrico Consalvi his secretary of state and a concordat was concluded with France. Concordats were reached with other countries, such as Prussia and Russia, and the Holy See's supranational status revived. It was recounted that, as eighty–year-old Pius lay dying in the Quirinal on the night of 15 July 1823, he dreamt of an imminent disaster. Some Romans already feared a disaster because they had noticed that in the basilica of St Paul's Outside the Walls there was no room for a portrait of Pius' successor. They asked if Pius, who had been a monk at St Paul's, was to be the last pope. However it was not the papacy which was in danger but the basilica: that night it was almost totally destroyed by fire. The news was kept from Pius who died on 20 July.

'A railway, a center for the needy are worth a hundred times more than St Paul's,' wrote Stendhal. 'After a century or two of useless efforts, the attempt to rebuild it will be abandoned.'

Devout Leo XII, who had succeeded Pius, could not have disagreed more. In March 1825 he announced his intention to rebuild St Paul's, the funds for which were to be raised through an international subscription. After this announcement, Father Gioacchino Ventura, a professor of moral theology and one of the most influential of Leo's entourage, commented on Rome in the journal *Diario di Roma*: 'because of its immortality,' he argued, 'which has made it more magnificent and beautiful than ever after its many disasters, it has won the title of Eternal City; because of the universality of its influence it can be called the Universal or Catholic City par excellence. In fact, it is the city where no one, particularly a Catholic, is a stranger, it is the homeland of all, and all have found here asylum, protection and defence under the peaceful sceptre of the Common Father, and it has nothing of its own which, in a certain way and under certain aspects, does not belong to all and which it is of universal interest to conserve and maintain.'

This was the manifesto of a group known as the Zealots, who wanted to repair the damage done to the papal heritage by two periods of French rule and by other factors such as tourism which were secularizing the city. The memory of the French outrages was kept alive by the installation in St Peter's in 1822 of an extant statue of the martyr-pope Pius VI kneeling in prayer in the sunken space below the papal altar and above St Peter's tomb.

In not quite twenty months of Republican rule from 15 February 1798, cardinals had been expelled, prelates dispersed and parish priests divided over whether to take the oath of allegiance to the Republic. Religious orders and confraternities were suppressed and their property seized. Many works of art were shipped to Paris. Soldiers, the French said, did not take orders from priests.

The new regime had numbered all buildings and introduced street lighting. Giuseppe Antonio Sala, a future cardinal, noted in his diary that these measures, together with information gathered by parish priests on the administration's orders, made it easier to convoke, tax, arrest and even conscript Romans.

The symbol of the revolution, the liberty tree topped by a Phrygian cap, garlanded with flowers, and draped with the Republican colours of red, black and white, replaced the cross in some public places; civic processions were held instead of religious ones and major sites were renamed: Piazza di Spagna became Piazza della Libertà; Piazza Venezia, Piazza dell' Ugualianza and the Sant' Angelo bridge Ponte della Repubblica.

The killing by pontifical troops of the French General Duphont had provided the pretext for the invasion. In February a huge monument in Duphont's honour was erected in St Peter's square. A pyramid on a rectangular base plus a column bearing an urn with Duphont's ashes, its severity contrasted with the magniloquent context. The following month a towering circular staircase was erected in the square, surmounted by three colossal figures of Rome, Equality and Liberty, while Bernini's colonnade was draped with the insignia of the Republic, military trophies and banners. In July the Register of the aristocracy was burnt in Piazza di Spagna along with papal records of trials of patriots. For the occasion, a structure was erected where three youths symbolizing Philosophy, Reason and Humanity defeated Superstition, Pride and Tyranny. Everything was done to underline that a new, anti-clerical administration was in power, but scornful Romans called it 'the burlesque Republic.' The Republican government, rather than the papacy, became the target of Pasquin's satire. In response to 'How's the weather?' he replied 'Weather for thieves.'

A more prolonged occupation, this time by the forces of Napoleon who now described himself as King of All Italy as well as Emperor, had begun on 2 February 1808, partly because the pope had refused to close papal ports to the ships of Napoleon's enemies, Britain and Austria. After looking back to an imperial model, papal Rome now had the uncomfortable experience of being a mere town in a department of an empire whose Caesar, Napoleon, never visited it.

Many of the Republican measures against the church were repeated. The Curia was abolished, the religious orders dissolved, the Holy See's archives taken to Paris. Of the 1200 lawyers attached to the Curia, 1156 refused to swear fidelity to the new regime; some were exiled to Corsica along with other citizens who refused to kowtow.

Because of its cultural riches, Rome was officially the second city of the empire. For the first time since ancient Rome, urban plans were made without any religious intentions. The redesigned Piazza del Popolo and the 'delicious view' from the Pincio Hill remodelled above it are examples of what the architect Giuseppe Valadier, a Roman who worked for the French, had in mind. Like architecture, archaeology was used to show there was a civic order independent of religion.

Unlike the papal administration, the French recognized the full civil rights of the Jews. Some intellectuals were in sympathy with the new regime and some aristocrats sought its favor, but for many Romans the French meant only rising food prices, the possibility of conscription and a holiday only every tenth day. Napoleon's defeat ended the French occupation.

The conviction that the temporal power was needed to ensure papal independence and its spiritual role was strengthened by the French occupation which traditionalists saw as a profanation. The Congress of Vienna in 1815 had restored legitimate monarchies and returned to the papacy nearly all the territories it had lost to Napoleon, which were the only prosperous parts of the Papal States. Subsequently in Rome there was an attempt to revive the glories of the early years of the Counter-Reformation, to assert an undeniable Catholic identity in all fields, to resacralize the city. There were saints such as Vincenzo Pallotti and Gaspare del Bufalo who founded new religious orders, scholars such as Gioacchino Ventura and artists such as Canova and Thorwaldsen, but they hardly bore comparison with Counter-Reformation figures such as Philip Neri, Ignatius Loyola, Robert Bellarmine, Bernini, Michelangelo and Palestrina. Moreover, Rome early in the nineteenth century was in a parlous economic and demographic condition whereas at the beginning of the Counter-Reformation it had been buoyant in both spheres.

But there was a similar determination to create an image of Rome as unchanging and also recapture the initiative after the Enlightenment had seized the torch of universalism. Rome was to be a bulwark against the corrosive ideas of the Englightenment, liberal individualism, religious indifference, Deism, naturalism and what, in his first encyclical letter of 1824, Leo called 'tolerantism'.

Annibale Sermattei della Genga had been born into a noble family near Spoleto on 22 August 1760, had studied in Rome, been private secretary to Pius VI, then a diplomat. In 1816 he was made a bishop and cardinal; in 1820 he became vicar for Rome. Once elected as Leo XII, despite his delicate constitution, he frequented sanctuaries, monasteries and charitable institutions. In May 1824 he left the comfortable Quirinal palace to transfer permanently to the Vatican although it was considered insalubrious. On 26 July he visited the new prison, tasted the inmates' soup and, disgusted by it, slammed a fine on the victualler.

As a lead-up to the Jubilee, for two weeks in August that year outstanding preachers gave a series of sermons in the main city squares. This initiative culminated with 15,000 people crowding Piazza Navona for a sermon. After it, Leo blessed them from Palazzo Pamphili, seat of the ambassador of the Czar of Russia.

An energetic attempt was made to moralize public life with ordinances against the sale of wine in public places except during meals; against dress contrary to modesty, 'the most precious ornament of the [female] sex'; against the letting of hotel rooms to prostitutes; against Freemasons and other sects, meaning subversives.

Maria Cristina, daughter of the King of Sardinia, Vittorio Emmanuele I, described the Jubilee opening ceremony in a letter to a friend: 'First the cardinals arrived, then the pope on his *sedia gestatoria*. He sat on a throne beside the Jubilee door, then hymns were sung and the pope went to the door. He hammered on it three times, saying prayers between the blows before returning to his throne. After a moment he gave an order that the door should fall. A little bell was rung and the door fell; they washed the jambs with holy water, the pope knelt for a moment in the doorway before entering the church accompanied by all the cardinals and bishops. We entered after the pope and went to the altar of the Confession where vespers were sung and so the ceremony finished.' As usual, simultaneously cardinals were opening the Jubilee door at the other basilicas but this time Santa Maria in Trastevere took the place of devastated St Paul's.

Leo was the protagonist not only of the opening ceremony but of the whole Jubilee. The future English Cardinal Wiseman gave an eyewitness account of Leo's activities amid the 'motley crowd of pilgrims arrayed in every variety of costume, from the sober, and almost clerical, dress of German peasants, to the rainbow hues of the Abruzzi or Campania ... For one of such delicate health and feeble frame it was no slight undertaking to walk from the Vatican to the Chiesa Nuova ... He was preceded by the poor, surrounded and followed by them. His look was calm and devout, and abstracted from all around. He reminded everyone forcibly of St Charles [Borromeo] of Milan.'

Sometimes Leo joined pilgrim processions. Each Friday he invited 12 poor people to share a meal with him; on Good Friday he washed the feet of pilgrims at the Trinity hospice and served them lunch. On the eve before the feast of St Peter he appeared unexpectedly at the Holy Spirit hospital to administer the sacrament of the dying. The following day he celebrated Mass in St Peter's and gave the *Urbi et Orbi* blessing. That evening the basilica was illuminated and there were fireworks at Castel Sant' Angelo.

It was one of the few festive occasions, although the architect Valadier did stagemanage a spectacular open air party at the Villa Medici. Among the nobles who came for the Jubilee were the Infante of Spain, Don Carlo; the Duke of Wurttenberg; and Francesco, the Bourbon King of the Two Sicilies, with his wife and son, who wore the confraternity habit (there was a branch of the confraternity in Naples) when he visited the Holy Trinity hospice and gave a coin to every guest.

The Jubilee ended at Christmas but Leo decreed that, if the prescribed conditions were fulfilled, except the visit to Rome, it was available to the whole Catholic world for the following six months. His aim had been to put Rome in touch with the world once more through the Jubilee and he had devoted himself wholly to the task.

An estimated 300,000 attended, fewer than at previous Jubilees, but this was not the main problem. Rather it was that the harder Leo tried, the less response he achieved. The French occupations had opened up new perspectives but there still seems to have been a store of goodwill for the papacy on Leo's return. Leo did not manage to tap it, however, partly because of reliance on fussy, legalistic methods and partly because of his fear of subversion. He obtained outer conformity but there were signs of rancour, not least in the vernacular sonnets of Giuseppe Gioacchino Belli which gave voice to the plebs. Largely unpublished during the lifetime of Belli, a papal employee, they show the crass ignorance of ordinary Romans at that time, their cynicism about the papacy but also their ingenuous faith. One called 'Holy Year' could have made Leo despair. The last two verses read:

> The bolt is off the gate of Purgatory
> And as for hell, by Christ,
> for this year only
> No one goes down, do or say what he likes.
> Just jaunt,
> Psalm-singing in the seven churches,
> Scatter some ash on your head
> And you hold
> Purgatory in your palm.

A 27-year-old Piedmontese liberal aristocrat, Massimo D'Azeglio, wrote in his 'Memoirs' that during the Jubilee Leo transformed Rome into a 'factory of spiritual exercises. No theatres, no parties, no balls, no receptions, not even puppet shows in the squares but instead sermons, missions, processions and religious functions.'

Even those without fervor felt constrained to pretend. 'That melancholy spectacle, or worse, that universal hypocrisy, made little appeal to me,' continued D'Azeglio. 'The young people, the soldiers, the clerks complained they had a choice of singing *Miserere* or losing their jobs.'

D'Azeglio escaped to his parents in Turin but on his return in 1826 found that his acquaintances, who had had to conform to expectations during the Jubilee, 'still with many undigested sermons, processions and religious ceremonies on their stomachs; all who suffered under duress were angrier than ever against the priests and their system.'

As vicar of Rome before his election, Leo had emphasized obedience to regulations rather than persuasion. A similar lack of psychological subtlety and pastoral flexibility damaged his pontificate which increasingly had recourse to police controls. His attempts to install morality by decrees, such as restrictions regarding wine shops, caused widespread disaffection.

The most striking example of the severity of Leo's regime occurred during the Jubilee. On 23 November two members of the subversive Carbonari organization, who were accused of assassinating a companion, were executed in Piazza del Popolo. The cardinal secretary of state decided it was only necessary to have moral certitude, rather than evidence, of their guilt. There were pleas to Leo for mercy but he decided on an exemplary punishment. One of the two died invoking justice.

In foreign affairs Leo collaborated with conservative rulers in an attempt to stem the advance of liberalism. He showed more flexibility than in Rome and the Papal States, and successfully encouraged emancipation of Catholics in Great Britain, which came with the Catholic Relief Act two months after his death. To head the Missionary Ministry he even recalled Cardinal Consalvi, whom zealots considered responsible for shameful compromise with secular governments and whom they also criticized for commissioning a statue from Bertel Thorswaldsen for St Peter's; the Danish sculptor was the only Protestant asked to work for it. However Leo partly reversed the attempt which had been made by Pius VII and Consalvi to update the Papal States, reinstated the feudal aristocracy and the ecclesiastical courts, and halted the employment of more laity. Inevitably this caused

a reaction which was interpreted as subversive. The result was employment of more spies and more repressive measures.

The atmosphere discouraged trade. The Papal States became
increasingly backward. Those aware of developments elsewhere in
Europe were restless but even those unaware of alternatives were
sourly resigned to a pontificate which tended to make religion a synonym for repression.

Leo's narrow clericalism thwarted his aim of re-establishing
contact between the papacy and Catholics worldwide. Belli watched
his funeral procession:

> Yesterday evening the dead Pope passed
> In front of our very eyes at Pasquin's corner,
> His head bobbing on the pillow
> He seemed a dozing angel.
> First came the muted trumpets
> Then the muffled drums,
> Then the mules with a canopied bed
> And the keys and the papal tiara.
> Priests, friars and nuns
> Grooms with lighted torches
> And then the useless Noble Guard.
>
> The bells of all the churches began to toll low
> As soon as the dead man left the Palace:
> We sure know how to put on a good show.

Rome's knack for staging ceremonies was unrivaled. But some
Romans lit bonfires to celebrate Leo's death.

BUILDING ON RUINS

For the 75 years from 1825, effectively there were no Jubilees because that promulgated by Pius IX in 1875 took place behind closed doors: there were few pilgrims, not even the Holy Year doors were opened and there were no public ceremonies. But the reshaping of Rome's image continued. As Carolyn Springer demonstrated in *The Marble Wilderness*, a culture war was fought over archaeology, which had seemed to provide evidence of papal Rome's continuity with the imperial past but then was used by those claiming an anti-papal republican and democratic tradition.

Digs were conducted in piecemeal fashion until Charles III of Naples gave, from his Farnese inheritance, fragments of a Rome city plan engraved in the reign of Septimus Severus. It provided the first exact idea of Imperial Rome's topography and encouraged a search for structures rather than isolated artefacts. This tendency was strengthened by adoption of empirical research methods developed in other sciences.

Excavations in Pompei and Herculaneum in 1755 had increased interest in digs in Rome, the world's richest archaeological site. Foreign powers had representatives exporting as much of the findings as they could. For this purpose, Gustav III of Sweden made Francesco Piranesi, the son of the engraver, his consul; Catherine the Great employed a sculptor; Frederick the Great had a similar arrangement, while the English were the most avid of all.

Export of antiques had always taken place but its rapid growth in the second half of the eighteenth century threatened Rome's archaeological patrimony. Spurred by his treasurer Giovanni Angelo Braschi, in 1770 Clement XIV established a Museum of Antiquities and when Braschi became Pius VI he greatly enlarged it. In the first years of his pontificate he also supervised 120 excavations and added just on 600 'marbles' (sculptures) to the Vatican collection. It was further enriched by purchases and grants, including Etruscan, Greek and later Egyptian material, until it became one of Europe's greatest museums whose architecture was a model for others.

The concern to transmit the heritage of ancient Rome intact showed that the papacy saw itself as its heir and perhaps also that it considered archaeology the least subversive of sciences. Framed on a wall of what is now called the Pro-Clementine Museum is a poem Vincenzo Monti wrote in 1779 which describes the classical world finding its fulfillment in the contemporary papacy. Whereas Augustan England tended to look at classical ruins as signs of decay, in Rome they were seen as evidence of survival into a Christian context which was the culmination of the ancient world's aspirations. The claim to links with distant and noble sources, in this case Pericles, made in the poem legitimated the papacy's temporal possessions which were being questioned.

Like the papacy, the French revolutionaries looked to ancient Rome: Karl Marx was to write that the Revolution had been enacted 'in Roman costume'. But the revolutionaries looked to Republican Rome rather than to the empire. The past in which the papacy had sought legitimation had become ambiguous. In 1797, under the terms of an armistice with the French who had invaded the Papal States, the papacy had agreed to cede 100 works of art and 500 manuscripts. Caravans of carriages took this loot from the Pro-Clementine Museum and the Vatican Library and Archives to Paris. It was a cultural *blitzkrieg*.

The first two works to be seized were a bronze bust of Lucius Junius Brutus, the legendary founder of the Roman Republic, and the marble head of Marcus Brutus, who had killed the tyrant Julius Caesar. They were heroes to those who had destroyed the old regime of throne and altar.

Archaeological settings and props were crucial to the revolutionaries' activities in Rome. On 15 February 1791, for the first time in many centuries, people met in the Forum for a civic celebration. They heard a speech inviting them to overthrow the papacy and abolish the emblems of oppression and despotism. They marched to the nearby Capitoline Hill where consuls were nominated and the flag of the new republic was raised. (The revolutionaries revived the consulate, a political office of republican Rome.) That same morning, the sixteenth anniversary of Pius VI's election was celebrated in St Peter's square. But Pius, allegedly sick, did not attend, nor did the majority of cardinals. The seven who did were arrested immediately afterwards.

One of the consuls nominated at the Campidoglio was the philologist Ennio Quirino Visconti, who revealed Vespasian's *Lex de impero* tablet, long hidden behind an altar in St John Lateran, which stated that sovereignty lay with the Roman people. Cola di Rienzo had made a similar claim in the mid-fourteenth century but the papacy had allowed only token civic representation under the bishop-sovereign. Republican authorities encouraged a cultural revolution by inviting people to demolish all coats of arms and insignias. There was such violence that after five days the consuls took over the task. Christian symbols were replaced by those of the Republic: on the column in Piazza Colonna a cord tied around the neck of St Paul supported a statue of the goddess of Liberty.

When newly-elected Pius VII reached the Vatican from Venice on 3 July 1800 he found that, before their departure, the French had stripped the palace and the museums. Elsewhere too the city had been plundered as never before. Pius did not despair. He made severe laws forbidding export of archaeological findings, financed excavations and research at Ostia, and at the Forum where he restored the arches of Constantine and Septimus Severus. Moreover, although the Pio Clementine museum was depleted, he ordered extensions to it. He could not overlook archaeology when he was restoring the papacy's pre-French Revolution status.

Pius VII took cultural politics seriously. So did Napoleon. In 1808 his troops invaded Rome. Over 2000 workers were hired to clear rubble from monuments and it was claimed that only Napoleon could restore Rome's 'ancient grandeur'. In fact, now that Napoleon was emperor, he was competing with the papacy and continued many of its archaeological projects.

He had an architectural project of his own, however, which exceeded those of any pope: a palace which would extend from Piazza Colonna to the Colosseum with Palazzo Venezia as its administrative wing, the Aracoeli church as its chapel and the Forum as its inner courtyard. Another was a plan to replace the narrow streets leading to

St Peter's with a broad ceremonial avenue. More modestly, he renovated the Quirinal palace; Pius VII was to enjoy its Sèvres porcelain,
Gobelin tapestries and paintings celebrating Napoleon's triumphs
when, at the next swing of the pendulum, he returned to Rome.

Archaeological activity continued under Pius VII but historical
scholarship was questioning the historicity of Romulus. Vatican officials felt obliged to defend the conventional wisdom on this and other
archaeological questions because of their claim to a providential continuity between pagan and Christian Rome.

Another aspect of the official mind-set was evident in an address
by the Vatican philologist Angelo Mai to the Pontifical Academy of
Archaeology in 1837. He compared missionaries in India, on the borders of Tibet and in Sri Lanka to Roman legions, with the difference
that they were destined to spiritual rather than military victory. It was
a spatial more than a historical image, in which Rome expands to the
limits of the world: *Urbi et Orbi*. Implied was the unchanging nature
of Rome, proven by archaeology, in which ancient and papal Rome
shared a universal mission. In this image there was no place for Italy
but some Italians resented that the papal states divided the peninsula
and prevented unity.

When the advocates of Italian unity gained control of Rome in 1846,
ruins and their interpretation remained crucial to the image of the city.

For a brief moment it had seemed that Pius IX (1846–1878)
might lead the movement for Italian unity, the Risorgimento.
Giovanni Maria Mastai-Ferretti, only 54 and extremely sociable, had
been a surprise choice to succeed Gregory XVI. Shortly after his election he granted an amnesty for all political prisoners, reformed the
state administration and set up city and state councils. These innovations triggered enthusiasm among those, including some Catholics,
who hoped that a reformist papacy would lead a federalist Italy. The
nationalist leader Giuseppe Mazzini wanted to exploit the situation to
seize the initiative for democrats and spark a war of national liberation
against Austria, which controlled much of north Italy.

On 14 March 1848 Pius IX granted a Constitution. Nine days
later, in support of King Carlo Alberto who, from Turin, had declared
war on Austria, there was a huge meeting in the Colosseum addressed
by a renegade priest who invited the crowd: 'Before that symbol of
the cross, an emblem of liberty, on this ground hallowed by the blood
of saints and martyrs, let us all pledge never to return to Rome until
we have slain the last of the barbarians.'

The cross had been transformed into a symbol of liberty in whose name enemies were to be slain. The following day Pius agreed to send troops north, specifying however that they were only to defend papal borders. But they marched beyond them to join forces with Carlo Alberto. Unwilling to be involved in a war against Catholic Austria, Pius publicly denied any participation in the Risorgimento. He fled to Gaeta, south of Rome and some thought he had been wise to avoid becoming a nationalist leader. However a Polish poet wrote that in the future there would be a Polish pope who would never betray his people. On 9 February 1849, followers of Mazzini took possession of Rome and formed a republic.

The rhetoric of the republic claimed that a new edifice had to be built on the ruins of imperial and papal Italy. Soon the ruins of republican Rome were added to these because, on 3 July 1849, French forces 'liberated' the city of the Pope.

As Mazzini had foreseen, the bloody resistance against French forces invigorated Italian patriotism and the ruins created on the Janiculum Hill near the Vatican became its sacred ground. After describing the smoking ruins, in the *New York Tribune*, the American journalist Margaret Fuller appealed to her fellow citizens 'to acknowledge as the legitimate rulers or leaders these men who represent the people, who understand their wants, who are ready to die or to live for their good.' Photography helped to spread the image of new Roman ruins caused by a pope relying on French forces.

The papacy was discovering how treacherous were Roman ruins. It was not surprising, therefore, that early in the 1850s Pius suspended excavations in the Forum, established the Commission for Sacred Archaeology and directed funds to digs of early Christian sites. In future, papal archaeology would be Christian archaeology. The papacy would care for its own traditions, which demonstrated that the church survived all kinds of persecution.

Pius used an ancient Roman column to convey another message. In 1777 a thirty-foot shaft of veined *cipollino* marble had been found in the Field of Mars. Nearly eighty years later, Pius used it for the monument to celebrate the dogma of the Immaculate Conception which he promulgated in 1854. It became a soaring pedestal for a statue of Mary in Piazza di Spagna. There was no ambiguity about that monument, the second last raised in papal Rome.

VISITING THE
PRISONER

Rome had changed radically by the time Leo XIII promulgated a Jubilee for 1900. He was a prisoner but in the palatial Vatican. It had more to do with dudgeon than dungeon. He was a self-proclaimed victim because Italian forces had broken into the papal city in 1870.

It was the fourth incursion in less than a century. The psychic wound was deep. When French revolutionary forces entered the city in 1798 it had been 271 years since the previous incursion of 1527. But the next incursion, again by French forces, came only a decade later and they remained for six years. Mazzinian democrats had established a republic 35 years later. Humiliation of popes by imprisonment and deportation was becoming frequent.

The invasion of 1870 was a particularly bitter draught. The forces of the Savoy family, which had been recognized as royal by the papacy, had produced saints and had pledged to defend Catholic Rome, overran the city once its French protectors withdrew to fight Prussia. Secret service funds had been spent beforehand by the invaders in a fruitless attempt to convince the Romans to rise against the pope. In the assault 41 Italian soldiers and 19 pontifical troops had died. A few days before the invaders arrived the Vatican Council, which had just approved the dogma of papal infallibility, was suspended largely because of the Franco-Prussian conflict.

Pius IX refused to hand over the keys of the Quirinal Palace which became a royal residence. Pius, who previously had frequently visited monasteries outside the city walls and often walked along the central Corso, had closed himself in the Vatican. For over a millennium the Holy See had expended great efforts to hold the Papal States as a guarantee of its independence. Now it had lost them and Rome itself by what it saw as betrayal. 'The barque of Peter won't sink,' said Pius, coming up for air, 'but the crew has to take many mouthfuls.'

Pius had blessed Italy but deplored its rulers' hostile measures as well as their bullying way of taking Rome. Because Italy had been united against the church, leadership of its unity struggle was in the hands of anticlericals; some were militantly anti-religious. They restricted the activities of religious orders, seized monasteries and convents, and removed the cross from the Colosseum and the Town Hall.

In its last decade as a papal city, tourists accounted for a quarter of Rome's income. Many came for the ten wild days of Carnival when Arab steeds raced along the narrow central Corso and masked revels continued far into the night. There were also fox hunts unrestricted by property rights, the theatrical-opera season, and impassioned card gambling in the palaces.

The population was only 240,000, little more than a tenth of that of Paris. The cow market was held on the Palatine Hill, agricultural day labourers were hired in Piazza Montanara, woods covered much of the Esquiline and Viminale hills near the city center. There were no smokestacks and little trade; half the male population of working age had no fixed occupation and showed little desire for any, but the tradition of skilled craftsmanship continued. Awareness of civil rights was feeble but social solidarity was attested by countless charitable institutions which helped the needy, the aged, orphans and single mothers. In 1868 the American poet Henry Wadsworth Longfellow had remarked to Cardinal Giacomo Antonelli that Rome seemed frozen in time. 'Yes,' responded Antonelli, 'and we never cease to thank God for it.'

Some enjoyed the *dolce vita*, others *dolce far niente* or doing nothing, but there was a darker side to papal Rome represented by short, stocky Giovanni Battista Bugatti, known as Mastro (Master) Titta, executioner for the Papal States. He began his activities in 1796 at the age of 17 and concluded them only on 1 August 1864. In 68 years he carried out 514 death sentences. He hanged, decapitated and, if required, also quartered and burned victims. There was no denying his versatility: he could decapitate with either axe or guillotine. He cut heads for a succession of popes but also for the French and, if he had not died in 1869 at the age of ninety, could have offered the same services for the Italian government. It would have been more appropriate that he execute for secular rulers than for the vicar of Christ.

Life imprisonment was prescribed for offences as minor as trying to kiss an 'honest' woman in public, being in possession of a pasquinade or writing graffiti. Often the bark of the lawmakers was worse than the bite of the judges but no clemency was shown to those guilty of political crimes.

Under Gregory XVI (1832–1846) trains had been considered inventions of the devil; he punned that railways (*chemins de fer*) were paths to hell (*chemins d'enfer*). Under Pius IX trains had been introduced but, when he became increasingly reactionary following the Roman Republic interlude, he condemned freedoms such as those of the press and religious tolerance which were already advocated by many Catholics elsewhere. He denied that the pope could or should come to terms with 'progress, liberalism, and modern civilization.'

Many outsiders had deplored conditions in the Papal States and were pleased that with their demise it was possible to buy foreign newspapers in Rome and for Protestant churches to be erected there. But some inhabitants did not welcome the invaders, called both 'the Italians' and 'the Piedmontese'. Several of the papal aristocrats closed their palaces in mourning and refused to receive the Savoy princes or others they considered usurpers. The palace of Prince Sacchetti was reopened only in 1929 when an agreement on contentious issues was reached between the Holy See and Italy.

Frederick Gregorovius, a German whose books had recreated medieval Rome, left the city after living there for 14 years. A month after the occupation he noted that Rome had lost its world status to become merely the capital of the Italians who, he adjudged, were not equal to the occasion.

In December 1870 the Tiber flooded disastrously. Since the sixth century BCE, when Etruscans had made settlement possible in what was to become the Forum area by draining it through the still functioning Cloaca Maxima, autumn–winter rains made the Tiber overflow almost yearly. Further, on an average, every 35 years it flooded badly. On such occasions it surged like a tidal wave through where Porta del Popolo now stands. It was several meters deep, as is attested by indicators on many buildings such as the San Rocco church in Piazza Augusto Imperatore.

Papalists claimed that the December 1870 flood was God's punishment on the Italians for seizing the city two months before. For their part, the occupiers claimed it was further proof of the ineptitude of the pontifical government which had not built defences against the river. Apartment houses, palaces and the Apollo Theatre overlooked the river; there were few embankments. At least from the time of Bramante there had been plans to control the river but nothing had come of them. The ancient Romans had not done much either, although they had built canals near the outlet at Ostia. The Tiber is not easy to control because of the considerable difference between its minimum and maximum levels, which is almost double that of the Seine. One factor is that the turbulent Aniene tributary, from the valley where Subiaco is situated, joins the Tiber near Rome and can abruptly increase its level.

General Garibaldi proposed to divert the Tiber around the city but, instead, 15-meter high bulwarks were built which 'buried' the river. There was overkill in this response but it ended flooding and the bastions created on either side of the river after the destruction of countless buildings are major arteries of Roman traffic.

Other initiatives were less successful. Within a few years some foreigners deplored the changes. F. Marion Crawford, an American novelist who knew Rome intimately, noted with regret 'Old Rome has disappeared. The narrow streets have become broad arteries, the Jewish quarter is a dusty building lot, the fountain of Ponte Sisto has been destroyed, one by one the magnificent pines of Villa Ludovisi have fallen under the axe and a mediocre, uninhabited quarter has replaced that enchanted garden.'

Emile Zola provided a memorable portrait of the new ruins of Rome when an economic downturn in the 1890s halted construction of the Prati quarter alongside the Vatican. It had been developed by carpetbaggers from the north and its street pattern was designed to prevent a view of St Peter's dome from any point. Zola said that the fields around Castel Sant' Angelo with their poplars had formed a green foreground to the dome of St Peter's but now had been replaced by 'massive buildings, stone cubes, all the same ... suggesting convents, barracks or hospitals.'

Some papal aristocrats and Vatican officials, such as the Belgian Monsignor François-Xavier de Mérode, joined forces with the 'usurpers' to exploit rising property values. It was another sack of Rome as buildings began to cover the Viminal and Esquiline hills; as F. Marion Crawford had noted, superb gardens were destroyed to create the via Veneto area. Guilt about the disreputable way Rome had been taken, greed and rhetoric combined dangerously: the new masters of Rome felt obliged to build bigger than the popes but it was an unhappy period for architecture as the Altar of the Fatherland and the ponderous Palace of Justice were to show early in the new century.

Perhaps Leo looked with nostalgia across Rome from the Vatican and recalled when, as a newly-arrived 15-year-old seminarian, he had frequented the Cafe Greco, which was a favourite venue for artists and aristocrats, many of them foreigners. He did not have first-hand knowledge of how Rome had been reshaped since 1870 but was one of the few who could still remember the Jubilee of 1825. He recalled it 'as if it was still before my eyes,' contrasting the favorable conditions then with the adverse contemporary ones when, ignoring pessimists and those preoccupied by his age, he promulgated a Jubilee for 1900.

Gioacchino Pecci, who had been studying at the Roman College in 1825, was the gifted son of minor nobility of Carpineto, a hill-town south of Rome. Entering papal service, he had been governor of Benevento and Perugia before becoming a diplomat in Belgium. While stationed there he visited Cologne, Paris and London. In 1846 he was made bishop of Perugia, emulating St Ambrose who had governed Milan before becoming its bishop. He wrote pastoral letters advocating Catholic rapprochement with contemporary culture which was to be the leitmotif of his pontificate.

Elected pope at the age of 68 in 1878, he was considered a stopgap appointment because of his delicate health. He was crowned in the Sistine Chapel itself; there was no public ceremony because the government feared demonstrations in his favor if he gave a blessing from the loggia of St Peter's.

He continued some of Pius' IX's policies: convinced of the injustice of the seizure of the Papal States, he demanded their restitution and also renewed the ban on Catholics voting in Italian national elections. But he recognized that any form of government was legitimate provided it promoted the common good and accepted the need for the church to dialogue with society and not merely condemn it. In his encyclical *Rerum novarum*, while defending private property, he championed the just wage, workers' rights and trade unions, which won him a reputation as the workers' pope. He was the scholars' pope too, because he fostered the study of Thomas Aquinas, biblical research, astronomy and natural sciences. He recommended that Catholic historians write objectively rather than polemically and opened the Vatican library to all scholars.

In 1892 he appointed the first Apostolic Delegate to the United States and seven years later censored 'Americanism' as a slavish attempt to adapt the church to contemporary trends. He set up regular hierarchies in Scotland, North Africa, India and Japan. The first to use the expression 'separated brethren', he encouraged Christian reunion, but accepted a commission's finding that Anglican orders were invalid. In 1879 he made John Henry Newman a cardinal.

The Jubilee was part of Leo's policy of showing that the papacy was not a quaint fossil. In 1896, to mark the beginning of the twentiethth century, a committee of laity in Bologna began preparing a celebration for Christ the Redeemer. Leo made it the Jubilee Committee.

The Italian government, after its successful aggression against the Papal States, sought an agreement with the Holy See which, however, was unsatisfied with the terms proposed. The government saw the Jubilee as an opportunity to convince world opinion that the self-proclaimed prisoner of the Vatican enjoyed freedom.

Catholics throughout the world rallied to the pope: the staff of the North American College, which had been founded in 1859, was kept busy making arrangements for United States visitors to attend Jubilee functions. Bishops around the world contributed to the expense of the golden hammer which was used to open the Jubilee door of St Peter's to the music of Palestrina's *Jubilate* directed by the composer Lorenzo Perosi. To celebrate the new century, in his chapel Leo said Midnight Mass.

It was more difficult to celebrate the Jubilee than when Rome was a papal city. Many institutions had been closed, the Trinity hospice could no longer be used but was partly replaced by that of St Marta within the Vatican. Some anticlericalist publications announced that there were few pilgrims because free thought had triumphed over religion.

In fact there were more pilgrims, about 350,000, than in 1825. The most spectacular ceremony occurred on Ascension Thursday, 24 May, when Leo XIII canonized John Baptist de la Salle, the eighteenth century French founder of the Christian or De La Salle teaching Brothers, and the fifteenth century Italian Augustinian nun, Rita of Cascia. The huge crowd in St Peter's was asked to refrain from shouting 'viva' to the Pope. Two hundred bishops and twenty cardinals entered the basilica first, then silver trumpets announced the arrival of Leo on his portable throne. The crowd could not restrain itself at the sight of Leo, vivas and applause accompanied him like a wave as he proceeded down the central aisle in what was the sixth canonization ceremony of the Jubilee and the last he was to perform. Even for the Romans such rich ceremonies made a deep impression for they had not seen anything like them in the previous thirty years.

Leo, like Pius IX, was keen to promote the canonization of Christopher Columbus but, probably because of his second, de facto, wife or his willingness to enslave indigenous people, his case is still becalmed. Many congresses were held: the renowned scholar Monsignor Duchesne presided at one on Christian Archaeology, there were others of Catholic Youth, University Students and the Franciscan Third Order of laity.

Oscar Wilde had returned to Rome. Three years before he had been photographed on the steps of St Peter's and inscribed it 'a young unmitred bishop *in partibus*' (*in partibus infidelium*—among the infidels). The young 'bishop' was 42 at the time. That year he had written *De Profundis* and in 1899 *The Ballad of Reading Jail*.

From Rome on 16 April 1900 he wrote to his Canadian-born journalist friend Robert Ross in London: 'Yesterday I appeared in the front rank of pilgrims in the Vatican and got the blessing of the Holy Father ... He was wonderful as he was carried past me on his throne, not of flesh and blood, but a white soul robed in white, and an artist as well as a saint; the only instance in History, if the newspapers are to be believed.

'I have seen nothing like the extraordinary grace of his gesture, as he rose, from moment to moment, to bless—possibly the pilgrims but certainly me ... I was deeply impressed, and my walking stick showed signs of budding' (a reference to Tannhauser's pilgrimage as a penitent to Rome mentioned in *The Ballad of Reading Jail*: 'Since the barren staff the pilgrim bore/Bloomed in the great pope's sight').

A few days later Wilde wrote to Ross that the pope's blessing had completely cured his mussel-poisoning, which had lasted five months. But also that when the king had driven past as he was taking an iced-coffee with gelato outside a coffee-bar, he had stood and bowed low 'to the admiration of some Italian officers at the next table.' He appealed to Ross: 'You know the terrible, the awe-inspiring effect that royalty has on me.' After his low bow Wilde may have wondered if he had a vocation for flunkeydom; at least, he remembered that he was, as he put it, *Papista*. Mindful of the antipathy between his two idols, he added 'I hope the Vatican won't hear about it.'

He could not get enough of Leo XIII's blessings. 'I do nothing but see the Pope: I have already been blessed many times, once in the private Chapel of the Vatican. He is no longer of flesh and blood: he has no taint of mortality: he is white [Leo was pallid] and robed in white. I spend all my money on getting tickets for, now, as in old days, men rob the pilgrims in Rome. The robbing is chiefly done by hotel porters, or rather by real robbers disguised as hotel porters, and it is perhaps right that heretics should be mulcted, for we are not of the fold.

'My position is curious: I am not Catholic: I am simply a violent Papist ... I have given up bowing to the King. I need say no more.' That was a form of repentance.

On Friday 2 April he visited the Vatican Gallery and, on leaving it, transformed himself into a Bohemian pilgrim which had a certain appropriateness: 'coming out of the Gallery ... I found that the Vatican Gardens were open to Bohemian and Portuguese pilgrims. I at once spoke both languages fluently, explained that my English dress was a form of penance, and entered the vast, desolate park, with its faded Louis XIV gardens, its sombre avenues, its sad woodland. The peacocks screamed, and I understood why tragedy dogged the gilt feet of each pontiff. But I wandered in exquisite melancholy for an hour. One Philippo, a student, whom I culled in the Borgia room, was with me: not for many years had Love walked in the Pope's pleasaunce.'

Early in May he was at it again, this time with Dario rather than Philippo: 'I have again seen the Holy Father. Each time he dresses differently; it is delightful. Today over his white and purple a velvet cape edged with ermine, and a huge scarlet and gold stole. I was deeply moved as usual.

'I gave a ticket to a new friend, Dario. I like his name so much: it was the first time he had ever seen the Pope: and he transferred to me his adoration of the successor of Peter: would I fear have kissed me on leaving the Bronze gateway had I not sternly repelled him. I have become very cruel to boys, and no longer let them kiss me in public.

'The pilgrims arrive in great black swarms: I am sure that Pharaoh was punished by a plague of them: some of them, however, go mad. Three cases yesterday. They are much envied by their more sane brethren.'

At the end of July, King Umberto I, who had so excited Wilde, was assassinated. An anarchist shot the king near Monza, but there was tension in Rome which cast a shadow on the Jubilee. Leo reaffirmed the papal right to Rome; the new king, Vittorio Emanuele III, responded that it had to remain the capital of Italy. On 20 September, when the entry of the Italian troops to Rome through Porta Pia in the Aurelian Walls was always commemorated, the Freemason Grand Master Ernesto Nathan said that the four laicist basilicas (the Pantheon, the Janiculum, Porta Pia and the Campidoglio) were 'certainly more majestic than those where a tribe of nomads is seeking pardon for their past and future sins.'

However the Jubilee was able to close on 24 December without further incidents. Leo extended it for the following year to the rest of the world and said he was now ready to die but lived for a further three years. He had reason to be pleased because he had proved it was possible again to hold a Jubilee.

There were still unresolved issues with Italy; the Holy See remained convinced that it was the victim of an injustice. But the Jubilee had confirmed that both papal zealots and anticlericalists had been wrong, that the Papal States were not essential to the papacy. One pointer was the fact that diplomatic representation to the Holy See had increased since their loss. Now there was no need for a Mastro Titta or rules to regulate prostitution. The occupation was really a liberation, the Papal States had taken too much of the Holy See's time and energy. They had been a millstone.

THE BIG PICTURE

The Jubilee of 1900 had taken place three years before the end of Leo XIII's pontificate and summed up his efforts to re-establish contact with the world at large. That of 1925 came three years after Pius XI's election and illustrated his program. Leo had shown that Jubilees were possible again, Pius that they could have universal aspirations.

Leo became pope after a century of assaults on the papacy which left it isolated and he built bridges to overcome this. Pius became pope after World War I, which had convinced him that the only hope for society worldwide was for greater church influence.

Benedict XV (1914–1922) had denounced World War I impartially as 'useless slaughter', which antagonized both sides in the conflict, and spent his own money and that of the papacy to help its victims. But, because of opposition from Italy, the Holy See was excluded from the Peace Settlement at Versailles. Its international standing was still not recognized, although during Benedict's reign the number of countries with representatives at the Holy See had grown from 14 to 27.

On his election on 6 February 1922, Pius XI announced his intention of strengthening the Holy See's international status and reaching reconciliation with Italy. 'I wish my first blessing to go out,' he continued, 'as a pledge of that peace for which humanity is yearning, not only to Rome and to Italy, but to the whole church and the whole world. I will therefore give the benediction from the outer balcony of St Peter's.'

Peace was to begin at home by healing the rift with Italy as a precondition for reaching the world as a whole. An hour later, on that cold, rainy morning, he appeared on the balcony as no pope had done since the election of Pius IX in 1846. The crowd in the square, which had increased since the white smoke signaling the election had risen above the Sistine Chapel, responded warmly. And, for the first time, Italian troops presented arms to a pope. The end of the conflict between the Holy See and Italy was in sight.

It is said that Benedict's lethargic intestines were the reason that Achille Ratti became pope. Born near Milan on 31 May 1857 to a silk factory manager, as a youngster sturdy Achille was called a 'little old man' because he was so self-contained. He took three degrees at the Jesuit Gregorian university in Rome, taught at the Padua seminary, and worked as a palaeographer—interpreter of ancient writings and inscriptions—at the Ambrosian Library in Milan. In 1911 he transferred to the Vatican Library, becoming its prefect three years later. He lived in the prefect's apartment above the library and, the anecdote goes, most mornings on his way down to his office crossed the path of Benedict XV who was pacing the corridor trying to coax his intestines into activity. The two often chatted. Benedict was impressed by the wide knowledge and tenacious intelligence of the librarian who, moreover, knew German and had travelled extensively in central Europe.

Whatever the truth of the anecdote, Ratti had a surprising career shift: Benedict sent him as the Vatican's man to Warsaw, where he had experience both of a chivalrous dictator, Marshal Jozef Pilsudski, and of a Soviet Bolshevik attack. In June 1921 he was made archbishop of Milan and cardinal when the Fascist movement was becoming increasingly powerful there. Eight months later he was elected pope.

In less than four years he had been elevated from librarian to pope, the first ex-librarian to hold the position. A mountaineer who said 'mountains are to be climbed, not to be looked at,' as pope he was a dynamo. He wrote thirty encyclicals on subjects ranging from marriage, including a condemnation of artificial contraception (*Casti connubii*), to reunion of other Christian denominations with Rome, in which he ridiculed ecumenical gatherings (*Moralium animos*), and social questions (*Quadragesimo anno*). He busied himself with minute details of the

Vatican administration and, while pope, for a time ran the Congregation for Seminaries and Universities himself. In his pontificate the huge San Callisto pentagon, where the post-conciliar Vatican offices are now housed, was built, as were the Vatican City Governorate, railway station and post office, and a new Gregorian university. He allocated large sums to his former bailiwick, the Vatican Library, established there a school of librarianship where the European Union now sends scholarship winners, and sent out two priests in plain clothes to buy books and manuscripts through East Europe and the Middle East. He established the pontifical Academy of Science, whose members are not confined to Catholics, and for its headquarters assigned the delightful Renaissance Casina of Pius IV in the Vatican gardens. He even followed the details of building plans and it was at his suggestion that a spiral staircase, modelled on the steps in the deep 'St Patrick's well' of Orvieto, was installed at the entrance to the Vatican Museums.

His first encyclical *Ubi arcano*, of December 1923, in which he said there would be a Jubilee in 1925, recommended that laity collaborate in the hierarchy's mission through groups called Catholic Action. He likewise encouraged the Young Christian Workers (Jociste) Movement, both indications that he wanted to form a Catholic laity for public life now that Catholic values were no longer transmitted by society.

Christianity had to be rebuilt but also disseminated. He announced a mission exhibition in the Vatican during the Jubilee, with material sent from missionary territories. And he expressed the hope that Catholic bishops from all over the world would come to Rome in 1925. In other words, the Jubilee was to show the church's muscle and underline its worldwide task. These seem to have been more basic aims than those mentioned when it was promulgated a year later: as well as individual amendment of life, its goals were listed as peace, reunion through the return of other Christians to the Catholic Church and settlement of the problems of the Holy Land. The war had ended Muslim control of the Holy Places but the Zionist movement was making claims to Jerusalem and Pius was concerned for Catholic rights there.

Pius had always been reserved but after becoming pope isolated himself. He allowed his relatives to enter the Roman nobility, as was the tradition, but did not enrich them and they had to make requests through the normal channels before being allowed to visit him.

Short but imperious, he could become a wrathful table thumper. When the French Jesuit theologian Cardinal Louis Billot wrote a letter of sympathy to the right-wing, nationalist movement Action Française after Pius condemned it, he stripped Billot of the cardinalate. He was to frighten even Hitler's Number Two, Hermann Goering, who recounted his first impressions of an audience with Pius: 'before that little figure robed in white I felt my heart jump as never before. For the first time in my life, I believe, I was afraid.'

Pius sought contact with pilgrims. Aristocratic Leo XIII had rarely received pilgrimages until the latter part of his pontificate, when he occasionally held audiences in St Peter's attended by as many as 20,000 at a time. He was carried on a litter and would talk to pilgrims for as long as six hours. The main contact of Leo's successor Pius X (1903–1914) with pilgrims was expounding catechism in the St Damasus courtyard within the Vatican on Sundays. The First World War had limited Benedict XV's contacts, but from the beginning of his pontificate Pius held daily public audiences running from about midday to as late as 4.00 pm. During the Jubilee but sometimes outside it, he also held evening audiences from six to ten.

At the end of each audience he gave a talk, and the severe scholar-diplomat found the wavelength of simple folk. He kept all their gifts until, during the Jubilee, they overflowed every room in his apartment. His secretaries wanted to throw out the junk but he objected that the gifts had been given with much love and should be kept; a room was found for them in the Vatican Library.

He also kept material which had been sent for the extensive and successful Missions Exhibition; ancestral poles from Melville Island, off Australia's northern coast, masks from Africa, jade statues from China, 50,000 objects in all which became the basis for the Vatican Ethnological Museum. His predecessor Benedict had recognized that nationalist missionaries were counter-productive and encouraged indigenous clergy. Now that colonial empires were breaking up, Pius intensified this trend. He pushed for indigenization of church personnel and consecrated the first native Chinese and Japanese bishops, and native priests for other missionary territories, doubling their number and also the overall number of missionaries by requiring that all religious orders provide them. He established a faculty of missiology at the Gregorian University. Incidentally, during the Jubilee, he took the Italian priest responsible for raising national mission funds and despatched him as his representative in the Balkans. His name was Angelo Roncalli and he was to become John XXIII.

Pius had a particular devotion to the Carmelite nun, Thérèse of the Child Jesus, who had died as recently as 1897, and canonized her during the Jubilee, along with others including the great confessor Jean Vianney, known as the Curé d'Ars, John Eudes who had established a religious order to spread devotion to the eucharist, and the sixteenth century Dutch Jesuit preacher, Peter Canisius; and he beatified Bernadette Soubirous, the visionary of Lourdes. He dedicated the world to Christ the King, as he wanted the peace of Christ in the reign of Christ. Just on 600,000 attended the Jubilee, 400,000 of them from Italy. Several pilgrim groups came from Australia, one of them led by Archbishop Daniel Mannix of Melbourne. At the closing ceremony on 14 December there were people from Great Britain, France, Germany, Poland, Switzerland, Austria, Yugoslavia, Hungary, Canada, the United States, Brazil, Argentina, Uruguay and Guatemala. *The London Quarterly Review* commented that the Catholic Church was the only one which could look to the future with tranquillity because it was without schisms, without a corrosive theology or changing religious values.

Pius told a visitor that, far from feeling the need for a rest after the Jubilee, he felt lonely. That may be why he held two further extraordinary Jubilees in 1929 and 1933. Previous popes had also held special Jubilees, particularly in the seventeenth century. They could last from a few days to a year and often related to an emergency. For instance, the first, promulgated by Leo X in 1518, had been in support of the Poles against the Turkish threat. Leo XIII, as if making up for lost time and gearing up for the Jubilee of 1900, had held Jubilees in 1879, 1881 and 1886. The year 1929 was the fiftieth anniversary of Pius' ordination but was also special for the Holy See because finally reconciliation was achieved with Italy.

It was the Italy of Benito Mussolini. After 1870 governments had proposed a Law of Guarantees for the church but the Vatican rejected the proposal. As the passage of time and difficulties shared with others during the First World War had reduced the rift within the nation, the Vatican had not objected when, in 1919, a Sicilian priest, Luigi Sturzo, founded a party of Christian inspiration, the *Partito Popolare* (People's Party). The boycott on Catholic participation in national politics ended. In the elections held that year, the *Partito Popolare* became the second largest party.

Benito Mussolini came to power in 1922. Several of his measures favored the church and some Catholics saw him as the 'Man of Providence'—that is, the man who would finally heal the rift between the church and the nation. Liberalism was still seen as the main enemy and many churchmen had a low opinion of parliamentary democracy. Unlike the *Partito Popolare*, Mussolini had the power to ensure acceptance of an agreement with the Holy See. The Holy See abandoned the *Partito Popolare*: Pius encouraged the laity but did not trust its political nous. With a Vatican passport the *Partito Popolare* leader Luigi Sturzo left for London, then went on to the United States. He was replaced by Alcide De Gaspari but the *Partito Popolare* expired a year later. (In 1933 the Vatican likewise abandoned the Catholic Centre Party in Germany to achieve a concordat with Adolf Hitler. But, in both Italy and Germany, concordats proved inadequate to protect the church and dissuaded Catholics from speaking up for human rights.)

The Lateran Treaty, signed in 1929, consisted of a Concordat and an Agreement. For the first time, the Holy See recognized Italy, with Rome as its capital. The Treaty established the Vatican as a city-state even though its area, 109 acres, is smaller than some golf courses. The secretary of state, Cardinal Pietro Gasparri said 'the Vatican, even with its gardens, is a palace, not a state.' The Vatican received 1750 million lire, which was the basis of its future finances, as compensation for the loss of the Papal States. The Treaty recognized Catholicism as the official religion and provided for automatic acceptance of church law in Italy in matters such as matrimony and the denial of employment in public office of ex-priests. Ecclesiastical corporations were exempted from taxes and once more legal personality was recognized for religious orders.

After 1929 there were many clashes over Catholic Action as the regime claimed it was engaged in hostile politics even though the Vatican had guaranteed that it would not be politically involved.

In 1931 Pius issued an encyclical condemning fascism, *Non abbiamo bisogno* (We have no need), in which he virtually admitted that the government had gained more from the treaty than the church. That was during a period of tension between the regime and the Holy See but later there was some church support for the Fascist interventions in Ethiopia (Ildefonso Schuster, Archbishop of Milan, blessed the Italian forces which 'at the cost of blood open Ethiopia to the Catholic faith and Roman civilization') and for General Francisco Franco in Spain; the jurist Arturo Carlo Jemolo said that anti-Fascist Catholics felt increasingly isolated.

The second special Jubilee of Pius XI's reign was held in 1933 to commemorate the conventional year of Christ's death. It was just over a century since Gregory XVI had condemned trains but now the church had updated: in 1931 Guglielmo Marconi, the inventor of radio, helped establish the Vatican Radio which allowed the pope's voice to be heard worldwide. After opposing revolutions of all sorts, the Vatican was drawing abreast of the communications revolution. In this Jubilee of the Redemption, Pius took part in ceremonies outside St Peter's, the first time a pope had done so since the Italian takeover in 1870. An estimated 300,000 attended the ceremony in St Peter's when he canonized the founder of the Salesian Order, John Bosco, whom he had met when a young man.

That year Hitler came to power. The Holy See had reached a concordat with Germany beforehand but eventually Hitler, who was no Pilsudski nor even a Mussolini, was to bring Pius' policy of pursuing concordats into question. Pius said that he would be prepared to make a concordat with the devil. He meant that if there were disputed issues between church and state, it was best to have them clarified by a binding agreement. In these he hoped to obtain the best possible conditions regarding ecclesiastical administration, religious teaching, matrimonial legislation and economic provisions for ecclesiastical institutions. Presumably he believed that, thus ensured, the church, the 'perfect society', would gradually bring about the sovereignty of Christ 'inclining men and peoples to its law of justice and peace.' (He was suspicious of the League of Nations as unrepresentative of the true community of peoples.) However concordats, while creating a space for the church, also limited it and tended to inhibit the initiative of local bishops and episcopal conferences.

In 1937, Pius, who had never suffered even a headache, became ill for the first time; myocarditis and diffused arteriosclerosis were diagnosed. He commented that until then he had been an ignoramus in the great and holy science of suffering. This may have been a factor in the issuance in March, within a few days of one another, of his three greatest encyclicals: *Mit brennender Sorge* on the difficult situation of the Catholic Church in the German Reich; *Divini Redemptoris* against atheistic Communism; and *Nos Es Muy Conocida* on religious persecution in Mexico. When Hitler invaded Austria the following year and Cardinal Theodor Innitzer, Archbishop of Vienna, declared himself satisfied with Hitler's provisions for the church, the Holy See disavowed him.

Hitler came to Rome shortly afterwards but, in disapproval, Pius left for his villa at Castelgandolfo. On 28 July Pius spoke out against Nazism and exaggerated nationalism; shortly before his death he made a moving appeal for peace, which he had made his goal.

Previously he had protested against violation of the rights of the church, of its personnel and property which were guaranteed by concordats, but towards the end showed a growing awareness that fundamental human values were threatened by the exaltation of race, ideology and state. Pius' courage was undeniable but perhaps he should have heeded the old saying: When you sup with the devil, use a long spoon.

A ROMAN TRIUMPH

Early in the century James Joyce had compared Rome to 'a man who lives by exhibiting to travellers his grandmother's corpse.' Then it had been small enough for its ruins to bulk large, but by the time of the Jubilee of 1950 it was spreading well beyond its ancient walls. At the beginning of the century there had been vineyards and vegetable gardens around the Vatican but now there were apartment blocks, and ribbon development crept along the consular roads. Industries were still scarce but the bureaucracy grew apace as politicians provided sinecures for their electors. In 1935 its population had reached a million, as it was in ancient times, and by 1950 it was a million and a half.

Cigarettes were still sold in ones or twos as well as in packets, the miseries of the last years of Fascism still smarted, but there was a miracle in the air: the economic miracle, whose first sign was swarms of motorscooters. Neo-realist films such as *Bicycle Thieves* showed that there were already many changes from the immediate postwar years, but change itself was contradicted by Pius XII who was an image of fixity, an icon. Tall and slim, his arms often spread like a cross, his every gesture hieratic, he seemed not so much a pope as an idea of the papacy.

The first pope in more than two centuries who was a Roman, he conformed to a view of Rome he described in a speech before his election: 'The destiny of Rome is subject to the Vicar of Christ, and through the Vicar of Christ it is directed to and fixed upon a goal that is not of this world ... Rome remains the city of God, the city of wisdom incarnate, the city that has the *magisterium* of truth and holiness.'

Exceptionally, in 1943 he had visited victims of the Allied bombing of the railway station near St Lawrence Outside the Walls but normally he was not seen in the city of which he was bishop. Somehow this behavior, a heritage of the sixty years when popes considered themselves prisoners of the Vatican, was accepted as normal. But although Pius rarely visited the city he was totally identified with it, particularly by non-Italians. The pope was immobile, the world could come to him, as he invited it to do in 1950.

Pius XI had done everything possible to ensure that his secretary of state, Eugenio Pacelli, became his successor, telling the other cardinals that he would be a fine pope. In preparation he sent Pacelli on many trips, including an extended private visit to the United States in 1936. Earlier Pacelli had been tempted to leave the diplomatic corps to teach canon law at the Catholic University in Washington. When he visited London people were intrigued by his dignified bearing, his reserve and his habit of finishing meals with three stewed prunes.

Born on 2 March 1876, Eugenio Pacelli was of a third-generation Roman family which had always worked with the Vatican. His father was a lawyer, as was his brother, who was involved in preparation of the Concordat with Italy. In 1917 Benedict XV made Eugenio Pacelli nuncio in Munich and six years later he became nuncio to the new German Republic. Named cardinal in December 1929, he was appointed secretary of state in 1930.

After strenuous efforts to prevent World War II, he declared his impartiality once it began. He did not endorse the Axis powers' attack on the Soviet Union and deplored the Allied demand for unconditional surrender. When Hitler occupied Rome in September 1943 he opened the Vatican to refugees, including many Jews, but was criticized later for not speaking out more clearly against Nazi atrocities.

By the end of World War II the Holy See had acquired greater international status, as attested by visits from leading world figures and many papal audiences for Allied servicemen. Pius proposed guidelines for a new world order. Shrewd investment of the Italian indemnity received as a result of the Lateran Treaty had greatly strengthened Vatican finances. The Savoy monarchy which had booted the papacy out of the Quirinal Palace was no more: a referendum in 1946 had gone in favor of a republic. Not only the monarchy had been defeated but also the Communists. In the immediate postwar years, the

Communist Party, the largest in Western Europe, had voted for incorporation of the Lateran Treaty in the new constitution and governed in coalition with the Christian Democratic Party, of Catholic inspiration, and other smaller groups. But there was fear of a Communist takeover as in Czechoslovakia. The 1948 election campaign was presented as a choice between Moscow and Rome, with priests recommending a vote for a party which they did not name but described as Christian and democratic. Cartoons warned 'In the election booth, God sees you but not Stalin.' The results enabled the Christian Democrat leader, Alcide De Gaspari, to govern without the Communists. A priest from Cracow, Karol Wojtyla, who was studying at the Dominican Angelicum university, observed the dramatic election campaign.

As well as success in these spheres Pius had another motive for confidence as the Jubilee approached. On Pius XI's death, he had lowered the floor of the crypt of St Peter's to provide more space for the tomb of his predecessor. As portions of pagan and Christian tombs emerged, Pius ordered further excavation in an attempt to locate Peter's tomb. Tradition held that this was the site of the Roman cemetery where Peter had been buried after crucifixion upside down in Nero's nearby chariot racecourse.

Papal documents were issued 'from the tomb of Peter' but polemicists had questioned whether he was buried there or even that he had come to Rome. The excavation was a risk if nothing convincing was found, but also because the sturdy columns which bore the dome rested on the basilica floor immediately above the dig. The risk paid off: as convincing as possible circumstantial evidence was found that it was Peter's tomb. After ten years of work excavations were completed in 1949. The scientific report was not made until 1951 but Pius announced the discovery at Christmas 1950.

To celebrate the Lateran Pact of 1929, in 1936 two old, narrow streets leading from the Tiber to St Peter's and the buildings between them were destroyed. No longer would visitors emerge from the confined streets into the expanse of St Peter's square. Instead there was to be a broad avenue, via della Conciliazione, whose message was, 'You-are-now-approaching-something-important.' Baroque surprise had been replaced by pomposity.

When Napoleon Bonaparte had asked the sculptor Antonio Canova why more trees were not planted in Rome, he replied, 'In Rome we don't plant trees, we plant obelisks.' That was what the architect Marcello Piacentini did after World War II when he realized that via della Conciliazione was so broad it drained the impact of St Peter's square. He installed a series of cement obelisks, but he might have done better to plant trees, as had once been planned.

The street was completed for the Jubilee but not the two buildings for Vatican Ministries at the end of it. That left Bernini's colonnade looking incomplete. But the buildings were finished early in 1950 in time for them to house exhibitions of modern religious art and missionary activities.

The only grave damage to a monument during the war was when Allied bombs hit the basilica of St Lawrence Outside the Walls. The basilica was restored splendidly for the Jubilee which avoided troubling war memories when Rome was inundated with visitors. Other troubling evidence was hidden by attaching fig leaves to the giant nude statues of athletes at the Mussolini sports complex, the Foro Italico, and removing advertisements for treatment of venereal disease. Rome was almost ready for its test as a sacred city. Church interiors gleamed: Jubilees meant spring cleaning of baroque convolutions which otherwise gathered dust, retouching gilt, salvaging stucco. Pilgrims were advised that a visit to the southern Italian Capuchin, Padre Pio, who had a reputation as a miracle worker, was not part of the Jubilee obligations.

The Holy Trinity hospice and others which offered free accommodation for pilgrims had been closed when Italy took over the Papal States. The Vatican vetted *pensiones* and families offering paid accommodation. Seminarians engaged in this work scored some magnificent meals from people anxious for Vatican approval. There were complaints that the Jubilee was a money-spinning affair. Religious institutions offered paid accommodation which offended those aware of the older tradition of free hospitality. But there was pressure to cover costs: the Milanese confectioner Motta paid handsomely for permission to put a large panettone advertisement opposite St Peter's but at the last minute was persuaded not to do so.

Visitors came by plane and tourist buses, some with HAIL VIRGIN MARY placards on their radiators. The buses filled St Peter's square, which had never occurred before, but even more surprising were the thousands who arrived on foot, which had not happened in 1925. The Catalan industrialist Jose Chapes Majmo walked from Barcelona to Rome in 37 days; Kurt Herming Drake left Helsinki in July and reached Rome in November. A seventy-year-old, Angel

Baufils, took three months to arrive from Paris. Baron Fritz von Cumpenberg, 29 and almost blind, walked alone from his castle near Munich. Others came on bicycle, by horseback, hitchhiking or, in the case of Bailot Siovatter, 61, from Paderborn, propelling a wheelchair.

The canonization of Maria Goretti drew criticism but also a crowd estimated at 300,000. She was an 11-year-old in a poor Pontine Marches village who, in 1902, had resisted rape by a young man who stabbed her to death. Before dying from the wounds, she had forgiven him. Among her unofficial miracles were that her murderer had repented after she appeared to him in prison where he was serving a thirty-year sentence.

Some criticized the Vatican for highlighting too obvious an example against sexual laxness. But it was also a story of repentance and forgiveness appropriate for a Jubilee. Maria's ninety-year-old mother was present, the first mother to see her daughter canonized. Years before the canonization the killer had written to her from prison asking forgiveness and she had offered it. After his release he became a monastery janitor. One Christmas Eve he had arrived unexpectedly at the house of Signora Goretti in a village where his name was a synonym for violence. He knocked on her door and, after they had talked, she cooked him a meal. Later they went together to Midnight Mass, sitting near a chapel dedicated to the child he had stabbed to death.

Another high point of the Jubilee was promulgation of the dogma of the Assumption of Mary into heaven, the first and only exercise of papal infallibility since the 1870 definition. Although there was grassroots pressure for it, there seemed an element of defying Protestants in the promulgation which, it was claimed, would help society.

During World War II, Pius had issued encyclicals on the church as the Mystical Body of Christ and on the liturgical movement, which encouraged those seeking a renewed Catholicism, but during the Jubilee he issued *Humani generis*, warning against theological errors. It was used to castigate French theologians such as Yves Congar, Marie-Dominique Chénu and Henri de Lubac whose work was to prove fundamental for the Second Vatican Council. Pius also issued a document expressing reservations about the French worker-priests' attempt to re-establish contact with the working class.

Theologians such as the French trio and philosophers such as Jacques Maritain were making it possible to justify developments in Catholic teaching in spheres from ecclesiology to the socio-political.

They laid the basis for a Christian humanism comfortable with democracy which had not been available to earlier popes. But Pius XII was becoming more restrictive. Perhaps the success of the Jubilee reinforced his authoritarian, triumphalistic tendencies.

The Jubilee basilicas were thronged once more, the Catholic kaleidoscope was on display: Indians in saris, an Australian group complaining that they had been robbed, Irish who were the best represented in proportion to their population, serious Germans who made the Italians seem, by contrast, chatty and casual. It was the last Jubilee in which a quaint practice took place. Only in St Peter's, confessors placed a long stick like a wand or fishing rod over the head of those who stood near confessionals. It looked magical but, in fact, derived from the medieval faculty of bishops to grant an amnesty to public sinners at Christmas and Easter by touching them with their crozier as they stood outside a church door. The modern practice meant the granting of a 300-days indulgence but was abandoned because it frequently interrupted confessions in course.

In 1350 the Jubilee had taken place with the pope in Avignon, in some other Jubilees the pope was an intermittent presence, but Pius was always at the center of applauding crowds; he granted audiences to cyclists, mayors and countless other categories. He had a formidable card index memory but also an unfortunate desire to show he was better informed and more up-to-date on any subject than the experts he was addressing.

Conspicuous by their absence were Catholics from Central and Eastern Europe. Pius had coined the phrase 'Church of silence' for them. He had protested when the Yalta Agreement consigned millions of Catholics to the Soviet sphere. In his Christmas radio message of 1950, he rejected Soviet claims that the church 'collaborated with imperialists for war,' recommending instead peace. Some non-Catholic participants found the Jubilee moving proof that a variety of peoples could unite for something which transcended narrow national interests.

The Jubilee had begun with the prolonged tolling of Rome's church bells and then Pius banging on the walled-up door of St Peter's with a hammer donated by Spanish Catholics. It ended with him wielding the customary trowel to plaster bricks into a screen which was to last until 1975. He was well satisfied that about 3,500,000 people had come to Rome for the Jubilee.

Rome as a city could be satisfied, too, because as postwar tourism gathered momentum it had received a boost as a venue. The

Holy See had received a still greater boost: it had decisively proved itself capital of something more extensive than Italy.

The Jubilee took place 11 years after Pius' election, eight years before his death, just over mid-point in his pontificate, and perhaps was its high point. By comparison, his last years were sombre. He had not appointed a new secretary of state after 1944 and, following the despatch of his closest collaborator, Giovanni Battista Montini, to Milan as archbishop ten years later, it seemed that the whole Vatican, the whole church depended on him. Illness and his taste for isolation eventually put him at the mercy of unscrupulous individuals in his entourage. The world press reported his alleged supernatural visions, his injections to forestall ageing, the details of the sale of photographs taken at the moment of his death.

Towards the end of his life the German novelist Thomas Mann had a private audience with Pius XII. 'The unbeliever and heir of Protestant culture,' he wrote in a letter after it, 'without the slightest spiritual inhibition, bent his knee before Pius XII and kissed the ring of the Fisherman, since it was no man nor politician before whom I knelt, but a white idol which, surmounted by the most formal spiritual and courtly ceremonial, meekly and a little sadly, represented two thousand years of Western history.'

For some Pius was, and remains, the archetypal pope, a remote ascetic figure of immense dignity. When he died, they felt an epoch had ended. They were right, but not quite in the sense they intended.

CONVERTING THE JUBILEE

To have or not to have a Jubilee: that was the question for Paul VI. He asked whether it was not anachronistic, both too Rome-centered and with a devotional style inappropriate for the 1970s. Certainly Pius XII's vision of sacred, unchanging Rome was challenged when blue movies were being shown close to the Vatican.

But in a talk in 1960, Giovanni Battista Montini, who was to become Paul VI, had asked, 'Can Rome be true to itself if it remains merely a national capital? For there has survived another Rome, at another level, the Rome of the Catholic faith.' Although Paul VI was not triumphalistic, as was Pius XII, and knew some would say that the center of the church was not Rome but the eucharist, he decided it should continue the Jubilee tradition, no longer as an exemplary city but as a typical First World city faced by countless social problems. When Rome had staged the Olympic Games in 1966 its population topped two million; in 1975 a survey showed that only thirty per cent of Romans attended Mass each Sunday and figures were lower still in the periphery where drugs were making inroads among youths who lived in shanty towns.

Changes were made for the 1975 Jubilee: it could be celebrated the year before at a designated church in each diocese with people converging later on Rome. And interiority was emphasized: 'We have to remake man from inside,' said Paul. 'It is what the Gospel calls conversion, what it calls *metanoia*.'

It was an attempt to reshape the Jubilee for a church and society which had changed profoundly in the previous 25 years. John XXIII (1958–1963) and the Vatican Council had transformed the church. John was the antithesis of Pius XII: whereas Pius was reserved and remote, John was warm and expansive; whereas Pius had a dire outlook, John was hopeful; whereas Pius seemed to bear the weight of the world and the church on his shoulders, John knew he was only a vicar. He did not have Pius' pretensions to encyclopedic expertise but his historical studies gave him a long perspective. And he showed confidence in his fellow bishops by convening a council which was to round out the one interrupted, after promulgation of the dogma of papal infallibility, almost a century before. John did not want it to condemn errors but open windows. He said at the opening that he was tired of hearing prophets of doom, he wanted a new presentation of the faith for contemporaries.

The Second Vatican Council changed the church's self-image. One of the paradigm shifts was from a mystical body, with the hierarchy as the head, to that of the pilgrim people of God. The council endorsed dialogue with contemporary culture; rediscovered the collegial links between the bishop of Rome and other bishops; proposed greater attention to the Bible and use of the vernacular in the liturgy; endorsed religious liberty and ecumenism; and inaugurated new relations with the Jews. In other words, it ended the siege mentality due partly to the Counter-Reformation and partly to subsequent events such as the French Revolution and the Italian seizure of the Papal States.

A factor in this change was that, in resisting totalitarianism, many Catholics had collaborated with Protestants and secular humanists and each group abandoned its former diffidence. This experience contributed to the theology which encouraged Catholics to 'collaborate in the construction of the earthly city.' The agenda accepted at the council was largely drawn up by German and French theologians, which gave rise to the expression that the Rhine had flowed into the Tiber. But the confluents lost some of their identity when they reached the secular sea.

Paul VI had been elected in 1963 and opened the second of the council's four sessions. The son of a lawyer-editor who was also a *Partito Popolare* parliamentary representative, Giovanni Battista

Montini was born in Brescia on 26 September 1897. He had entered the secretariat of state in 1922 and spent seven months in the Warsaw nunciatures the following year but, because of his delicate health, returned to the secretariat. He served also as chaplain to the Italian Catholic University Students' Federation where he influenced many future leaders of the Christian Democrat Party.

In 1952 he became pro-secretary of state, which meant that he did the secretary's work without having the title. In 1954 he was made archbishop of Milan, but not cardinal, which strengthened speculation that he had fallen out with Pius XII. John XXIII, shortly after his election, elevated Montini to the cardinalate and he helped prepare the council.

Just before the council, in a speech at the Rome Town Hall, Cardinal Montini acknowledged that the Italian occupation of Rome, by allowing the Holy See to concentrate on spiritual aims, had been a blessing. It was the first time in ninety years that a high-ranking church official had recognized this in public.

He had translated *Three Reformers* by Jacques Maritain and defended him and other innovative Catholic thinkers against censorious curialists. In other words, he was not fighting rearguard battles but nevertheless found the postconciliar period trying.

Some considered the task of the council was to correct the church's defects and delays, as was implied by the word John XXIII had used about it, *aggiornamento*, updating, but others thought it an invitation to remake the church entirely. When it concluded, some wanted to set a date for Vatican III whereas others wanted to apply what had been decreed.

Few Catholics were prepared for the changes it introduced. They produced different effects in different countries: in Anglo-Saxondom the invitation to dialogue with society coincided with Catholics' upward social mobility, leading to abandonment of many Catholic structures and consequent loss of identity.

The English anthropologist Mary Douglas commented that the council was about how the church could stop mangling people. But there was no defence against the immaturity uncovered in its wake. Many favorable to the conciliar changes were dismayed by the postconciliar 'silly season' when those intoxicated by change, in an institution which had prided itself on being unchanging, ran wild.

There were also those revolted by the changes, particularly cancellation of the previous form of the Mass in Latin. They found a leader in the French Archbishop Marcel Lefèvbre, whose threatened schism preoccupied Paul.

That was a lesser problem, however, than that caused by the debate over artificial contraception. In 1963 Paul had appointed a commission to study the question. A majority of the commission favoured approval of artificial contraception in certain circumstances but in 1968, in his encyclical *Humanae vitae*, Paul reaffirmed the ban. As there had been five years of debate and the majority report had been leaked to the press, there was expectation of change and the decision caused a crisis in papal authority.

It also increased Paul's reputation for indecisiveness; many, as confirmation, cited a curial comment that he was like Hamlet. However this seems to have been not so much a literary citation as a reference to similarities with Cardinal Amleto Cicognani who had been appointed secretary of state in 1961 and was reconfirmed by Paul.

The criticism of Paul was not altogether warranted but it is true that he lacked energy in his later years. It was easier for popes to appear decisive before the council, when initiative was in their hands. Everything was in their favor because any unpopular decision was attributed to the supposed villain, the Curia. But Paul was overshadowed by the council. He had not convoked it, had to attempt to obtain as wide a consensus as possible before closing it and then had to apply it while being sensitive to those who could not understand its spirit. John XXIII, in contrast, won credit by convoking it but died before facing the subsequent problems.

Paul had refused to be crowned like a sovereign and sold the papal tiara, devolving the proceeds to the poor. He did much to internationalize the Curia and to simplify curial style, abolishing the long train of cardinals' robes and the ostrich feather fans, deriving from the Byzantine emperors' court, in papal ceremonies, as well as the portable throne (which however enabled those on the outskirts of crowds to see the pope). He took advantage of conciliar criticism to reduce the power of the curial cardinals, which had been a counterbalance to that of the pope, without providing an alternative, which would have been possible if the Synod of Bishops had been allowed to have a deliberative vote. The result was unprecedented power in the hands of the secretariat of state and rupture of the tacit agreement whereby popes defended the Curia in exchange for all defects of a pontificate being attributed to it.

Paul was the first modern pope to make international trips, ten in all, touching all continents: in 1964 to the Holy Land, Bombay and the United Nations headquarters in New York, in 1967 to Istanbul, Geneva and Uganda, in 1970 to South-East Asia and Australia. In his encyclical *Populorum progressio*, he pleaded for greater justice for developing countries; he called for a new evangelization and convoked a series of synods of bishops.

But by 1975 he seemed tired, after 12 years of trying to prevent the energies unleashed by the council from fragmenting the church. Probably he was also saddened by the failure of high hopes and disturbed by hints of the future. Pier Paolo Pasolini, poet and filmmaker, expressed similar preoccupations in 1975, although in his case it was as if he had a premonition of his own death at the hands of a youth he had picked up for homosexual purposes. Pasolini identified the emergence of a post-Christian culture, a consumerism which promoted hedonism, encouraged banality and exalted violence. He attacked the Christian Democrat regime which had produced a ruling class tainted by scandals and which, in Rome itself, had profited from land speculation, along with elements of the Vatican. The Christian Democrats presented themselves as a barrier against Communism but ignored consumerism which was to prove insidious.

Paul could hardly avoid reflection on the difference between the idealism of the Catholic renewal movement of the 1930s and 40s and the results, both in the socio-political and church spheres. Nevertheless, during the Jubilee, earnest Paul issued a reminder that it was an occasion for 'Christian joy, the joy of the Holy Spirit,' adding that education was also needed to appreciate 'the many human joys the Lord gives us.'

Paul saw the Jubilee as an opportunity to refurbish the council's message of reconciliation, fraternity and solidarity, particularly with the Third World. In fact, it was the most ecumenical of Jubilees, during which Paul granted audiences to Orthodox, Anglicans, Protestants, Jews and even Tibetan Buddhists.

On 14 December a Catholic-Orthodox ceremony was held in the Sistine Chapel for the tenth anniversary of the revocation, by Paul VI and Patriarch Athenagoras, of mutual excommunication between the two churches. At its conclusion, Paul VI threw himself down and kissed the feet of Metropolitan Melitone, who represented Athenagoras' successor. It was a sign, perhaps too emotive, of Paul's desire for reconciliation and it upset some curialists.

Critics had seen the Jubilee as a nostalgic occasion, but attendance was such that, for the first time, audiences were held in St Peter's Square as only it had sufficient capacity. In all, 8,700,000 attended, including this time some from Central and Eastern Europe where restrictions on religion had been slightly relaxed. The closing ceremony, held in St Peter's and its square on a cold evening, 24 December, was seen by a television audience of 300 million. Paul said that the Jubilee would serve as preparation for Jubilee 2000 and the third millennium of Christianity.

JUBILEE 2000

A WIDER DOOR

None of his predecessors put such emphasis on Jubilees as did John Paul II. And no predecessor had prepared for a Jubilee which coincided with a millennium. He called the twenty-sixth official Holy Year the 'Great Jubilee', adding that the Holy Door 'should be symbolically wider than those of previous Jubilees, because humanity, on reaching the goal, will leave behind not just a century but a millennium.'

Why has he loaded it with such importance, saying from his first encyclical that preparation for it is the key to his pontificate? Whereas he inherited the council, he was able to shape the Jubilee as the completion of his pontificate. His statements suggested that he felt an urgency about achieving, through it, certain aims such as significant advances in ecumenism, inter-religious dialogue and purification of the church through acknowledgement of errors.

He showed little sign of apocalyptic worries for the end of the millennium. When he visited Fatima in 1991, to thank the Virgin Mary for saving him from the assassination attempt in St Peter's Square ten years earlier, some expected him to pronounce an apocalyptic message but, instead, he spoke of a new dawn for humankind and the church. Likewise in *Tertio millennio adveniente*, the encyclical announcing the Jubilee, he did not make dire predictions but drew attention to signs of hope, including 'scientific, technological and especially medical progress in the service of human life, a greater awareness of our responsibility for the environment, efforts to restore peace and justice wherever they have been violated, a desire for reconciliation and solidarity among different peoples, particularly in the complex relationship between the North and South of the world.' In church matters he mentioned 'a greater attention to the voice of the Spirit through the acceptance of charisma and the promotion of the laity, a deeper commitment to the cause of Christian unity and the increased interest in dialogue with other religions and with contemporary culture.'

No, he was not predicting the end of the world in the year 2000; surprisingly, *Tertio millennio adveniente* did not present the Christian vision of it, although this will be of increasing interest in the year 2000. It did not even say that the further one moves from the death of Christ the closer one moves to the Second Coming. 'It is certainly not a matter of indulging in a new millenarianism,' John Paul wrote, 'as occurred in some quarters at the end of the first millennium.' But he looked with expectation towards the year 2000, perhaps because towards the end of the first millennium Christianity was accepted in Poland, Hungary and the Rus of Kiev. John Paul has pointed out that celebration of the millennium of these events preceded the collapse of European communism which he still believes, despite the subsequent disappointments, makes possible a resurgence of Christianity. He made a significant contribution to that demise, not least by his visit home in 1979, which inspired peaceful mass demonstrations in which the participants found that they were not alone in their desire for change. The Jubilee could have a similar effect, convincing the participants that they are not isolated and that, despite the doomsayers, the world can be improved. As a survivor of nazism and communism, John Paul seems convinced that the horrors of the century have led to a diffuse desire for a new beginning.

Throughout his pontificate he seems to have challenged God to give a sign so that people might believe. In his eyes the collapse of European communism was one such sign and the advent of the third millennium can be another, provided people prepare for it properly

In other words, he wants people to concentrate not on the end of the second millennium but on the beginning of the third. He would like the barque of Peter to ferry the church and humankind into it.

Some who shaped the modern world predicted the death of God, the demise of the papacy and the end of religious belief which was considered superstition. True, much of the context of religion has changed, but God survived, even in gulags; religion persists, even if believers are often wary of institutions; and, far from disappearing, the pope is considered the prime voice of Christianity. Although the Catholic Church is in a minority position, it claims a public role to prevent religion being confined to the private sphere. Its interest in public policy and social justice are part of its identity but still more basic is its sense of the meaning of life and time which helps Christians face suffering and look beyond idols, even those topping popularity charts. These characteristics underlie its aspiration to ferry humankind into the third millennium.

Attempts to discern God's hand in history are tricky and never more so than when the calendar is involved. And does not talk of special years run counter to the sanity which considers all days good for living or dying and no years holier than others? Is there not a danger of augmenting millenarian mania and of encouraging crazy cults? Traditionally, the church is cautious about attempts to conflate history with salvation history and wary of perfervid religiosity. St Peter's, with its poised dome, is an image of sobriety. Catholicism can seem a lightning rod designed to earth religious cranks.

But John Paul evidently wants both to channel the excitement which will mount towards the year 2000, and not leave the millennium to Mammon. Although purists at the Greenwich Royal Observatory have pointed out that the year 0 must be taken into account and the new millennium will not really start until 1 January 2001, tourist agencies are competing for those who want to see, at dawn on 1 January 2000, the first light of the third millennium. Islands near the International Date Line, such as Pitt and Caroline, are competing with Tonga and Fiji for the honor. Gisborne and other places on the east coast of New Zealand are competing among themselves, while Byron Bay and Sydney each claim to be the first part of the first continent to receive the light of the new millennium. Mountains also compete: Buddhists will go on pilgrimage to Mount Fuji in Japan for the dawn light but New Zealand Maoris say that, as the god Maui foretold when he raised Mount Hikaurangi from the sea, it instead will receive the first light. Many aspire to the most extravagant party: to mention only a few, a Greet-the-Millennium Party at the pyramids, a champagne-fuelled Concord flight from London to New York, and concerts at the Eiffel Tower, Trafalgar Square and Times Square.

It is difficult to party for a whole year, which is what the Jubilee will do in the spiritual sphere, but it has one signal advantage over private initiatives and national celebrations: it can channel universal aspirations, particularly as the impoverished United Nations seems unlikely to stage anything comparable. And, as for the first Jubilee of 1300, it can mobilize more people than anything else, including the Olympics in Sydney. Jubilee 2000 will be a spiritual Olympics in which all, including the halt and the lame, can participate.

The Bible maintains that all days are good but some days and years should be specially dedicated to God. For the Bible, time is not cyclical, nor just one-damned-thing-after-another, but God's gift which provides an opportunity for humanity to meet its Creator.

In this perspective, the expulsion from the Garden of Eden meant humans falling under material necessity. But in acknowledgement of a higher destiny, the Sabbath was consecrated to God, as was each sabbatical or seventh year, when it was recommended that land be left fallow, slaves be released and debts remitted. The year after seven such sabbaticals had even more ample provisions; for instance, it was recommended that alienated land be returned to its original owners. It was a levelling of the economic playing field to enable everyone to start afresh. It was called the Jubilee. Some trace the origin of the word to the Hebrew *jobhel*, the trumpet or ram's horn which was sounded to announce this time of joy.

Chapter 25 of Leviticus explains the Jubilee: 'on the Day of Atonement you shall sound the trumpet through the land. You shall declare this fiftieth year sacred and declare the liberation of all the inhabitants of the land. This is to be a Jubilee for you: you will not sow, you will not harvest the ungathered corn, you will not gather from the untrimmed vine. The Jubilee is to be a holy thing to you, you will eat what comes from the fields. In this year of Jubilee each of you is to return to his ancestral home. If you buy or sell with your neighbor, let no one wrong his brother ... Let none of you wrong his neighbor, but fear your God: I am Yahweh your God.'

The Jubilee was an affirmation of God's suzerainty, and its recommendations an assertion that even the economy should obey higher laws, that equity was more important than market forces. Its civic aspect is suggested by the inscription of a passage from Leviticus on the Liberty Bell in Philadelphia: 'Proclaim liberty through all the land to all the inhabitants.'

Scholars disagree on whether the Jubilee law was applied or remained merely a utopian ideal. It may have been suitable for giving new energy to an agrarian society with a limited amount of land, for ensuring that no Jew remained perpetually in bondage, for indicating that the ritual aspects of the Jubilee were tied to the ethical. But it is difficult to apply in an urban society.

The Jubilee is a live issue for some Jews today, as Raphael Jospe has indicated: 'From a religious Zionist perspective, the ingathering of the exiles, the rebuilding of the Land of Israel, and the restoration of Jewish sovereignty in the State of Israel did not represent the messianic fulfilment of Jewish history but (at most or at least, depending on the point of view) "the beginning of the flourishing of our redemption." The renewal of the Sabbatical year is a feature of the messianic era, according to Maimonides. The question is whether its revival should be initiated now, by us, or whether, like other features of the redemption, it should be postponed indefinitely, until the messianic era. That is precisely what Jews debate every seven years in the State of Israel. Has the time of the Sabbatical come?'

Of course Christians believe it came with Christ, that he was both the Messiah and the Jubilee, as he announced in the Nazareth synagogue after quoting Isaiah:

> The spirit of the Lord has been given to me,
> for he has anointed me.
> He has sent me to bring the good news to the poor,
> to proclaim liberty to captives
> and to the blind new sight,
> to set the downtrodden free,
> to proclaim the Lord's year of favour.

He told his audience, 'This text is being fulfilled today even as you listen.'

Release from the types of bondage listed was a sign that a new era had begun. Jubilee 2000 will again assert Christ's suzerainty over time but there is awareness now that the conventional date for Christ's birth was mistaken. The latest scholarship indicates that Christ was born from four to six years before the conventional date: the third millenium began about 1995. But although the date is mistaken, its significance is unaffected: for much of the world the advent of Christ is the watershed between eras. The British member of parliament Ann

Widdecombe forcefully underlined that the millennium is fundamentally a Christian event: '2000 years does not mean a sausage unless it is 2000 years AD.' It is an acknowledgement of the sense Christ gave to time; the Jubilee will attempt to project this into the third millennium.

Christian dating may be considered an imposition. What is the year 2000 for Christians for Jews will be 5760–1; and, for Muslims, will be 1420–21, as they date from Mahomet's flight from Mecca to Medina. Dating is a relative matter, but the Jubilee will try to show the universal relevance of Christ's advent.

While concentrating on Jubilees it is easy to overlook the fact that pilgrims came to Rome for over a thousand years before the first Jubilee and would still be doing so in the year 2000 even if the event had not been invented. The institution is not known by the Orthodox and other Christian denominations but its Jewish prefiguration makes it appropriate that in 2000 it will be tied to the Holy Land.

Jubilees have been protean within the constant aim of providing the joy of pardon which implies acknowledgement of sin. Their ceremonies have given some continuity while devotional practices have varied. The intervals between Jubilees have altered, as has their reference point from Leviticus to Luke. Originally Rome claimed a monopoly of the Jubilee indulgence but a gradual globalization has been attempted without this stopping pilgrims coming to Rome, partly because of its evidence of the early church. Jubilee 2000 will hint at what future awaits Rome's past when electronic communications tend to make the present ever more present, hiding the past which means greater difficulty in projecting a future.

Jubilees as an institution have no permanent structure: each Jubilee Committee starts from scratch. It is not always easy to integrate the programs Jubilees propose with those already in course. They spawn much hot air, endless promotional guff and mini-Jubilees for categories such as, in 2000, sports people, military personnel, children, the sick, the aged, clergy and members of religious orders, deacons, industrial workers, farmers, police, scientists, university teachers, public authorities, parliamentarians, crafts people and those in show business.

Contemporary accounts of the first Jubilees testify to the participants' fervor but subsequent ones have never quite captured that fine, careless rapture. Some have been mired in indulgence abuses, others frittered away a spiritual opportunity in ostentation.

Jubilees have had a palpable impact on Rome as a city because public works were undertaken for them such as the building of Ponte Sisto, the widening of streets and the sprucing up of palaces and churches. In addition, the Pietà of Michaelangelo, the Spanish Steps, the fresco in the dome of St Andrea della Valle and countless other works of art were completed for Jubilees.

Has the church of Rome been reshaped as well as the city? To the extent that Jubilees alter the church's self-image, they have shaped it. Some rose to the challenges of their era, others evaded them. That of 1950 influenced the reigning pope through the proof it furnished of his drawing power and hence had an effect on the church. The increasing emphasis on spiritual preparation for a Jubilee has influenced ever greater numbers of Catholics.

To judge from the events of 1525, Jubilees are a poor substitute for a council, but can they be an effective follow-up? In *Tertio millennio adveniente*, John Paul affirms that the Second Vatican Council was a 'providential event whereby the church began the more immediate preparation for the Jubilee.' The originality of the council, he wrote, was that it 'focused on the mystery of Christ and his Church, and at the same time was open to the world.' It presented God, 'in his absolute lordship over all things', but also as 'the one who ensures the authentic autonomy of earthly realities.' He asserted that the best preparation for the Jubilee was to apply the council but did not specify in what spheres its application has been defective nor how the Jubilee could remedy this.

John Paul II had a trial run for the celebration of the year 2000 with the special Jubilee of the Redemption from 25 March 1983 to Easter 1984, which brought nine million visitors, and with the Marian Year of 1983–84. But there are those who think that if Jubilees are worth continuing, they should be done in a new way, Giovanni Franzoni, formerly abbot of the Benedictine community of St Paul's Outside the Walls and now leader of a left-wing Catholic group, suggested a 'possible Jubilee'. He proposed anniversaries and subjects for reflection in the lead-up to 2000: for 1998, that attention be given to Girolamo Savonarola, the friar who was a fierce critic of Alexander VI, as it was the seventh centenary of his killing, and also to Mahatma Gandhi, the prophet of non-violence, as it was the fiftieth anniversary of his assassination. For 1999, he proposed a reflection on the reconquest of Jerusalem by the Crusaders 'who believed they could gain plenary indulgences by slaughtering Muslims and Jews.'

Finally, in 2000, for the fourth centenary of the burning at the stake of Giordano Bruno, he recommended that the pope pray at the site in the Roman market of Campo dei Fiori.

Franzoni claimed that Boniface VIII and later popes abandoned the social aspect of the Jewish Jubilee 'to reinforce the centrality of the Roman church and the papacy.' For him the Jubilee should come to grips with social problems: Third World debt, nuclear contamination, feminist issues, the quality of life, indigenous peoples' rights. He did not say how to do this, although he mentioned that Bishop Samuel Ruiz of San Cristobal del Las Casas used the Christian Jubilee as a basis for protesting against injustice in the Chiapas region of Mexico. He concluded by asking why people should come to Rome 'from lands drenched in blood, hate and desperation, where ethnic groups and factions have torn each other apart' when they can ask pardon on the spot. He advised them to stay at home to discover their neighbours.

At the other end of the spectrum, Cardinal Giacomo Biffi, archbishop of Bologna, saw dangers in the Jubilee. In his pastoral note *Christus hodie* he warned that it might encourage irrational expectations which obscure the fact that the fullness of time has already come and salvation has been achieved. The second danger Biffi foresaw was that the year 2000, a Christian date, be totally banalized as has occurred, in his opinion, with Christmas and as is happening with Easter.

Moreover, he feared that the Jubilee could accelerate the tendency to substitute values such as peace, solidarity, defence of nature and love of animals for belief in Christ, rather than their being a consequence of it. He would like it to correct the tendency to use 'people of God' as a synonym for the church in favor of the 'mystical Body of Christ'. According to Biffi, the 'people of God' image has led to a sociological-juridical stress on questions such as who commands in the church at the expense of awareness of the church's salvific mystery and believers' participation in it. As a result, the faithful are robbed of the 'joy, the gratitude, the pride of belonging to the church; and, without this, it becomes difficult, except perhaps for intellectuals, to live the life of faith.'

Indeed Biffi would like reassessment, during the Jubilee, of postconciliar ecclesial culture and its consequences on 'Christian coherence, the vitality of ecclesial communities, on the choices for special consecration, on evangelical action, on the church's impact on contemporary humanity and so on.'

The Jubilee will provide a measure of the changes in the past 700 years. Indulgences were the main attraction in 1300, and there is no more effective pointer to the shift in religious sensibility than their reduced contemporary significance, even for the devout. Many consider them an embarrassment. It is important to revive an understanding of the Jubilee indulgence as acceptance of spiritual sharing which indicates also a willingness to be redeemed. In other words, it implies a step towards conversion which enables people to go beyond crippling guilt. The Bull of Indiction of Jubilee 2000, which spoke of the indulgence rather than indulgences, attempted to renew the approach, but its rules still seem somewhat mechanistic despite worthy innovations such as that visits to the sick, the handicapped and others in need are considered worthy of an indulgence because they are 'a pilgrimage to Christ present in them [the needy].'

Pilgrimage, fasting, not only from food, and almsgiving all remain valid means towards conversion or remaking in Christ, which is the aim of the Jubilee. It could hardly be otherwise when non-Christian religions also recognize some form of self-denial as a preliminary to dialogue with divinity. In the religions which look back to Abraham, Judaism, Christianity and Islam, fasting is considered a way to become worthy of receiving divine revelation. Following the example of Moses on Mount Sinai, Jesus fasted for forty days in the desert, although he also compared the time he had inaugurated to a wedding feast. But fasting contributes to conversion only when it entails solidarity with the needy. This aspect of fasting was sometimes ignored in the past when it and similar disciplines were seen mainly as a means to interior perfection. Now such disciplines are put more directly in relation to the community, with an emphasis, moreover, not so much on self-denial as on meeting Christ.

In inviting to a journey of conversion, John Paul wrote that it includes 'both a "negative" aspect, that of liberation from sin, and a "positive" aspect, that of choosing good, accepting the ethical values expressed in the natural law, which is confirmed and deepened by the Gospel. This is the proper context for a renewed appreciation and more intense celebration of the Sacrament of Penance in its most profound meaning. The call to conversion as the indispensable condition of Christian love is particularly important in contemporary society, where the very foundations of an ethically correct vision of human existence often seems to have been lost.'

Conversion is needed both because of the internal situation of the church and the state of society. The signs are not all negative but it is not a symptom of moral panic to recognize the down-side of certain developments. In much of the world, economic rationalism provides many goods, except for members of an underclass, but loosens social cohesion, as is indicated by the figures for divorce, abortion, single parent families and violence; loneliness is rife and the social costs could become crippling. Democracies are uncertain of any ground for values other than majority opinion, which encourages efforts to cancel the distinctive Christian elements from society's moral code. Technological development triggers change at a disconcerting pace and fewer persons are needed for productive processes.

The social changes have been felt within the church. Although in some countries the decline has levelled out in recent years, in the past four decades in the western world figures for regular Mass attendance and other standard criteria for testing church allegiance have nose-dived. There is massive detachment from the institutional church. Moreover, in some countries, polarization within the church is acute. Often this is seen in progressive-conservative terms but there is also a significant rift between those satisfied with an intellectual faith and a smoothly-running institution and those for whom religion means feeling the eruption of the divine in their lives. John Paul has tried to close this gap. He represents both the Polish tradition of popular devotion, of processions, of Marian piety, and the intellectual Catholicism of the French personalist movement and the philosophy he taught. Insertion of the bullet which wounded him in St Peter's square into the crown of Our Lady of Fatima, during his visit there in 1991, showed how far he is prepared to go to dramatize himself as part of a story with which people can identify. He wants a Catholicism which has intellectual substance and social outreach but is also popular, palpable and public. In other words, he wants a faith which shapes culture.

It may not be fanciful to see this as a result of a Polish background, because there many of the asperities which marked the relations of the church and culture elsewhere in Europe were avoided. In contrast to Galileo who campaigned for his views, Copernicus advanced his as a hypothesis and avoided a science-faith clash. Casimir of Poland allowed his subjects freedom of conscience whereas Western European rulers insisted on their subjects following their religious choices. Poland was tolerant before tolerance became a cause in Western Europe. In Poland the Counter-Reformation did not entail an Inquisition or burning at the stake. Polish patriotism was not sundered from religious sentiment as in Italy and elsewhere. Opposition to communism led to extensive collaboration between Catholics and those who did not share their beliefs or culture. There are qualifications to be made but there are grounds for John Paul II to believe that certain fractures in Western societies were not inevitable and may still be mended.

But some claim that Catholicism nowadays finds convincing embodiment only in vanishing, traditionally Catholic societies. The crowds which greeted John Paul at Jasna Gora during a World Youth Day seemed to confirm this, but he drew them likewise to Denver and Paris when it was held in those cities, one typical of postmodern society, the other the capital of the laicist Enlightenment. In both cases, youth responded warmly to an act of faith in their aspirations. Many of all ages might do likewise for a Jubilee which signifies neither bland optimism nor the end-is-nigh. It will function through pilgrimage, which was mistakenly thought to be a only a medieval phenomenon. It sparks a synergy between sweat and symbols, it works from the feet upwards, involving the whole person, and can still convince people that life itself is a pilgrimage, even though this was more likely when visiting holy places required more time and effort.

Huge meetings, such as rock concerts, where people enjoy a shared experience which can be dilated to world scale by television, have marked recent decades. Some regard such events as fulfilment of Vladimir Soloviev's vision of the reign of Antichrist, a pagan humanity in which it is assumed that Christian characteristics are irrelevant. And it is worth recalling that Hitler and Mussolini both successfully organized vast meetings with striking scenographies. Obviously, in attracting crowds to a Jubilee the church aims at something different, using its religious savvy to shape spiritual impulses. The concert held at the Eucharistic Congress in Bologna in 1997, where Bob Dylan performed in John Paul's presence, indicated an attempt to plug in to the energy of rock culture; the church may have enough continuity to do this but it could also be a victim, as the quip has it, of déjà vu all over again.

Can occasions such as Jubilees convey a lasting message effectively? There are several innovations for Jubilee 2000 which should make this more likely. For one thing, John Paul announced it in 1994, allowing three years of preparation focusing on the Trinity: 1997 devoted to Jesus Christ; 1998 to the Holy Spirit; 1999 to God the

Father. A series of synods of the bishops of each continent will be part of the preparation. A Synod of Bishops, a Eucharistic Congress, a World Youth Day, a World Family Day, Marian Lay Apostolate and Missionary meetings will be held in Rome during the Jubilee. Pride 2000 is likely to have a different tone: gays, lesbians, bisexuals and transsexuals have received approval from the City Council to hold their world meeting in Rome from 1–8 July 2000.

From the beginning, there was a relationship between Jubilees and the Holy Land, with Rome as an alternative to occupied Jerusalem, but for the first time Jubilee 2000 will re-establish the link. John Paul said he wanted to visit 'the places on the road taken by the People of God of the Old Covenant,' starting from those associated with Abraham and Moses, through Egypt and Mount Sinai, as far as Damascus which witnessed the conversion of St Paul. He said also that he would like to arrange meetings in places of 'exceptional symbolic importance', like Bethlehem, Jerusalem and Mount Sinai, as a means of furthering dialogue with Jews and followers of Islam.

By 1997, in Jerusalem, the prospect of the Jubilee was improving relations between Christian churches which had been notorious for their squabbles and jealousies. A Coptic Orthodox/Greek Orthodox/Armenian Orthodox/Catholic/Protestant commission was preparing joint initiatives for the year 2000. For the first time, representatives of all the Christian churches of Jerusalem prayed together at the inauguration of the newly restored and decorated dome of the basilica of the Holy Sepulchre. Previously it had been the site of scandalous physical clashes between the three churches which own it. This harmony was achieved in the light of the Jubilee, but was rendered urgent because of the steep decline in the Christian presence. In the 1920s, Palestinian Christians were 52 per cent of the inhabitants of Old Jerusalem but by 1997 they were less than three per cent.

Jubilees celebrate the gifts Christ has bestowed. Jubilee 2000 may be saved from the triumphalism which marked that of 1950 because John Paul's most significant innovation has been to encourage scrutiny of Christians' historical shortcomings. If it does not pretend that all mistakes are confined to the past, it will be a spur to continuing reform.

A YEAR-LONG
SABBATH

Jubilee 2000 is an idea whose time has returned. The idea is that
time is sacred and that unless this is recognized, at least for certain periods, humankind is endangered. Pol Pot, Stalin and other
dictators tried to abolish the traditional day of rest in their societies in an attempt to turn them into work camps. The day of rest was
an inconvenient reminder that humans have other purposes than to
work for a party-state.

Even outside totalitarian regimes, people can be seduced by the
allure of consumerism, while television and communications tech-
nology make it increasingly difficult to have time for oneself. People
can be harried also by the chronological concept of time and the pressure to achieve. The resultant stress abrades family life.

The Sabbath mentality, the idea that there is a Sunday or sacred
day of rest, subverts encompassing economic demands. On the
Sabbath all are equal in not having to work; all have time to worship
God, a reminder not to bend the knee to idols.

As extended Sabbaths, Jubilees have had important implied social
messages, not least of which is the need for stewardship of creation,
which now finds expression in ecological concerns. Some Jubilees
have also had an explicit social aspect, such as the release of prisoners
in Rome or an armistice to facilitate the passage of pilgrimages. A

further social aspect was the network of hospices established on the pilgrim routes and in Rome itself.

However, whereas the Jewish Jubilees made socio-economic recommendations, the Jubilee of Rome had a largely devotional character. The socio-economic recommendations may have been utopian but that provided inspiration; the devotional practices aimed to convert hearts. The corollary of solidarity with the needy was expressed through almsgiving which funded social initiatives such as orphanages and hospitals. This was admirable, but there was an etherialization of the biblical recommendation to release people from burdens which could be socio-economic or concern other spheres. In Roman Jubilees, for centuries, the biblical injunction was given an overwhelmingly spiritual interpretation.

When the Holy See no longer had its own territories to govern, it became more alert to the need to change iniquitous social situations and not merely succor its victims: Leo XIII's encyclical *Rerum novarum* began the revival of Catholic social teaching. His successors developed it, as did the Second Vatican Council, but subsequently there has been controversy over whether the spiritual springs of social action have been abandoned in favor of political activism. It has proved difficult to be prophetic rather than directly political, to challenge without being confrontational, to avoid simply accepting the media's agenda of relevance, to recognize that social analysis can determine perceptions. Some felt that new concepts such as social sin and structures of oppression undermined a sense of individual responsibility. Superficial Third Worldism was as much a danger as complacency about the status quo.

In *Tertio millennio adveniente* John Paul said that Jubilee 2000 should pursue the Old Testament aim of restoring social justice. Later he reaffirmed the church's preferential option for the poor and outcasts. He mentioned one specific instance: '... reducing, if not cancelling outright, the international debt which seriously threatens the future of many nations.'

In Lusaka, Zambia, in 1989, John Paul said, 'Is it merely rhetorical to ask how many woman and children die in Africa every day because resources are being swallowed up in debt repayment?'

Aware that Third World countries' loan repayments to the West are about three times as much as they receive in aid, in the encyclical *Solicitudo rei socialis* he pointed out that the loans designed to aid development have become, instead, a hindrance: 'The instrument chosen to make a contribution to development has turned into a counter-productive mechanism. This is because the debtor nations, in order to service their debt, find themselves obliged to export the capital needed for improving or at least maintaining their standard of living. It is also because, for the same reason, they are unable to obtain new and equally essential financing. Through this mechanism, the means intended for the development of peoples has turned into a brake upon development instead and indeed, in some cases, has even aggravated underdevelopment.'

Again, in *Centesimus annus*: 'The principle that debts must be paid is certainly just. However, it is not right to demand or expect payment when the effect would be the imposition of political choices leading to hunger and despair for entire peoples. It cannot be expected that the debts which have been contracted should be paid at the price of miserable sacrifices. In such cases it is necessary to find—as in fact is partly happening—ways to lighten, defer or even cancel the debt, compatible with the fundamental right of peoples to subsistence and progress.'

Third World countries are often accused of irresponsible borrowing, but there also seems to have been much irresponsible lending. In the Vatican, in June 1997, officials of the Vatican Justice and Peace Commission plus Latin American, United States and German bishops met for the first time with World Bank President, James Wolfensohn, the International Monetary Fund Director, Michel Candessus, and Enrique Iglesias, President of the Banco Interamerican para il Desarollo.

The church representatives argued that loan repayments are distorting development possibilities and that proposals for structural economic changes should take account of their effect on education, health care and other social policies. On the grounds that people are the most important resource, they wanted to prevent essential social expenditure being reduced for debt servicing.

Early in the 1990s attempts to obtain legislation against land mines were considered mere emotional appeals which had no chance against governmental armament manufacturing interests. But the pressure was maintained, public opinion became favorable, and by March 1999 a mini-ban convention had been signed by 134 nations. Major nations such as the United State, China, Russia, India, Iraq, Iran and Israel had not signed, but not only 110 million mines in more than sixty countries were being destroyed and mine victims being helped but also signatory nations renounced mine production and pledged to get rid of their own arsenals by 2009. Something similar may be happening for debt repayment because international banking institutions are taking measures to achieve a new balance between debt servicing and social expenditure. Politicians such as Gerhard Schroeder have shown concern, while Luciano Pavarotti, David Bowie, Annie Lennox and other singers have added their voices to the Stop the Debt campaign.

Some Christian groups aim at a one-time cancellation of the debt. A group founded in England, Jubilee 2000, which has the backing of all the Christian churches and aid agencies, aims to obtain remittance of the poorest countries' unpayable debts by the time of the Jubilee. By the beginning of 1999 it had gathered over two million signatures.

The Vatican Justice and Peace Commission is arguing instead for an adjustment of the burden on the grounds of re-establishing social harmony and equity. Easing of the debt burden would fulfil the Jubilee spirit and could encourage the many other groups of Christians working for social reconciliation and a more equitable society.

MARTYRS FOR A
GOOD CAUSE

lthough John Paul has described the ultimate goal of ecumenism as 'full visible unity among all the baptised,' for the year 2000 he hopes for a Christianity which 'if not fully united, is at least much closer to overcoming the divisions of the second millennium' (*Tertio millennio adveniente*). He hopes that the divisions among Christians, most of which came during the second millennium, will be healed in the third. But first Christians must make amends for the sins which wounded Christian unity, contradicting the will of Christ and causing scandal. John Paul has taken several initiatives in this direction. In Paris in August 1997 he deplored the St Batholomew Day massacre of about 3000 Huguenots by Catholic forces in 1572. He has offered many other apologies. One of the most striking was in the Czech Republic in April 1997 when he called the killing of John Hus and his followers 'execrable' and asked pardon for the wrongs Catholics had inflicted on non-Catholics: 'As Pope of the Church of Rome, in the name of all Catholics, I ask pardon for the wrongs done to non-Catholics.'

In his encyclical of 1995, *Ut unum sint*, John Paul said that he was prepared to put the exercise of the papacy itself up for discussion in order to further unity. He explained that he was seeking 'a way of exercising the primacy which, while in no way renouncing what is essential to its mission, is nonetheless open to a new situation.'

It is being discussed, not so much by other Christians, as John Paul intended, as by some Catholics who consider he has pushed ecumenism too far, too fast, has ceded too much without reciprocity, and has obscured the uniqueness of the Catholic Church. Why has so much effort been expended, critics ask, in attempts to reach understandings which, in human terms, seem highly unlikely? Before the Vatican Council, they continue, Rome expected other churches to recognize their errors and then reunite; since the council it has gone out of its way to attribute to itself errors, and other churches see this as a good reason for not reuniting with it.

Before the council the Catholic Church considered it had well-defined boundaries, but the council recognized that baptism means a real communion among all Christians, even if this needs perfecting. As a result, members of other Christian churches were called 'separated brethren', while ecumenism became not an optional but a dimension of the church. Some Catholics, however, were indifferent to ecumenism, and those who adhered literally to the idea of 'no salvation outside the church' were hostile. The hostility became intense when John Paul staged an international prayer meeting in Assisi in 1986 involving all religions. The presence of Shintoists, American Indians, African animists and representatives of other religions indicated that this was inter-religious dialogue, rather than ecumenism, which is confined to Christians. Nevertheless it roused fears that ecumenical intentions would lead to a syncretic mishmash. It was the straw that broke Archbishop Lefèbvre's back and some Roman curialists grumbled. But outreach to non-Christian religions is an aspect of Jubilee 2000.

The council raised hopes that centuries of separation between Christians could be overcome swiftly, but the path to reunion now seems endless and some are suffering ecumenical fatigue. 'The climb becomes slower as one nears the peak,' says the Australian Cardinal Edward Cassidy, head of the Pontifical Council for Promoting Christian Unity. Not only does it become slower but new obstacles can be encountered, as in the case of Anglican approval of women priests.

More progress has been made, however, than many realize. In the Western world, to a significant degree, rivalry between churches has been replaced by collaboration. The healing of fractures between

Rome and ancient churches such as the Coptic Orthodox, the Syrian Orthodox and the Assyrian Church of the East is well advanced, while theological discussions with the Presbyterians, Methodists and Lutherans have been fruitful. With the latter there has been substantial advance towards agreement on the crucial issue of justification, of how Christ saves people, which was the breaking point at the time of the Reformation.

The biggest disappointment has been the failure to achieve Catholic-Orthodox understanding after the demise of European Communism. The council recognized the Orthodox churches as sister churches of the Catholic, but the sisters squabble over their identity, over who owns what, and continue to nurse grievances over past tiffs. Sometimes it seems that Rome never remembers and the Orthodox never forget. Although the Orthodox churches are the closest of all to the Catholic theologically and sacramentally, culturally they are centuries apart. It was hoped that the sufferings of Orthodox and Catholics under communism would bring them together once it waned but instead old resentments acquired a new virulence, although at certain levels there is greater empathy. The difficulties were exacerbated by what some saw as a war between Orthodox Serbia and Catholic Croatia. A root cause of the difficulties is different ideas of the relationship between local churches and the universal church. Moreover, Rome finds itself caught up in internecine Orthodox strife: for instance, it can hardly make overtures to the Patriarch of Moscow without the rival Patriarch of Constantinople taking offence.

In the Western Ukraine, Belarus, Poland, Romania and the Czech Republic, Eastern-rite Catholics, called Uniates here for convenience, are a sore point for the Orthodox. At various times from the late sixteenth century, sometimes under duress, groups of Eastern-rite Christians accepted the authority of Rome while retaining their Eastern liturgy and customs, including a married priesthood. They saw themselves in continuity with Eastern-rite Christians of the first millennium who recognized the jurisdiction of Rome. But the Orthodox saw them as traitors, the edge of the Roman wedge.

During World War II the Orthodox absorbed these churches but most of their members remained loyal to Rome and, after the collapse of communism, the Uniate churches were allowed to function again. Immediately there were disputes with the Orthodox, often over return of church property that had been seized by the government but given to the Orthodox for their use. The friction was somewhat diminished by a Catholic–Orthodox agreement in 1993 which recognized the Uniate churches' right to exist but abandoned piecemeal 'annexation' of Eastern-rite Orthodox as a method to promote unity.

The problem persists, but there is yet another: that of Latin-rite dioceses in Orthodox countries. Although the Orthodox have dioceses in the West, particularly in Russia they resent the establishment of Catholic dioceses for Latin-rite Catholics. They are seen as an expression of the aggressive, invasive West. Catholic profession of ecumenical intent is suspect: communists called it 'expansion by dialogue' and some Orthodox likewise consider it merely a tactical ploy.

Several Catholic initiatives have worsened relations. The Orthodox were irritated by the way the Vatican appointed bishops in Russia. It had been recommended that the Orthodox be given prior notice of pastoral initiatives. Metropolitan Kyril of Smolensk had visited the Vatican only a month before the appointments were made but no one, from the pope downwards, had mentioned them to him. The embarrassed, unofficial Vatican reaction to Orthodox irritation was that it was not used to giving prior advice. To make matters worse, the Catholic Tadeusz Kondrusiewicz was sometimes referred to unofficially as Archbishop of Moscow; after protests, he was always given his official title as Apostolic Administrator for European Russia.

Some Catholic aid organizations provide financial support for the Orthodox as well as for Catholics. The Jesuits have been sensitive to Orthodox sensibilities, but representatives of some new Catholic movements have raised Orthodox hackles. They claim that Catholics are proselytizing as if they were bringing the Christian message to Russia for the first time. The Catholics concerned claim, however, that they are not trying to convert the Orthodox but those who have no religious convictions or knowledge. The Vatican secretary of state, Cardinal Angelo Sodano, seemed to support them when he said that the important thing was that Christ be preached. The implication was the ecumenical chips could fall where they might.

Subsequently, guidelines were prepared to ensure that Catholic activities did not upset the Orthodox, but still in mid-1997 John Paul was blessing statues of Our Lady of Fatima for Catholic churches in Russia, even though Orthodox bridle at the Fatima campaign of prayers for the conversion of Russia. In September 1997 in Russia a law on religious freedom was passed which seemed to restrict it. Although said to be directed against the most disruptive sects, it could also be applied against Catholicism and other mainline churches—except the Orthodox.

The Jubilee could serve as a reminder of the suffering which other Christians shared with the Orthodox under communism. It will pay tribute to witnesses of all denominations who already share full communion in heaven. Perhaps the living will learn from the dead.

In an improvized talk after the Stations of the Cross in 1994, for which Patriarch Bartholomew of Constantinople prepared the meditation, John Paul compared the Colosseum where the ceremony took place, to contemporary sites of martyrdom and the 'Mountain of Crosses' in Lithuania: 'I have thought of these other numerous Colosseums, these other Mountains of the Cross which traverse European Russia and Siberia … I want to say to all our dear brothers of the East that Rome, the Mountains of the Cross, the Solovki Islands and so many other extermination camps are united by these martyrs. We are united by this background of martyrs, we cannot be other than united.' The Jubilee tribute to twentieth century witnesses of the faith as an aid to ecumenism is not confined, however, to Catholics and Orthodox but includes those of other Christian denominations.

Could there be ecumenical canonizations? Before he became Benedict XIV, Prospero Lambertini recognized that other Christian martyrs were saints, though he called them saints of God rather than saints of the church. Canonization is an ecclesial act, a recognition that a person is worthy of inclusion in the canon or list of saints of the Catholic Church. Some Lutherans once suggested that the church recognize as a saint Pastor Dietrich Bonhoeffer who was killed by the Nazis but Rome did not want to poach. In 1964 Paul VI canonized 22 black Ugandan martyrs. When they were martyred, in 1886, 24 Anglicans had met the same fate. At the canonization ceremony, Paul said, 'We do not want to forget the others, who belonged to the Anglican confession, who met death for the name of Christ.' As the church recognizes that other Christians may be saints, there could be ecumenical canonizations if there were prior agreement on their significance.

The Jubilee 'New Martyrs' Commission (the others are Ecumenism, Theological-Historical; Inter-Religious Dialogue; Liturgy; Pastoral-Missionary; Art and Culture) asked Catholic and non-Catholic organizations and individuals to submit information on those in this century who have offered their lives for the Gospel. It aimed to help preserve the memory of the many twentieth century

Christian witnesses—'martyr' originally meant witness although its use with time was restricted to those who died for the faith.

In each case, the commission recorded biographical information, the context of the life, a description of the witness given and a list of other sources. By early 1999, approximately 5000 mini-biographies had been prepared. The largest group, 1700, was of those who had died in Spain during the Civil War; the bulk of the remainder were those who suffered under Nazism and European Communism. There were others from Africa, which, since the 1960s, has been the scene of most martyrdoms. At the beginning of the century missionaries were killed there, as were others at the time of decolonialization and the civil wars of the 1960s; from the mid-1990s there have been many martyrs in the Great Lakes area of central Africa and elsewhere. In Latin America missionaries were killed attempting to quell ethnic clashes early in the century, in the 1930s the Mexican government persecuted the Catholic Church and, more recently, outstanding witness has been given by Christians opposing dictatorial regimes, drug traffickers and terrorists.

The census will provide a geography of witness and a reminder that in this century more have been martyred than at any time since the first centuries of Christianity. Those martyrs were called the seeds of Christianity, in John Paul's view their contemporary counterparts are seeds of unity.

How will the catalogues be used, apart from the Jubilee ecumenical commemoration for new martyrs at the Colosseum on 7 May 2000? They can serve for paraliturgical ceremonies such as those which for some years have taken place each Easter Tuesday at Santa Maria in Trastevere basilica in Rome, where representatives of various denominations commemorate their martyrs. Moreover they could indirectly help the practice of saint-making by encouraging local churches in gathering records of witnesses. Some in the catalogues might later be investigated for beatification but that is not their purpose; rather they are a response to the appeal of *Tertio millennio adveniente* to preserve the memory of witnesses. John Paul, who has beatified and canonized more than any of his predecessors, has been seeking ways to find contemporary exemplars and the catalogues may be an answer.

The census for the Jubilee widens the idea of martyrdom beyond what is customary in the Congregation for Saints. Included are not only martyrs because of *odium fidei*—those who died rather than deny their faith, as was the original concept—but also those who gave their life for another person, martyrs of charity.

Largely because of John Paul, the Congregation for Saints has been moving in this direction: Father Maximilian Kolbe, the Polish Franciscan who, in Auschwitz concentration camp, volunteered to take the place of a married man condemned to death, was canonized in November 1982 as a martyr of a new kind. This tendency will be strengthened by the Jubilee catalogues which will demonstrate that many twentieth century Christians were ready to sacrifice their lives and that all Christians can unite in honoring them.

The attention to contemporary witnesses will be a link with the martyrs of the first years of the church in Rome, a source of its resilience. Far from being simply an anachronism, in an electronic era the catacombs, and Rome's other historical remains, could acquire a new importance. They comprise a significant part of the history of humanity and Christianity and have the authority of tangible memory. In Rome one can see Peter's tomb, where St Lawrence was buried after decapitation, and the remains of the first house churches. In an age where everything can be simulated, they speak louder than words. They should help the Jubilee be a celebration of the real as opposed to the virtual.

ONE TRIP TOO
MANY?

rips have been a thread running through John Paul's pontificate, but many cardinals advised him against a guilt trip during the Jubilee. John Paul proposed that the church admit its historical errors but some cardinals would prefer to await the Last Judgement. Even though he may have soft pedalled some aspects as a result of their opposition, John Paul still proposed an ecclesial *glasnost* or transparency.

In *Tertio millennio adveniente* he stated, 'the joy of every Jubilee is above all a joy based upon the forgiveness of sin, the joy of conversion ... the precondition for reconciliation with God on the part of both individuals and communities; ... as the Second Millennium of Christianity draws to a close, the church should become more fully conscious of the sinfulness of her children, recalling all those times in history when they departed from the spirit of Christ and his Gospel and, instead of offering to the world the witness of a life inspired by the values of faith, indulged in ways of thinking and acting which were truly forms of counter-witness and scandal.'

This set emergency signals flashing for Cardinal Giacomo Biffi, archbishop of Bologna, who in a pastoral note warned that the theme can cause 'ambiguity and spiritual malaise'. He pointed out that in Galileo's time most academic circles did not accept his arguments, but no contemporary university rectors are expected to apologize for the judgements expressed by their predecessors. The point he was making was not confined to the Galileo case, but he might have added that, at the time errors were admitted regarding Galileo, several newspaper reports were along the lines of the *Los Angeles Times*: 'It's Official! The Earth Revolves Around the Sun, Even for the Vatican.' And that some scientists regarded the arguments used in the revision of judgement on Galileo as a case of too little, too late. Many people take gestures such as the Galileo revision as entitling them to press for the modification of judgements on every question under the sun.

'Who will humanity send the bill to,' asked Biffi, 'for the many who were guillotined in France in 1793, killed for no other fault than belonging to the wrong social class? Who will humanity send the bill to for the tens of millions of Russian peasants killed by the Bolsheviks?' In other words, as no one has been held responsible for many mass crimes, why should the church rush to accuse itself for episodes about which there is still debate among historians.

Biffi clashed with Cardinal Joseph Ratzinger, prefect of the Congregation for the Doctrine of the Faith, on this theme at the Eucharistic Congress in Bologna in September 1997. Responding to Ratzinger, who had said that the burning of Giordano Bruno in 1600 should inspire repentance, Biffi claimed that it was ridiculous to put the church on trial. He is author of a book, *Chaste Harlot*, which claims that the church is not sullied even by its members' despicable conduct. 'The church is Christ's spouse,' he said at the Bologna meeting. 'Do you think Christ can marry someone ugly? Be careful bad-mouthing the church as Christ is of Mediterranean stock and jealous.'

Mary Ann Glendon, a Harvard law professor who led the Vatican delegation to the UN Conference on Women in Beijing, has written that for some people excuses are never enough because they really want Catholics to apologize for being such.

John Paul did not decide to apologize for the church's short-comings because of the Jubilee. Although more attention has been given to his affirmation of Catholic identity and certainties, a will-ingness to admit defects is a salient aspect of his pontificate. The Dutch pope, Hadrian V (1522–1523), often mentioned by John Paul, was the last pope for over 400 years to acknowledge that critics could be right: he admitted that the disorder in the pre-Reformation church was due mainly to the Roman Curia which, of course, did not increase his popularity with its members.

The Reformation threw the church on the defensive. Rome responded energetically; it removed causes of scandal but was in no mood to admit faults or ask excuses. One of the reasons that the church did not join the ecumenical movement until the Second Vatican Council was fear that it might be expected to admit past mistakes. That attitude changed with John XXIII, Paul VI and the Council.

Karol Wojtyla, with other Polish bishops, fostered postwar reconciliation with the German bishops and nation. Although the gesture was criticized not only by communists but by Catholics, it proved to be prophetic and may well have influenced his Jubilee project. After his election as John Paul II, on more than ninety occasions he has deplored the shortcomings of Catholics or asked pardon, to the chagrin of some other Catholic churchmen. Addressing the European Parliament in Strasbourg in October 1988, he pinpointed the limits of religious integralism which fails to 'distinguish between the sphere of faith and that of social life,' with the result that medieval Latin Christianity excluded from the temporal community those who did not profess the true faith. In 1995, referring to the Crusades, he said that nowadays it was realized it is better to engage in dialogue than resort to arms; in the same year, he asked women pardon for the injustices they have suffered. Among other things, he has asked pardon for offences against Protestants, indigenous people who suffered from colonialists, Negro slaves, and for Christians' behavior in wars and in the recent Rwanda slaughter. He seems determined to make up not only for four centuries of never offering apologies but also the shortcomings of the preceding six centuries.

His desire to make a collective examination of conscience, which is a leitmotif of *Tertio millennio adveniente* (one example: 'another chapter of history to which the sons and daughters of the church must return with a spirit of repentance is that of the acquiescence given, especially in certain countries, to intolerance and even the use of violence in the service of truth'), is similar to the approach found in an anonymous position paper which was presented to all cardinals when they were summoned to Rome in 1994. Entitled *Reflections on the Great Jubilee of the Year 2000*, it proposed that the church not only admit its members' sins but also 'in a certain sense, its own.'

The paper asked, 'How can one be silent over the many forms of violence perpetrated in the name of the faith? Wars of religion, tribunals of the Inquisition and other forms of violation of human rights ... It is significant that the coercive methods, which damaged human rights, were used by the totalitarian ideologies of the twentieth century and are still used by Islamic fundamentalists. The crimes of Hitler's Nazism and Marxist Stalinism arose from such coercive methods. The Declaration of the Rights of Man and, in the church, the Declaration on Religious Liberty of the Second Vatican Council were a proper reaction to this. In the light of what the Second Vatican Council said, it is necessary that the church, of its own initiative, reveal the dark aspects of its history and assess them in the light of the Gospels.' It went on to say that the church was holy but also a community of sinful people.

One participant said that the majority of cardinals disapproved of this approach. In particular, cardinals from Central and Eastern Europe disliked it. Probably, after years of hostility from communist regimes, they did not want to declare that the church's Inquisition was at the origins of Stalinism. In any case, a Polish theologian, Joseph Tischner, and others argue that Stalinism derived ultimately from a degeneration of Enlightenment rationalism.

The cardinals may have accepted an admission that Catholics erred but became edgy when it was suggested errors were made in the name of the church. Perhaps the only time these have been acknowledged in recent centuries has been with canonization of those who had clashed with church authorities. Biffi expressed concern that admission of errors will make the church seem no different from other organizations but the argument can be reversed: it is reluctance to admit errors which makes it seem like other organizations. The cardinals' cold reaction to the position paper seems to have had some influence on John Paul; in *Tertio millennio adveniente* there was no reference to the crucial concept of error committed 'in a certain sense' in the name of the church. Nor was the relationship beween the Inquisition and twentieth century totalitarian regimes spelt out. But before the Jubilee, symposia were held on the church and anti-Semitism and on the Inquisition or, rather, on the Inquisitions because distinctions are made between those held in various times and places.

Eamon Duffy, reader in Church History at Cambridge, one of the fifty scholars who met in the Vatican in November 1998 on the Inquisition, found that no attempt was made to whitewash it. However, he reported in the London *Tablet* that the final theological analysis condemned cases of violent enforcement of 'truth', but claimed that the church itself was not guilty. Duffy found this an example of the distinction, which some find illegitimate, between certain bishops and theologians and the church itself and also that it leaves open the question of the church's silence on these cases before the Second Vatican Council.

The cardinals summoned to the Vatican were probably aware of a draft document on 'Anti-Semitism, the Shoah and the Church' prepared by Professor Hans Hermann Henrix of the Catholic Theological Institute of Aachen, Germany, for a joint Vatican-Israel Commission. It said that the Catholic Church bears co-responsibility for the Shoah: many Christians together with their bishops were so prejudiced that they did not have the necessary clear-sightedness to recognize the evil of anti-Semitic persecution by National Socialism and, consequently, did not react against it. A similar attitude underlay the French Catholic bishops' declaration of contrition, on 30 September 1997, for their predecessors' failure to oppose the Vichy government's wartime anti-Semitic legislation. It seemed that they were fulfilling George Steiner's requirement for European culture 'to regain its inward energies, its self-respect'—by 'Christendom becoming answerable for its seminal role in preparing the Shoah.'

In March 1998, the Vatican Commission for Religious Relations with Jews issued *We Remember: A Reflection on the Shoah*. Ten years of preparation for this text of nine pages, to which was added a page and a half of introduction by John Paul II, indicated the difficulties of the undertaking which, among other things, had to take account of the reaction of Islamic countries, particularly those with Catholic minorities. The document claimed that Nazism was a modern paganism, hostile to Christians and others as well as to Jews. It asked if anti-Semitic prejudice had disposed some Christians to sympathy with Nazi measures but did not give an answer.

In an interview which coincided with the publication of the document, the German curial cardinal, Joseph Ratzinger, put the matter more clearly by saying that Christian anti-Jewish prejudices were 'not the root cause of the Shoah but facilitated it.' The document deplored, without naming any, those Christians who had collaborated with the Nazis or were indifferent to their crimes, but it did not blame the church itself. In a footnote, it cited Jewish organizations and personalities who, immediately after World War II, had praised 'the wisdom of Pope Pius XII's diplomacy.' Jews who consider he was culpably silent objected to this, and to the document's denial of any link between Christianity and Nazi ideology. An Italian Jewish historian, Carlo Ginsburg, maintained that Catholics, instead of offering ambiguous apologies, should express shame at some of their co-religionists' behavior.

Some churchmen fear that whatever the sorrow expressed and pardon requested, when the Jubilee penitential procession is held on Ash Wednesday, it will not settle controversial issues and that officially-sponsored revisionism will have no end: for instance, many historians now claim that, in the fourteenth century, the church acquiesced with the French King Philip IV who, it is claimed, successfully rigged a case against the Knights Templar on charges including rampant homosexuality and so seized their property. Should the church now apologize? And to whom? Should the papacy apologize for aiding the English overlordship of Ireland from the twelfth century? Similar historical cases are legion and, moreover, new evidence is always coming to light, not to mention claims by contemporaries, such as homosexuals, against the church. Revisionism is a Pandora's box. As Mikhail Gorbachov could tell the Vatican, one knows where it begins but not where it may end.

In previous Jubilees, participants have been encouraged to seek pardon for their own sins, but John Paul wants Rome and local churches to look back over their historical record to see where there has been departure from Christian ideals. This is not supposed to replace a sense of individual sin but in fact it might substitute for it.

The arguments against such an examination of conscience are cogent. Those who advance them might find their greatest consolation in Marshall McLuhan's remark that not even the best intentions can destroy the Catholic Church. The willingness to admit errors can seem an ecclesial version of political correctness or masochism. Many deny that contemporaries have any responsibility for what happened in the past and assert that returning to the scene of the crime can stir bitter controversy instead of healing wounds.

John Paul himself has asked why only the Catholic Church admits shortcomings, without others doing likewise. But, in fact, apologizing has become an end-of-millennium vogue. Those who have indulged include Tony Blair for British indifference to the Irish Famine, F. W. de Klerk for the policies of white South African governments, Nelson Mandela for the violence of the African National Council, Bill Clinton for the use, in the 1950s–60s, of Afro-Americans as human guinea pigs. The list is so long that practitioners are accused of seeking easy publicity and of reducing institutions to the level of weepy soap operas.

Some erroneously think that expression of regret implies acceptance of the victim's claims, but an apology for the burning of Giordano Bruno does not necessarily mean endorsement of his ideas. John Paul's admissions have not concerned doctrinal substance nor contradicted that the church Christ founded subsists in the Catholic Church. Most of his apologies have been inspired by an occasion such as a visit to a site where slaves were held in Africa before departure for the Americas.

His concern, in fact, seems not so much historic as spiritual. He is not only looking to the past but preparing the way to the future. He aims not to foster endless retrospective debate but, instead, to trigger a new beginning. He knows that sometimes it helps to say 'sorry' even though damage is irreparable. In preparation for the third millennium, he wants to detach the church from any suggestion of acquiescence with power or prejudice.

While ready to admit errors, he also advises not to dwell on them. He does not recommend permanent sackcloth and ashes. Recent Central and Eastern European experience suggests that the purification of memory is necessary to emerge buoyantly from the past because shifting the deadweight of sin opens up a future without lingering resentments. Admission of faults can be a prelude to pardon, reconciliation, thanksgiving and joy, a Jubilee.

REIGNING POPES DURING JUBILEES 1300–1975

	Jubilee Year	Pope	Dates of office
1	1300	Boniface VIII	1294–1303
2	1350	Clement VI	1342–1352
3	1390	Boniface IX	1389–1404
4	1400	Boniface IX	1389–1404
5	1425	Martin V	1417–1431
6	1450	Nicholas V	1447–1445
7	1475	Sixtus IV	1471–1484
8	1500	Alexander VI	1492–1503
9	1525	Clement VII	1523–1534
10	1550	Julius III	1550–1555
11	1575	Gregory VIII	1572–1585
12	1600	Clement VIII	1592–1605
13	1625	Urban VIII	1623–1644
14	1650	Innocent X	1644–1655
15	1675	Clement X	1670–1676
16	1700	Innocent XII	1699–1700
		Clement XI	1700–1721
17	1725	Benedict XIII	1724–1730
18	1750	Benedict XIV	1740–1758
19	1775	Pius VI	1775–1799
20	1825	Leo XII	1823–1829
21	1875	Pius IX	1846–1878
22	1900	Leo XIII	1878–1903
23	1925	Pius XI	1922–1939
24	1950	Pius XII	1939–1958
25	1975	Paul VI	1963–1978

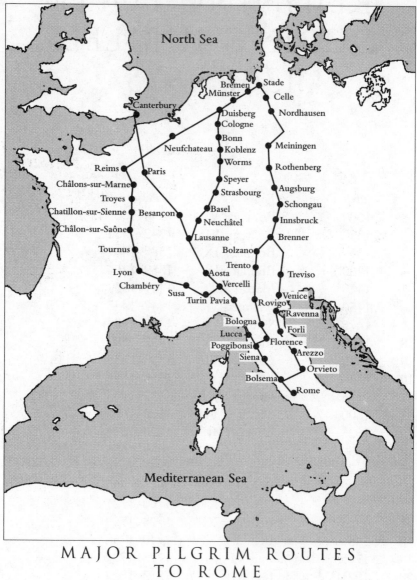

MAJOR PILGRIM ROUTES
TO ROME

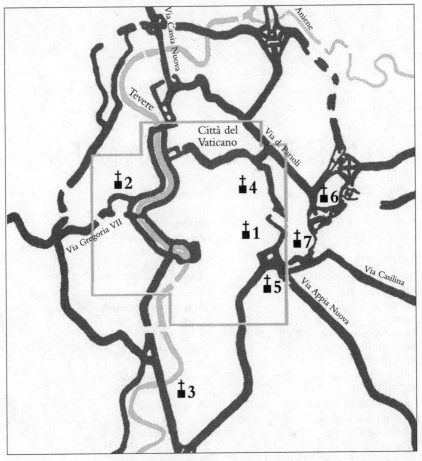

THE SEVEN PILGRIM CHURCHES OF ROME

The four Patriarchal Basilicas
1　St John Lateran
2　St Peter's Basilica
3　St Paul's Outside the Walls
4　Santa Maria Maggiore/St Mary Major

The three 'Jubilee' Basilicas
5　St Sebastian Outside the Walls
6　St Laurence Outside the Walls
7　Santa Croce in Gerusalemme

INDEX OF NAMES

Within the index, popes are designated
by (p) after their name, rival or
antipopes by (a)